ZOO STATION

ZOO STATION

ZOO STATION

Adventures
in East and West Berlin

IAN WALKER

THE ATLANTIC MONTHLY PRESS
NEW YORK

For Mary and Reg

First published in Great Britain in 1987 by Martin Secker & Warburg Limited
First published in the United States of America in 1988
Printed in the United States of America
FIRST EDITION

Library of Congress Cataloging-in-Publication Data

Walker, Ian, 1952–
  Zoo station.

  I. Title.

PR6073.A398Z39   1988   823'.914   87-31896
ISBN 0-87113-197-8

The Atlantic Monthly Press
19 Union Square West
New York, NY 10003

First printing

CONTENTS

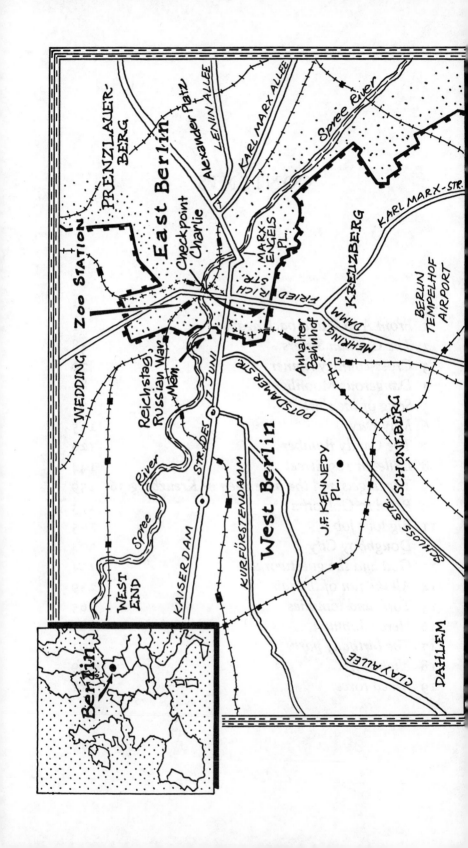

1 From A to B and back again

The maroon-and-caramel train ran all day back and forth between the systems, capitalism-communism-capitalism-communism, the rhythm of the iron wheels lent itself to any number of repetitive lyrics. I looked out the dirty window. A girl was waving. I waved back. There was something about trains that caused children to wave spontaneously at the passing faces, some idea that the strangers at the window were bound for adventure or romance, some idea about stories starting in trains.

I had waved myself to the steam trains running along a track at the bottom of our garden, one of many houses I lived in as a child, we were always on the move. I saw the Wall being built on the television at another house. It was my ninth birthday: 13 August 1961. My grandmother bought me a dog. My mother and father seemed sad and scared by the black-and-white pictures of tanks and barbed wire. It spoilt the atmosphere of my birthday. My father was a public health inspector (my mother was working at the checkout of the local Co-op). Sometimes my father had to go away for the weekend on civil defence courses. When war broke out, he said, we had to cover the windows with brown paper. I wondered then: why brown? Now, twenty-three years later, I was on this train about to pass through a hole in the Wall.

Going from west to east was quicker by underground, but I preferred the S-Bahn: the varnished wooden seats, the linoleum floor, the view from the window. The train clattered across an iron bridge.

Beneath that bridge was the third widest street in the world, empty of traffic, a ghostly highway lined with flags. It cut straight as a knife through the wooded Tiergarten, bulged around the golden angel atop the Victory Column and terminated at the Brandenburg Gate. Hitler named this street the East–West Axis.

Like other streets christened by the Nazis, its name had been changed. It was now called Strasse des 17 Juni in memory of the failed uprising of East Berlin building workers on that date in 1953.

'The seventeenth of June is kind of our May Day,' Captain Genser had told me on the telephone from US Army headquarters on Clay Allee. (General Lucius D. Clay had been the American commandant in Berlin after the war.)

Calendars, same as everything else, were open to interpretation. Every year on 17 June, that day and that street, American and British and French soldiers paraded their guns and colours along the boulevard devised by Hitler as one of two showpiece entrances to the city he dreamed would extinguish the glamour of Babylon and Rome. The East–West Axis was 400 feet wide. The North–South Axis never got built.

If it hadn't been for Johnny I would never have been smitten by this two-faced city, I thought, as the train swung right by Lessingstrasse. Four streets in the west and two in the east were named after Lessing, the dramatist who believed reason would overcome the eighteenth-century anti-semites.

Johnny was a friend of mine from London who had grown up in East Berlin. I had once shared a flat with him off the Old Kent Road. The flat received a steady trickle of escapists and ex-prisoners from the German Democratic Republic. Some of them were contemporaries of Johnny's at college in Weimar. Others were old friends from East Berlin. All of them had been forced for various reasons to flee the east, but none of them was starry-eyed about the west. They were special people, they had lived their lives under laboratory conditions: half in the east, half in the west. Two heads were better than one.

Johnny was also a traveller between the systems. His parents had blessed him with an Austrian passport. He was in East Berlin now, staying at his parents' house in Grünau, a plush suburb for intellectuals, nicknamed Intelligenzsiedlung. The train pulled out of Bellevue station. No one had got on or off.

Thanks to Johnny, I had friends both sides of the border, both sides of the argument. I had walked around John F. Kennedy Platz and drunk in the café on Leninplatz. In a stationery shop on Karl Marx Allee, formerly Stalinallee, I had bought some birthday cards embossed with the East German flag. Laura would be receiving those birthday cards for the next couple of years, hopeless attempts to jump-start her memory. Meanwhile, I was on this S-Bahn train, thumbing through the yellow index of my Falkplan, examining the distribution of genius on Berlin's streets. Einstein had one street in each system. Beethoven had two streets in the west and three in the east. There was a Dickensweg in the west, a Bertolt Brecht Platz in the east. The schizophrenic city had one Freudstrasse in West Berlin, one Jungstrasse in East Berlin.

God was poorly represented in both Berlins, Christ scoring only one street in the west. The train crossed the bridge over the Spree, the river which had bequeathed a phrase to English. Intent on having a good time, so the story goes, Berliners took to their boats on the Spree.

'I write as a citizen of the world who serves no prince,' wrote Schiller, whose name was nailed to the walls of seven capitalist streets and three communist streets. The princes were still in the driving seat. I remembered some years ago listening to the breakfast show on Armed Forces Network, the radio station run by the US Army. The DJ was giving out routine traffic information.

'Squatters and anarchists are assembling on . . . Karl Marx Strasse . . . in the American sector,' he stuttered, the comic-book thought-bubble above his headphones saying *holy shit*. After the next record he came on the air to say that Karl Marx Strasse was in fact named after a former mayor of West Berlin and not after the well-known communist.

This was a barefaced lie, but Berliners were inured by habitude to liars. Their radios broadcast a contradictory babble of propaganda in English, French, German and Russian twenty-four hours a day. People in the occupied city laughed at the illusions which propped up life in other places. Truth was neither here nor there. The train continued east along the banks of the Spree.

I tapped my chest, checking the sturdy oblong of British Passport no. 676352D was still there in the inside pocket.

It was 2.30, the last Sunday in April, 1984.

I sat opposite a teenage Turk. He was plugged into a Walkman, but he wasn't paying much attention to the music. Fidgeting with his fingers on the wooden seat, he glanced up and down the carriage, avoiding my eyes. He was en route to the Intershop at Friedrichstrasse, East Berlin, with three empty shopping bags. Guestworkers, punks, winos, the elderly and the thirsty poor made this journey regularly. You could buy a ticket for DM 2 at any U-Bahn or S-Bahn station in West Berlin, take the train across the border to Friedrichstrasse, walk along the platform to the Intershop, buy duty-free cigarettes and alcohol and hop back on the train to the west without ever showing your passport to a soul. Discovering this and other paradoxes, western tourists reared on the cold war were sometimes disappointed. What kind of iron curtain was this anyhow? Jesus, it was bad enough finding out Berlin was nearer Poland than West Germany. West Berliners do their shopping in East Berlin underground stations? Yes, you say, they buy enough vacuum-sealed packs of filter coffee to see them through the week. Coffee is expensive in the west. The alcoholics make the trip for the GDR vodka at DM 8 a bottle. Continually patrolling the Friedrichstrasse platforms are three members of the Volkspolizei whose job is to chuck western drunks on trains destined for the western sectors. Some of these cold war jobs are very dull. Not everyone can be a spy.

The Turkish boy on the facing seat was a smuggler. His shirt was one size too big. If he made enough trips a day to the Intershop he could supplement his unemployment money by selling the cigarettes and alcohol at a profit in the west. Lethargic western customs officers did occasionally board trains returning from the east, but the risk was minimal.

I was carrying a plastic bag full of records I was taking across to a friend who lived in a tenement flat off Schönhauser Allee, a friend who had learned to speak English by listening to the pop music shows on AFN and BFBS, who watched western TV stations at night and read *Neues Deutschland* in the morning. His name was Tommy. He worked as an architect and was married to a woman who modelled for East German fashion magazines. His main grudge against the west was that it had claimed most of his friends.

The train slowed down to about 12 m.p.h. as it crossed the border at Invalidenstrasse. Parallel to the concrete Wall at a distance of fifteen yards, steel crosses stood in double file like obedient schoolchildren on a freshly raked avenue of sand. They were giant versions of the steel jacks I used to toss in the air and try and catch on the back of my hand when I was a boy. I had no idea what security function those crosses performed, but these days anyway no one tried to escape by clambering over the Wall. That was passé as moptop haircuts and flowers stuck down the barrels of M16s.

Two guards were on duty in the watchtower, their feet up, having a smoke. Car boots, false papers, corrupt military and embassy staff, these were the main illegal modes of exit from east to west. The more money possessed by the would-be runaway the safer the method of escape. Escaping was a business run by gangsters in West Germany and Switzerland. Safe in this knowledge, the two guards in the watchtower occasionally lifted the binoculars to their eyes, a theatrical acknowledgment of their official purpose in life. Along the 66 miles of concrete Wall and the 35 miles of wire-fence encircling West Berlin there are 260 such watchtowers.

One such night in October 1979 I scaled a wooden watchtower in the British Sector. In a café on Olivaerplatz I had been drinking with Pint, a man who had spent the first twenty years of his life in East Berlin, the next ten in West Berlin. 'Two words that changed my life,' he said. '*Wolfgang Spielhagen*.' That was his name. Pint was his nickname. Part of a contingent from East Berlin that had been in Prague during August 1968, Pint had set about producing leaflets and dropping them on the S-Bahn trains after he returned to Berlin. When Pint's name was given to the Staasis by a comrade after some hours of interrogation, Pint had no option but to flee. Heading for Italy he was caught on the border between Rumania and Yugoslavia.

'It was a beautiful moonlit night,' he said. 'This guard came out. He was carrying a beautiful Kalashnikov. He said, stop. I said, okay. Better to be in the east with two legs than in the west with one.'

In due course Pint would give me his story in full, which was generous considering he was also a writer, but later that October night a West Berliner named Oliver drove us out to Spandau in his white German Ford. It was a one-hour journey to an isolated forest known as the Ice Keller, at the westernmost edge of the border. At four in the morning there were no MPs or soldiers to prevent Oliver from driving into the restricted zone. Skidding on the frozen snow, the Ford careered along the track that ran alongside the Wall. The Beach Boys were playing loud on the car radio. Pint made some joke about surfing all along the watchtowers.

Having dumped the car beneath a tree we mounted the disused wooden watchtower. The ladder was slippy with ice. Standing on the creaky platform, hands cupped round frozen mouths, we shouted out some things at the GDR guards in their heated glass cage just forty yards away. *Good fences make good neighbours.* Smiling, the guards on the nightshift trained their binoculars on us. I suppose they thought we were just another bunch of western drunks with nothing better to do on a weekday night than howl at the moon like frustrated dogs. I suppose they were right, too, but it was one of many nights in this city that seemed to mean something at the time, one of many nights blurring past the window of the S-Bahn train.

Pint's father had fought for the Wehrmacht and was captured by the Red Army during the Battle of Stalingrad. My father had been a signalman on warships escorting convoys across the North Sea. Was it ridiculous to think that they too could have been friends? I had met Pint's father just once, a year before he died. East German pensioners being permitted annual holidays in the west, Pint had brought his father to London.

'I hung out flags for the communists in the twenties,' Pint's father said, 'I hung out flags for the Nazis in the thirties. After the war I hung out flags for the communists again. Now it's all over with me and the flags.'

From a distance the flags of the two Germanies looked identical: gold, red and black horizontal stripes. Only close up could you see the motif of the compass and hammer encircled at the centre of the East German version. Flags, like guns, had an automatic glamour for me as a boy. I pored for hours over a book which had miniature colour reproductions of the flags of the whole world. My favourites were the rising sun of Japan and the yellow stars on red of China. I never much liked the Union Jack. I was wondering vaguely whether the Turkish boy opposite owed allegiance to any flag.

I doubt he had much enthusiasm for either of the German ones. Nationalist ghosts awoke at night to paint *Turks Out!* on the walls of West Berlin. Chancellor Kohl, elected voice of these ghosts, was currently encouraging the guestworkers to return to their homelands. Guests of the capitalist metropolis, the 130,000 Turks in West Berlin were mostly congregated in Kreuzberg in the American Sector. Kreuzberg, people said, was the third largest Turkish city in the world. Its young men still had to return to Turkey for their military service. I had a friend called Murat who had found God as a result of spending three years inside a British Chieftain tank in the American-backed Turkish army. The smuggler on the S-Bahn looked too young to have yet received his call-up papers.

Entering the steel-and-glass half-moon of Friedrichstrasse station, the train slowed in a series of jerks. The Turkish boy gripped the brass handles on the wooden door and pulled them apart like chest expanders. He jumped on to the platform and the momentum of the train sent him leaping towards the Intershop kiosk. Two green-uniformed policemen were escorting a drunk on to a train bound for Wannsee.

I walked along the platform, past advertisements for Praktika cameras and the East German railway company. In the window display of a newsagent's kiosk one whole shelf was devoted to books and magazines on philately. Stamps, like flags, triggered the imagination, their colours and designs providing clues to faraway lands and tongues. Philately was a cheap way to travel.

The travel restriction was probably the biggest single source of complaint among East Germans. Time and again people said,

Why won't they let us go to the west? I don't want to live in the west, everything I have, my family and friends, my job, my home, everything is here in the east and I have no wish to leave it, but I would like to see the west. We see the west every night on the television. We want to see it with our own eyes.

I was once told by an East Berliner (who came straight to London as soon as he had escaped to the west) that tourism for East Germans was like the Central Line: Bulgaria, Czechoslovakia, Hungary, Poland, Rumania, the Soviet Union, maybe Yugoslavia, a six or seven-country cycle endlessly repeated in a lifetime of holidays. Western tourists had the freedom, but not the desire, to visit the communist countries. Eastern tourists had the desire, but not the freedom, to visit the capitalist countries. Swings and roundabouts. Too much movement twixt the systems might dampen people's enthusiasm for threatening strangers with bombs. Demonologies flourish best in the dark.

Looking through the window of the newsagent's kiosk, at a beautiful hardback edition of Engels's *Dialectics of Nature* selling for 5.60 eastern marks, I lit a cigarette. The earth, Engels wrote, would one day become an extinct frozen globe circling the dead sun in an ever narrower orbit. The newsagent was closed on Sundays.

Next to Engels on the shelf were three volumes of Rosa Luxemburg's letters, 16 marks the complete set. The daughter of a Polish Jew, she came to Berlin in 1914 to escape the Tsarist police. Together with Karl Liebknecht, who had founded the German Social Democratic Party, she led the Spartacist insurrection of 1919. Walking home after a meeting one night, Liebknecht and Luxemburg were hustled into a limousine and taken to the Eden Hotel on Budapesterstrasse. They were charged and sentenced by three officers of the First Guards Cavalry Battalion. Liebknecht's corpse was found the same night on the Charlottenburger Chaussee. The next day Luxemburg's body was seen floating on the Landwehrkanal.

I couldn't remember Rosa Luxemburg figuring much in the history of the Weimar Republic, the way I was taught it at school. The republic was a brave experiment in democracy that was fouled up by Hitler, that was the general message. I joined the queue at the Intershop.

Having bought a bottle of whisky for Tommy and two packets of Club cigarettes, premier brand in the GDR, I proceeded towards the sign which said in black capitals EINREISE IN DIE DDR. I didn't need the sign, I knew the way. I walked down the stone steps, along a pedestrian underpass and up some more steps into Friedrichstrasse checkpoint.

Four queues about fifteen yards long stretched back from the four wood-effect Formica kiosks that were in operation. Metal signs, slid into slats like destination boards at railway stations, indicated the appropriate queue for citizens of West Berlin, citizens of West Germany, citizens of other states. There was another queue for transit traffic, westerners bound for foreign countries via Schönefeld airport or Ostbahnhof railway station.

I joined the queue for non-German nationals. Apart from one small group of Swedish tourists the line was composed of guestworkers. 'They are kings here,' Tommy once told me. 'Slaves in the west and kings in the east.' Their western money bought the kind of access and privilege denied the guestworkers in that money's home. One deutschmark, translated into four ost marks by a bank or a black marketeer, bought so many more things east of the border. And at the Palasthotel discothèque in East Berlin Turks and Yugoslavs were not snubbed by the girls the way they were in the western clubs. Friday and Saturday night between 11 and 12 was lovers' rush-hour at Friedrichstrasse. People would be back at the checkpoint in time to relinquish the visas which expired at midnight. They would cross back to the western zone of the station, do an immediate U-turn, queue up for another visa and be back in their lovers' arms at one o'clock. The system was well established. Tommy saw it as a kind of modern fairy tale: the east was the secret garden to which the slaves escaped at weekends.

The queues shuffled patiently towards the kiosks. Old women with relatives in the east hauled their loads of food and drink a foot at a time. Transit travellers dragged suitcases and rucksacks. A couple of Mohicans sat glumly on a bench while a policeman explained that they had been denied entry to the GDR. He didn't have to give a reason, but everyone knew that part-shaved heads and torn leather jackets were ill-received at the border. East

Berlin had its own community of nihilists and the authorities seemed reluctant to encourage fraternal relations with their counterparts in the west. Western punks with a serious reason to spend the day in East Berlin knew all about this and took the necessary measures, borrowed a dress or jacket, wore a hat, whatever. The sartorial requirements for day-trippers to the east were not so stringent. I was wearing blue Staprest GI pants bought in an army surplus store, a shiny green three-button jacket and a pair of sunglasses, which the guard told me to remove when it was my turn to stand before him in the kiosk.

I slapped a DM 5 coin down on the Formica next to my passport. This was the entrance fee, the price of a one-day visa. The border guard flicked a bead of sweat from his forehead. His green shirtsleeves were rolled up. Angled above head height in the narrow passageway was a mirrored strip facing the guard. Having glanced at the mirror to establish I was not concealing anything behind my back, he addressed my eyes.

The long hard stare from the guards had ceased to bother me. I had found it unnerving the first time, a uniformed stranger searching my eyes for a full ten seconds, but anything becomes normal in time. I remembered Pint telling me I must stare right back into their eyes and not be cowed. I adopted this method for a while, till it began to seem childish. The guards, like me, were only doing their job. In any case, were not eyes the window of the soul? The psychology of the ten-second glare was tainted by romance, I thought, standing before the guard for one more minute. He tapped the keys of his computer, then mumbled into a black telephone. The guard smoked his Club right down to its flimsy filter and crushed it swiftly in the Bakelite ashtray.

He stamped my visa and pressed a button which made a dull ring signifying the grey metal door could be shoved open. I walked along the corridor to another kiosk where a woman sat behind glass exchanging western money for eastern money. Day-trippers had to change DM 25. The 20 mark notes of both currencies were green. The eastern note was decorated with children holding hands and carrying satchels on their backs. The western note had a more formal arrangement of violin and bow and oboe. It was about twice the size of its eastern equivalent.

Eastern money was white, like thin typing paper. Western money was thicker, creamier, water-marked. To western hands it did feel more valuable. There were plenty in the east, too, who thought the money of the Deutsche Bundesbank was beautiful compared to the more paltry productions of the Staatsbank der DDR. Personally, I had never been much impressed by money's pretence to embody value, hopeless in its way as the clock's campaign to pacify time, but then again I was usually broke and late.

I had no strong feelings on the relative aesthetic merits of the paper money published by the competing systems, but I did somehow prefer the eastern coins, which were so light they didn't wear holes in your pockets or spoil the line of your jacket. The woman at the cash kiosk smiled pleasantly as she handed over my eastern currency in a plastic wallet. The final chore was to walk the twelve-yard gauntlet to the exit, past two guards picking on people at random to search and question. I had six records for Tommy I had bought in a record shop on the Kurfürstendamm. I carried them in a plastic bag. There was no point trying to conceal these things.

Shlepping pop music through the border, I had in the past been stopped and questioned. I always said the records were for Georg Karger, Johnny's father. He was the leading musicologist in the GDR and had written a number of distinguished books. Georg, I had told the guards on a number of occasions, was preparing a paper on new western music. The guards knew I was lying, but they didn't much care. The name of Georg Karger was an alibi for both myself and the guards. Such things were international.

Officially, it was illegal for citizens of the GDR to even talk to western journalists, but Georg was an august intellectual, a 77-year-old Party member who had founded East Berlin's first academy of music. He was not vulnerable to charges of subversive relationships with westerners. He had befriended Bertolt Brecht and Hanns Eisler after he came to Berlin from Vienna in 1929. He found a job as a choirmaster and in the evenings accompanied Helene Weigl, Brecht's wife, on the piano. One night in 1933 when they were performing at a workers' club in Wedding the SS arrived and broke up the show. Brecht and

Helene Weigl fled the next day. Georg was given the key to their apartment so he could rescue some of their belongings. He stayed a few more weeks before leaving for Vienna. Back in his home town Georg worked round the clock for the Communist Party. There were street-battles between the communists and the private army of Prince Starhemberg. Austria seemed on the brink of revolution. Kim Philby arrived in Vienna in 1933 and promptly fell in love with one of Georg's best friends, Lizi Friedman. The three of them were all involved in the Vienna uprising of February 1934. In four days of fighting 1,000 were killed, the left was defeated and Georg was slung in jail. He had to share a cell with two Austrian Nazis. (Dr Engelbert Dollfuss, the four-foot-eleven Austrian dictator, was taking the advice of his ally Mussolini and locking up both communists and Nazis.) Georg had his head stuck down the latrine by the Nazis and was made to sing the Horst Wessel song. Georg was a Jew. His parents bribed an official to secure his release and Georg was aided in his flight from Vienna by a glamorous young communist who wore a fur coat to deceive the cops. Georg escaped from Vienna through the sewers like in *The Third Man*. He never talked about his time in prison to anyone but his wife, Florence, whom he met in London.

I did not need to invoke the tumultuous life of Georg Karger that Sunday afternoon. A bottle of Johnny Walker in one plastic bag, the six LPs in the other, I walked past the two pairs of eyes paid to look suspicious. Two lines from the chorus of a song I had heard that morning on the radio had stuck in my mind: 'Wouldn't it be nice to be in your shoes . . . The grass is always greener over there.'

I didn't much like the tune, but I hummed it nonetheless.

Waiting for friends or relatives or lovers there was, as always, a small expectant huddle, three-deep, around the wooden barrier facing the last door between the west and the east. Like speeded-up film of plants inclining to the sun, the heads of the waiting crowd stretched towards each new emerging face, the way such gatherings do at railway stations and airports the world over. I strolled alone into the sunshine.

A tram the colour of vanilla ice cream was clanging its way down the centre of the street towards the hump-backed bridge across the Spree. It made a stop at Bertolt Brecht Platz and then disappeared in the direction of Wedding in West Berlin, Red Wedding as it was known in the twenties when Brecht was writing his Berlin poetry: 'A talk about trees is almost a crime. Because it implies silence about so many horrors.'

The street was wide and clean and, compared to the west, empty of cars. I kept my sunglasses in my pocket, I got stared at enough as it was. My clothes betrayed my identity: *westie*. A middle-aged man in a check jacket sidled alongside and asked if I wanted to change any deutschmarks. I shook my head.

'Alles klar,' he grunted, walking away.

Both kinds of Berliners, westies and zonies in the respective pejoratives, said 'alles klar' so much that its sense became somehow inverted. Nothing was very clear. I looked up at the Tele-Tower, the highest building in all Berlin. Its concrete pillar was like a symmetrical tree-trunk, topped by a glittering globe made from top-grade West German steel. Inside the globe was a restaurant that completed one revolution every hour and did a brisk trade among East European tourists. Its convex windows afforded the best view those tourists would ever get of the west, the stranded piece of the west that was the other half of the city, the swirling neon advertisement for the west in the heart of the GDR.

Another reason for not wearing the sunglasses was this absence of neon glare, the absence too of that blitzing array of self-satisfied white teeth and suggestive eyes that stared like whores from billboards in the west.

A red fire engine raced down the street ringing its bell. West Berlin fire engines were dayglo pink and possessed an electronic scream that stopped the heart. I must stop doing this, I thought. Every single thing was mirrored and echoed in an undeclared war of buildings, cars, clothes, flags, food, music and street-signs. But I must stop seeing two fire engines when there is only one.

I picked my way through the crowds of tourists milling around between Humboldt University and the Memorial to the Victims of Fascism and Militarism. Bayonets fixed in their rifles, two statuesque soldiers stood alongside two of the six stone pillars supporting the tomb's classical façade. The same dead soldier had embraced many causes in his time. Before the war this had been a tomb to the unknown warrior of the Third Reich. The dead were very adaptable.

Across the street two pigeons were perched on the roof of the Opera House, bombed in the war and rebuilt twenty years later. Pigeons could pick and choose between the systems, but overwhelmingly they chose the west and it puzzled me why any pigeons should remain in the much cleaner east. Perhaps these pigeons kept their homes in the east and went scavenging in the west, as many small businessmen did in the days before Ulbricht built his Wall.

Western trash was an important foreign currency earner for the GDR. Around four million cubic metres of rubbish was driven annually from West to East Berlin in a deal worth DM 1.5 billion to the state-owned refuse company. I had worked for twelve months as a dustman, I was interested in such matters. I knew that 100 million cubic metres of western shit was drained each year into the GDR at a cost of DM 12 million to West Berlin.

Crossing the Marx-Engels bridge to Museum Island, I decided those pigeons operating in the communist sector must have calculated that though the pickings were lean in the east, the competition was minimal.

Since the age of three I had had a phobia about birds. I could never associate flapping wings with freedom, much less with peace, and I hated all those corny photographs of birds flying across the Berlin Wall. Flapping wings, desperate and trapped, belonged to the nightmares of my childhood. Hawks and doves, the militarists and the pacifists, shared the same flapping imagery. When the Americans assumed control of Tempelhof airport they took down the stone swastikas but left the stone eagles standing.

I sucked the last drag from my Club and stuck the butt in one of the sand-filled maroon bins provided for such a purpose. When in Rome.

The baroque dome of the restored cathedral on Museum Island was reflected in the mirrored-bronze windows of the Palace of the Republic, nicknamed the lampshop on account of the multitude of lights suspended from its ceiling. The mirrored-bronze theme was further elaborated in the Swedish-built Palasthotel the other side of the Spree. It was a style of architecture I associated with American soap opera, fairy-tale millionaires, helicopter shots of Hyatt Hotels that shimmered like stars. *Dallas* was one of the most popular programmes in East Berlin. Since 1974 Honecker had abandoned the doomed project of trying to convince GDR citizens that they should not tune their televisions to the western stations.

I reminded myself I should ask Tommy what he thought about East Berlin's infatuation with reflecting-glass buildings. For the last ten years Tommy had been part of a team of architects working on a new town called Biesdorf-Marzahn that was being built on the outskirts of the city. The last I'd heard, Tommy was thinking of joining the Party. Whether or not I could also ask him about that depended on who else was at his house, I thought, hurrying past the Neptune Fountain. Children splashed naked beneath the gargoyles. A young soldier in shirtsleeves walked hand in hand with his girlfriend. She wore the kind of cotton frock I had seen my mother wearing in photographs. The couple recalled the romantic interlude of some war film, the lull before the storm. (The soldier would get killed in action, the girl would cry, but the cause would be won, the flags would wave and probably the girl would fall in love again.)

Farther along, beyond two oblong beds of red flowers, were two parallel water displays. Each pool had sixty jets of water in three stepped rows of twenty. The arcs of water rose and fell in perfect harmony. Around the pools were steel-framed chairs furnished with strips of white plastic. Some people sat gazing at the symmetrical cascade. Others, eyes closed, uplifted their faces to the sun.

Two skateboarders were showing off on the concrete slopes that buttressed the foot of the Tele-Tower. A portable tape recorder, propped up against a rubbish bin, was playing 'Relax' by Frankie Goes To Hollywood.

From a distance the figures strolling in the vast concrete plain of the Alexanderplatz looked like the stick-people in architects' drawings. Teenagers were skylarking around by the World Clock, the circular meeting place that told the time in a dozen different zones. In East Berlin it was 3.17. The Centrum department store was closed, but a party of Polish tourists was staring wide-eyed at a window display of stereo equipment. The GDR had the highest standard of living of any of the communist states and the five-storey Centrum showcased this superiority.

I once met a black GI from Michigan in the café at the Centrum. He said he had kicked a piece out of that fucking Wall to take back home. He couldn't have kicked a piece out of the concrete slab Wall so I suppose his memento had been extracted from that part of the border which was still comprised of house façades and garden walls. I walked into Alexanderplatz station. What had happened to the GI's fragment of brick or plaster? Was it standing on a mantelpiece in a Michigan apartment? Did the GI make a habit of telling all his friends the story behind the innocent-looking piece of Berlin debris? Did his friends make jokes behind his back? I paid 20 pfennigs for my U-Bahn ticket and boarded the yellow train bound for Pankow.

I tried to ignore the stares I seemed to be getting. Some of these stares were hostile, but most were just curious, especially as I had taken out the small black-and-red bound notebook that was made in China and bought in Kreuzberg. In it I wrote that the train had just left Rosa Luxemburg Platz, that the woman on the wooden seat next to me was reading a plain white paperback edition of *One Hundred Years of Solitude*, that I was helplessly in love with Laura and vaguely wished I wasn't. Laura was still in London. I spoke to her most nights in one of the yellow telephone kiosks, by the Imbiss dispensing various kinds of wurst with chips and mayonnaise, at the entrance to Gneisenaustrasse U-Bahn. Gneisenau was a general who also had a battleship named after him. The house where I was staying had no telephone and no television and the door was never locked, which had concerned me at first, till I decided an unlocked door was a good thief-fooling bluff. Unlocked doors meant the residents were home. Unlocked doors, the more I thought about it, were a more effective deterrent than locked doors. It's an upside down world. The inhabitants of this unlocked Kreuzberg house included two sisters from Heidelberg, a taxi driver who doubled as a dope dealer, an expatriate Tamil guerrilla, an actor, an orphan who worked as a magazine designer and a Peruvian woman who claimed to be pursued by magicians. Three punks from Copenhagen were also in temporary residence. Soon we would all be joined by Laura.

'The grass is always greener over there . . .' The syrupy synthesiser tinkle of that same seductive tune, haunting as an advertising jingle, caused my head to beat in time, my mouth to murmur the words. Everywhere I went I carried this luggage of western noise. The train gasped for breath as it came to a halt at Senefelder Platz. I gathered up my plastic bags.

Lining the walls of the underground tunnel were anti-war posters, the prize-winning entries to a nationwide competition. One showed a baby's face in a gunsight. Past all the other collages of missiles and mushroom clouds, I walked along the platform and up the steps into the fresh air.

Tommy lived in Kollwitzstrasse on the fourth floor of a five-storey tenement block overlooking Käthe Kollwitz Platz. In the square children were playing table tennis on concrete tables, swinging from the wooden climbing frame, sitting in the sandpit with their buckets and spades and sunhats. Bikes scrunched across the gravel. In a dozen different games yellow footballs marked with green octagons were thwacked by hand and foot.

Presiding over this Sunday afternoon babble was the stern black statue of Käthe Kollwitz, a member of the Berlin Secession school of artists at the turn of the century, the time when these tenements were hastily raised to house the labour required for Berlin's booming iron and steel works, electrical and chemical plants and textile factories. The year that Kollwitz died, 1945, was also the year these tenements received their bullet wounds. The buildings were most pock-marked at the street corners, where the fighting had been fiercest in the eleven days and nights of the Battle for Berlin.

Walking up the wooden staircase, I felt again the pangs of guilt. My friendship with Tommy had been useful to me. I had written about him before and I would do so again.

Tommy opened the door. His wan smile recognised the complications and temporarily cast them aside. He placed his arm round my shoulder and rubbed his cheek against mine. I handed him the plastic bags and he set them down on the floor without inspecting the contents. Tommy always felt ambiguous about presents from the west. He appreciated the records, but he had no intention of drooling over the shiny artefacts and it depressed him that so many of his compatriots demeaned themselves and their system by expressing excessive gratitude to westerners bearing gifts. He wiped the thin black hair from his eyes.

One of the records I had brought was by Nina Hagen, an old friend of his. She had made a name for herself in the seventies as the punk rocker from East Berlin. Like most of his friends, she had fled to the west, where she was managed by Johnny's ex-wife, a beautiful Bulgarian of gypsy ancestry.

Tommy enjoyed music and painting and films from the west. Yet unlike most of Johnny's old friends from East Berlin he had decided to remain in what was for him the better Germany. The west was such a force in his life, he had often said, but it was a force outside his control. More than hatred he felt frustration at the west. *Frust*. The word has more power in German.

Our friendship was tainted by this: I could come to see Tommy but he couldn't come to see me.

His wife, Vera, came dancing down the hallway. Her long brown curls fell loose halfway down her back. She wore a pink T-shirt and baggy white jeans. Though she had been to art college and had once hoped to become a sculptor, she was happy enough modelling for East German fashion magazines. The money was quite good and it left her plenty of time for the children.

'The house is full of westerners this afternoon,' Tommy said, smiling, to Vera.

'*Full* of westerners?' I said.

'Yeah. Johnny is here too. And Astrid,' said Vera, leading the way into the high-ceilinged living-room.

Its white walls were hung with Tommy's paintings, palaces in bright colours tottering towards the sky, psychedelic landscapes, empty yellow deserts. A series of lithographs called *Spiral City* showed three circular Babylons disappearing into the clouds.

The radio of the Hitachi stereo was tuned to British Forces Broadcasting Services. Posh English voices were droning on about this and that. An announcer interrupted the show to say there had been some excitement at Lords. Johnny shook his head in faint amusement.

It was no surprise to meet up with Johnny, I knew he was spending a few days with his parents in Grünau, fifteen miles away, but I had not expected to see Astrid. She had been a student with Tommy and Johnny at Weimar in the late sixties. Caught trying to escape to West Berlin on a train from Prague, she had spent eighteen months in prison and had then been bought out by the West German government. The GDR had no real use for people who wanted to flee to the west and, as a matter of routine, they were offered up for sale after eighteen months or so in jail. Doctors fetched the highest price. Astrid had been living in West Berlin for ten years. She wanted to be a photographer but meanwhile was working as a cinema usherette.

Asleep in a pram on the iron balcony facing Käthe Kollwitz Platz was Tommy and Vera's three-month-old son. The balcony was overgrown with potted plants. It looked out towards the maple trees shading the square. I remembered Johnny saying all his friends in East Berlin were married with children and all his friends in West Berlin were single and childless.

Their six-year-old daughter was rearranging the decor in the doll's house Tommy had built for her in the corner of the room. Stuck to the roof of the doll's house was a paper GDR flag on a lollipop stick.

'Why the flag?' I said to Tommy.

He shrugged and asked what I wanted to drink. Tommy never said much.

Looking again at his collection of beetles and butterflies, mounted behind glass cases, I wondered if Tommy still felt like an anarchist with brakes. That's what he said the first time I met him, in 1979. He went now to get more beer from the fridge. When he came back he thanked me quietly for the records. He was particularly pleased with the two LPs by King Sunny Ade, the Nigerian musician who had about thirteen wives. I said the Hawaiian guitars made it sound a bit like the music piped into the elevators of western hotels.

Astrid sat talking with Johnny about her latest photographic project, an exhibition on the theme of death for which she had

been photographing a sheep's skull against a number of Berlin
backdrops: the shelves of supermarkets and the seats of cars, in
beds and rubbish bins, on buses and trains. Since leaving East
Germany she had been back just twice to see her family, who lived
in a small town called Gotha near the border with West Germany.
Her father was a history teacher.

With her broad shoulders, slim hips and aquiline face, Astrid
resembled one of those models that artists sketch for the fashion
pages of newspapers and magazines. Her red hair was cut short
and asymmetrical. Her boyfriend in West Berlin had also studied
architecture with Tommy and Johnny at Weimar. He had been
with Astrid on that train from Prague twelve years ago. He had
also spent eighteen months in jail.

This was Astrid's first visit to East Berlin in ten years. She was
entertaining the company with stories about the boredom
attendant on being a cinema usherette, stories too about the other
shitty work she had done in the west, cleaning, waitressing, the
usual kind of jobs women did to subsidise some other aspiration,
writer, artist, actress, whatever.

Listening to these anecdotes was a friend of Tommy's I had
never met before. He was a film writer. In a whispered aside
Astrid hinted he was not to be trusted, but the stranger seemed
friendly enough. His name was Wolfgang. He wore a blue zipped
jumper, white jeans and baseball boots.

'Easterners in West Berlin stick together. Same as the Turks,' he
said, running a finger across his stubble. 'Or so I've heard.'

Astrid said most of her friends in the west were originally from
West Germany.

'West Berlin is full of exiles anyway,' she said. 'Whether from
East Germany or West Germany, it doesn't make much difference. Most of the people I know there don't know where I come
from. My story's not important. It doesn't matter where I come
from.'

Astrid neglected to mention that her lover in the west was
originally from the east. It did matter where people came from,
even in West Berlin, which was a sort of halfway house between
the two Germanies. (The first conversation I ever had in Berlin
was with a taxi driver who said he came to West Berlin from West

Germany to escape the German in himself.) I had met East Berliners exiled in West Berlin who had never been to West Germany, though they had all been to London and Paris. And Wolfgang was right. The eastern exiles did stick together. For the last ten years Astrid's boyfriend, Pius, had shared a flat in the west with a man he met on the Praktika camera production line of an East German prison.

I said the escape from nationality was as doomed in its way as the escape from class. We could only remake ourselves from the existing materials. We were all prisoners of our past.

'Here there are no classes,' said Wolfgang. 'It's beautiful. In the state built upon the philosophy whose central tenet is contradiction, it is now officially proclaimed that contradictions no longer exist.'

This was one of the reasons people suspected Wolfgang. He was too outspoken. He criticised the GDR too often, too loudly, and he was being too friendly with me, a westerner he had never met before. Paranoia was functional in East Berlin: the suspicion of a spy was effective as a spy. Anyone like Wolfgang, seemingly untouched by paranoia, was automatically under suspicion. By his own account Wolfgang had nothing to lose. It had been five years since a screenplay of his had been made into film. He had applied officially to leave the GDR. He said the state continued to pay him, 1,000 marks a month, because the state did not want to lose its intellectuals to the west.

Tommy had no appetite for such discussions. He was in the kitchen preparing the dinner. In the five years I had been coming to visit, Vera had never yet cooked dinner. Tommy enjoyed cooking. He slowly stirred the vegetable soup with a blackened wooden spoon.

Like Wolfgang, Tommy had suffered his disappointments at work. Designs he had prepared for the shopping centre at Biesdorf-Marzahn had been quashed by his superiors, much of his time had been wasted, but he had stuck to the task and he was still pleased enough with the results. Biesdorf-Marzahn was going to be a significant advance upon all the ten-storey blocks built in the sixties from prefabricated parts. Architects in the east were fucked up by bureaucracy, he said, but architects in the west were fucked up by money and competition. Tommy didn't see the point in exchanging one form of sadness for another. Tommy was staying put.

The view from the kitchen window was of a Jewish cemetery, beautifully overgrown. The one synagogue in East Berlin was also in this neighbourhood, just round the corner from Käthe Kollwitz Platz. Since 1969 it had been without a rabbi. Only 400 orthodox Jews were left in East Berlin and most of them were pensioners. There was one kosher butcher's. Tommy inspected the progress of the curry. In the living room Wolfgang was railing against the apparatchiks who controlled the arts, but Tommy preferred to thicken and spice the yellow sauces that ran like quicksand round the chicken pieces. Tommy had eyes for the dark gaps between people's words and thoughts. He knew that friends of his with a yen for the west spoke of freedom and daydreamed of BMWs. Tommy thought the west was a well-dressed whore seeking out people's lowest common denominator. I respected his sadness, his disgust.

The overgrown Jewish cemetery visible from the kitchen window reminded Tommy of another reason for his choosing this Germany. On 30 June 1946 there was a referendum in Saxony, in the Soviet zone, in which 77.7 per cent of the electorate voted to expropriate the war criminals and the Nazi industrialists. In that same year in the western zone Dr Hans Maria Globke was released from jail. A civil servant in the Ministry of the Interior, Globke had risen quickly through the ranks after the Nazis came to power. He drafted the Nuremberg Race Laws. In 1948 Konrad Adenauer appointed Globke as his state secretary. Born-again Nazis flourished everywhere in the West German civil service and judiciary. The convicted directors of Krupp and I. G. Farben were not detained overlong in Landsberg jail. As far as the Americans were concerned, releasing Nazi industrialists at the end of the forties was a small price to pay in the fight against communism. The unbroken chain of Nazi command in West Germany had been well documented in books, but had somehow never received the publicity it deserved in the west. Tommy knew all this.

I had read somewhere that those preparing the next holocaust should be tried now, for there would be no courts of law in the world they would create. *The war criminals of the future should be tried now.* I mentioned this notion to Tommy. He nodded slowly.

'Why not?' he said, smiling.

Johnny poked his head round the door to say that he, Astrid and Wolfgang were going for a stroll and did I want to join them? I left Tommy alone in the kitchen.

All along the street silvery perms craned out of the tenement windows. Some of the old women were settled in for a long afternoon's street-gazing and had made themselves nice and comfortable, their elbows propped on cushions by the window-sills. They drank coffee and smoked cigarettes and held brief conversations with passers-by. It was just the same in the old neighbourhoods of West Berlin. Both halves of the city had disproportionately high numbers of pensioners, mostly war widows. (Between 1939 and 1945 the population of Berlin shrank from 4.3 million to 2.8 million.)

Johnny and Astrid walked ahead.

'These buildings haven't been touched since 1900 and now it's too late. They're damp from the basement up to the first floor,' Wolfgang said.

Faded signs for bars and shops, painted advertisements for beer and cigarettes, were still legible on the ground floor of these ashen tenements. Out on the road maroon skips were piled high with coal bricks, shining like gems in the sun.

Wolfgang was born in Leipzig, which he said was one of the dirtiest cities in the world. He was the father of a four-year-old girl called Lilli, but he had never married. Conscripted into the National People's Army, he was discharged after three months because he was allergic to the leather rim of the helmet, he said. An injury sustained when he was a child made him unable to wear anything wrapped tightly round his head. Somehow the story sounded too good to be true.

'Last night I dreamt that London was destroyed by bombs,' he said. 'I have always thought that nothing can happen to me which I have not already imagined. Perhaps the dreams are a kind of psychological preparation.'

I was having apocalyptic dreams about twice a week in those

days. Which amounted to saturation pre-publicity, I thought. Was a time I dreamed innocently of scoring goals in football matches.

Twitching with electricity, the overhead cables announced the arrival of another tram down the centre of the street. Berlin was the home of the streetcar, the first electrical model having been tested here in 1881, eleven years after the city became the capital of the new nation called Germany.

In West Berlin the tramlines had all been dug up, but the east was more poor and less fashion-conscious. Steam trains still in service on the East German railway system were a tourist attraction. The four-day sightseeing holidays were particularly popular with British enthusiasts.

I had often thought it would make a good magazine feature, the western buffs armed with cameras and tape recorders, riding the communist trains. It had good headline potential: GOING LOCO IN EAST GERMANY? STEAM RISES BEHIND THE IRON CURTAIN? Thoughts of trains were interrupted by Johnny asking if I fancied an ice cream. Yes please.

The ice-cream parlour was at the corner of Prenzlauer Allee and Sredzkistrasse. The two servers wore red and white frilly frocks with matching caps. One of the servers was in her forties, her dyed blonde hair stacked in a bouffant, a style from the same period as the decor: the net curtains, the stainless-steel counter, the five orange lights encased in black buds. Outside, teenage couples licked their ices astride motorbikes parked on the cobblestone street.

'Brilliant, this commie ice cream,' I said to Johnny. Johnny agreed. Ice cream in East Berlin was still made from traditional recipes. Astrid said she didn't much care for the ice cream produced in either system. We wiped our mouths clean and headed back to Tommy's. Chatting to Wolfgang en route, I said Tommy sometimes made me feel guilty. He was so honourable, he made me feel dirty by comparison.

'Oh, he makes me feel guilty too,' Wolfgang replied, offering me a cigarette. 'Sometimes I go round there and we just sit for hours, hardly talking. But he is really one of my best friends. He's someone you can trust. But, you know, when I told him I had applied to go to the west, he cried. I didn't know what to do.'

If it was true, Wolfgang should not have told me that, some things should remain private between friends. In any event I found the story hard to believe. Tommy was not the sort to make a public exhibition of his grief.

A wooden caravan of the kind gypsies once lived in had been abandoned near Käthe Kollwitz Platz. On its side Pink Floyd was written in drippy white paint.

'Pink Floyd,' mused Wolfgang. 'The east is always ten years behind the west, right?'

I nodded without enthusiasm, but it was true: journeying east was like retracing your steps. You remembered as a child drawing cars like these with curved roofs, bulbous bonnets, enamel radiator grilles like jagged smiles.

These Trabants and Wartburgs were luxury items in the GDR. Only people who were well connected, or who had access to western money, could purchase cars as and when they wished. Most East Germans spent years on the waiting lists. Of the 200,000 motor vehicles registered in East Berlin half were motorcycles or mopeds. West Berlin, with twice the number of people, had more than four times as many cars, 465,981 at the last count. In 1977 road accidents accounted for 123 dead and 3,758 injured in East Berlin, 286 dead and 17,342 injured in West Berlin. Why were these events still called accidents when there were only slight annual variations in the rate of death?

Dinner that night was eaten off white plates bearing the Meissen cross. Most of the china made in that medieval town was painted in an unimaginative range of baroque designs, but Jimmy's father was a potter at Meissen and these plain white plates were seconds. Much nicer than the painted ones, everyone agreed. We ate the soup and curry, drank Bulgarian white wine, chilled. Johnny proposed a toast to international friendship. He was only half-joking.

'Deutsch-Amerikanische Freundschaft,' murmured Tommy. German-American Friendship, this was the name of a West German pop group. Humming a snatch from one of their tunes, Tommy collected his thoughts.

'The west can afford the arms race,' he said finally. 'But the east can only keep up by being on a permanent war economy. It's sucking us dry. Even in East Germany, the richest of the socialist countries, we have all these shortages. The west knows the arms race will eventually bankrupt the east. The Soviet Union has a *material* interest in disarmament. Nothing to do with idealism, it's a practical necessity. Otherwise there will eventually be nothing to eat in the socialist countries. The Americans must know that. Why else do they start Star Wars now?'

Tommy's little speech must have been gestating for quite some time, but he had delivered it in his usual downbeat way, his tobacco-cut voice low and monotone, his fork rearranging the yellow remains of his curry. He left the table to fetch some more wine from the kitchen. Wolfgang said he had never heard Tommy talk so much.

Vera was adamant that the rest of the evening should not be overshadowed by talk of war. She brightly announced we were all going to a party. People would go mad if they dwelt too long on the horrors of this world. You're a long time dead. Che sarà, sarà. Clichés, in both systems, comforted like babies' dummies. Friendship, Vera said, should be a matter for celebration. Our own friendships, she implied, constituted a little victory.

Conversation meandered pleasantly enough through jobs, books, television, music, holidays, clothes, children. Vera breast-fed her baby son while Johnny told an East German joke, about an NVA regiment on parade. For the purposes of the joke a general was striding along the ranks, inspecting his men, when one of the soldiers farted. The general glared at the farter and said, 'Hey you!' Obeying the beckoning finger of his superior, the soldier marched towards the general, who then whispered in his ear, 'Where did you get the beans?'

Wolfgang laughed more loudly than Tommy. It was just gone nine. The baby-sitter was due any minute and Vera went to get changed. A radio news bulletin was announcing the latest list of countries to join the boycott of the capitalist Olympics in Los Angeles.

Tommy felt sure Honecker was most distressed at having to toe the Russian line and withdraw from the Games. East Germans were proud of their athletes, who they had fully expected to win more gold medals than either the USA or the USSR. Where athletics was concerned the GDR was a match for the super-powers. By way of smalltalk I mentioned I had been in Moscow for the 1980 Olympics. A few frayed memories were replayed. Getting drunk on the overnight train from Kiev to Moscow. Watching the Olympics on the black-and-white TV in my hotel room. Playing football with some university students up at the Lenin Hills. A strange night drinking Budweiser at a disco in the American Embassy. Another night almost getting beaten up by a burly Muscovite who emptied my packet of Winston on the floor and squared up to me at the bar. Being stood up by a ballerina in that same bar. Being harangued by a soldier outside the Lenin Stadium. He said I could not sit on the step and eat ice cream. I could stand up and eat the ice cream or else I could sit down without my ice cream. I could not sit *and* eat ice cream. At the time the soldier made me mad. In retrospect he was probably fed up with all the arrogant westerners flaunting their disrespect for Soviet protocol, sneering at the Russian way, ostentatiously crossing roads when the red man was lit on the pedestrian traffic signals, that kind of thing. The soldier was about the same age as me. I still sometimes wondered why the ballerina never turned up.

Red Army soldiers in East Berlin were no more popular than GIs in West Berlin, but the jokes told about the respective armies of occupation reflected jarringly different prejudices. The Russian soldier was a five-foot-six peasant standing on street corners trying to sell his watch for the price of a bottle of vodka. The American soldier was an ignoramus with a drug habit and a flashy car. All GIs in West Berlin were entitled to ship over one car from the USA and the army footed the bill for the freight costs, a fact which told its own story about the anthropology of the American automobile, its power and beauty, its death-dealing sex appeal. The baby-sitter arrived at 9.30. In two and a half hours I would have to be back at the border.

Walking to the party, Tommy was describing a gig he had recently attended at the Church of Our Saviour in Rummelsburg, a few miles away. Gigs in churches were always unofficial, advertised by word-of-mouth only. Although the security police never arrested anyone inside the church grounds, there were always plenty of Staasis at such events, mingling with the audience and maybe taking photographs.

'In the front row of pews there were about twenty Staasis,' said Tommy. 'You know how they always stick out a mile in their tight white T-shirts and moustaches? Well there was this group playing a mixture of R&B and soul and one of the Staasis got really into it, jumping up and down and singing along. The other cops kept trying to restrain him, but eventually they had to escort him from the church.'

Johnny chuckled. He had been something of a pop star himself in East Berlin in the sixties. And he had been with me at that same Lutheran church the previous spring. 'Remember that night?' he said.

'Of course,' I said, thinking back to the band called Klassenkrampf (it means class cramp but sounds like class war) performing a song whose chorus went, 'No Nazi pigs, Nazi pigs, Nazi pigs in East Berlin.' The lead singer wore a leopard-skin leotard and fishnet tights.

Tommy led the way up the polished wooden staircase and into the party. It was in another of those tenement blocks that had been partly colonised by intellectuals. Like Tommy's flat, it had high ceilings, tall windows, pre-war furniture salvaged from junk shops and dead grandparents. The white walls were hung with paintings. Wallpaper, for the intellectuals of both Berlins, was a *faux pas* commited by the less fortunate. Intellectuals preferred their walls to advertise the talent of friends and associates.

For a birthday present Tommy had brought the hostess an old silver teaspoon tied with a frayed fragment of yellow silk. He presented this gift with mock gravitas, bowing like a subject to a queen, and she placed it on an oak table with all the other birthday presents: the bouquets of flowers, the hardback books, the signed paintings and photographs, the bottles of sparkling white wine.

Everyone shook hands with everyone else, another custom which had died out in West Berlin, at least among the circles in which I had been moving since that first innocent visit in 1979. (Why were people always described as moving in circles?) All the guests were in their twenties and thirties. Mostly they were dressed in black. With the exception of Tommy and Wolfgang the men had short hair. A couple of them also wore black eye-liner and eye-shadow. The women's hair was cut in bobs, short at the back and longer at one side than the other. What differentiated the party from similar gatherings in the west was an absence of the cultivated moodiness that seemed the natural accompaniment of black clothes the other side of the border. Smiling was less unfashionable in East Berlin. People helped themselves to sausage soup and spargel fricassee from the kitchen and afterwards they washed up the plates.

I needed all these clues, washing plates and smiling at strangers. No city could be judged by what its rulers said or what was written by the scribes who were in the pockets of the rulers. Recruiting the same words to their cause, both capitalists and communists spoke of freedom, democracy, justice, words were adaptable as dead soldiers. Critics on both sides used different combinations of the same words, too. Oppression. Injustice. Brutality. Inhuman. Imperialist. Warmonger. I had been chanting the slogans since I was about seventeen, but now I needed more detail. A song by the Doors was playing on the Japanese stereo. It was followed by the West German novelty single, 'Da-da-da'.

'Fifty per cent more surrealism,' Wolfgang said.

The party was warming up, the guests starting to dance on the varnished wooden floor. The tongues were loosened, the voices louder. The music was turned up. The neighbours didn't complain.

For Astrid the party had brought back too much too quick. Her eyes kept fastening on another familiar face. Another embrace would ensue, another slightly embarrassed conversation. Everyone knew she had gone to the west many moons ago, but no one asked how or why. To these East Germans who had once known Astrid, she was like someone whose life had been taken prematurely in a car crash. She might reappear in East Berlin maybe twice a lifetime, but for all intents and purposes the friendship was dead. Faced with this ghost of their friend, the party guests asked Astrid polite questions about her work, her flat, the kind of music she was listening to these days.

Astrid replied as cheerfully as she could and only occasionally did her eyes meet theirs in expressions making nonsense of the words, like former lovers who talk about the weather while their eyes smuggle messages.

Johnny was lucky, possessing an Austrian passport. Of all the Berliners I knew, he was the only one who could have his cake and eat it. As a small boy he had flown each year to England with his mother. Alone among his peers, he was able in later life to shop for records and clothes in West Berlin. Johnny had the best of both worlds. There had always been those who had envied him this privilege, but his friends had long since accepted he was a special case. When Johnny went to the west his friends in the east did not feel bereaved. They knew his parents still lived in East Berlin, they knew he would be back for a few weeks every year, and it remained a possibility that one day Johnny would return to the east for good.

He stood now in animated conversation with Tommy. Architecture, romance, politics, Johnny spoke of all three with equal erudition. Sometimes I envied him his sane sophistication, his measured appetites for art and pleasure, his ordered progress through the capitals of Europe. He had, too, his small private income, an inheritance from a grandfather who had composed light operas that were still performed in Austria. Johnny was an only child who had never wanted for anything other than a first language and a home. For him I was a link between his Berlin life and his London life. By befriending his friends I had become attached to the web spun by Johnny. Strung out across the nations and the systems, people stayed in touch through telephone calls, letters, occasional visits. Some strands became so thinly stretched they faded into nothing, but there were always new strands being spun, new people, new telephone numbers.

While people danced to 'Pretty Vacant', the Sex Pistols song which sounds somehow like the Beach Boys, Wolfgang was feeding me more information about himself. If he was some kind of agent, his qualifications for the job were most strange. He had been assistant director on *Mephisto*, which had won all manner of prizes at western film festivals Wolfgang had been unable to attend.

He said he was currently compiling an anthology of poetry written in praise of Stalin. It would be published in West Berlin, by the same small imprint which had recently published an anthology of contemporary German poetry containing three contributions from Wolfgang himself. He had not yet seen the book and he asked if I would mind bringing over a copy some time. No problem, I said.

'Okay. You must contact this friend of mine in West Berlin called Udo,' said Wolfgang, scribbling an address and a telephone number in my notebook. 'Udo used to be a member of Kommune II. Now he's a taxi driver.'

A household of militant students from the Free University of West Berlin, Kommune II was founded in 1967. Another of its six original members was Jan Carl-Raspe, who later went underground into the Red Army Fraction.

'I have no telephone. But when you've got hold of the book from Udo you can ring this number,' Wolfgang said, writing down another seven numerals. 'She's a friend of mine. Tell her when you're coming over. Just say a place and time and I'll see you there.'

Telephone connections between East and West Berlin were re-opened when the Four Power Agreement was signed on 3 September 1971. It was a compromise in the battle of interpretation over the status of Berlin. The three western powers argued that all Berlin was still subject to Four-Power control. The Soviet Union maintained that this should apply only to West Berlin and that the west should recognise East Berlin as the capital of the GDR. The Four Power Agreement established that western soldiers could come and go in the eastern sector without being subject to passport or customs control, that western aeroplanes could fly the airspace above East Berlin in a radius of thirty-two kilometres from the Allied Air Security HQ and that East Berlin citizens could participate in GDR elections. Before the Four Power Agreement the telephone lines had been cut. These days there were 417 cables connecting the two halves of the city. About 22,000 calls were made daily across the border. I told Wolfgang I'd be in touch.

I looked around the room. The food was all finished, as was the polite conversation. The place was teeming with noise and bodies, the Sunday night celebrants too far gone now to worry about Monday morning. Alcohol was a sacrament in both Berlins. I danced to 'I Can't Help Myself' by the Four Tops, sang along with the words.

At 11.45 Astrid tapped me on the shoulder. Standing behind her, Johnny was examining his watch.

'Time to go,' she said. 'Vera's going to drive us to Friedrichstrasse.'

Johnny was staying put. He would remain at the party till around three then drive the fifteen miles to Grünau in his father's white Lada. I shook hands with Johnny, Tommy and Wolfgang and raced after Astrid down the stairs. Vera was waiting in the cream Trabant, the engine running, a high-pitched low-powered splutter.

I felt sick in my stomach, as I always did on these Cinderella chases back to Friedrichstrasse for midnight, having to leave one part of the city for another at a particular time for no particularly good reason, having to flee friends, leaving drink and conversation unfinished. It always made me mad, the tap on the shoulder at a quarter to twelve. I suppose I resented the dash to the border because it reminded me I was a victim too, a victim of my passport, a victim of all the sins committed in my name and others by the people who ran the show, the people who said *we* and presumed to speak for the nations, the people who regulated movement on maps where heroic countries and villainous countries were demarcated by iron curtains. I sat in the back seat of the Trabant, dribbling oaths, breathing deep.

Flat out at 65, the car bumped down the hill towards the Tele-Tower, its mighty concrete pillar lit up like a shaft of sunlight through a break in the clouds.

Winding down the window, I shut my eyes and tasted the cool breeze. It was two minutes past midnight.

'Don't worry,' Vera said. 'The guards don't fuss over the odd minute.'

I wasn't worried. I knew day-trippers from the other side had to be at least thirty minutes late before they were interrogated, asked to supply the names and addresses of those with whom they had been socialising. I wound up the window so Astrid and I could light our cigarettes.

On the pavement outside Friedrichstrasse checkpoint, a steel-and-glass construction known locally as the glasshouse, two grandparents were giving their small grandson a last kiss goodbye. As the old couple took their place in the queue at passport control the mother grasped her son's arm and waved it up and down like a flag. Turning round, the grandparents smiled and waved back. Lovers embraced. Friends solemnly shook hands. Hugs and tears and see you soon. The routine pathos of Sunday night at the border. Kissing Vera, I thanked her for the dinner, the party, the lift, the day. Astrid did the same. Digging passports from pockets, we took our place in the queue.

Going back to the west was always much quicker than entering the east, particularly in these minutes after midnight when the queues reeked of alcohol, unshaven men shouted out loud and the guards, dog-tired in the Formica booths, extracted visas from passports and, after a cursory examination of the face against the photograph, pressed the buttons that opened the grey metal doors. Within five minutes Astrid and I were down on the U-Bahn platform, waiting for the yellow underground train.

Farther along the platform a man in a leather stetson was singing country and western songs on an acoustic guitar. He sang well, except he was drunk and slurring the sibilants. God didn't make the little green applesh. It don't rain in Minneapolish. In the shummertime. As the train charged into the station two green-shirted policemen grabbed him and a third held open the doors when the train was at a standstill. The singer was slung into the carriage, a performance that was repeated with four other winos slumped at different points in the fluorescent-lit tunnel.

The train had come from Tegel, by the lakes in the north, and was bound for Alt-Mariendorf in the south. This was Line 6, coloured purple in the western underground maps. After leaving Tegel the train makes ten stops at western stations and then travels beneath the border, past three stations that are closed down and patrolled by East German border guards. These disused stations still appear on all the U-Bahn maps, the only clue to their non-operational status being the nature of the purple square next to their names. Whereas the western stations are marked by solid squares of purple, the eastern stations on Line 6 are marked by purple squares framing a white blank space, as if the map designer had acknowledged an unfortunate but temporary state of affairs, leaving it so the blank spaces could be coloured solid purple at a moment's notice when the city was re-united. On these same maps the Berlin Wall is an elbow-shaped black line, hatched in grey on the eastern side.

Within this black elbow Friedrichstrasse was the only station on Line 6 coloured solid purple. Its platforms were a piece of the west beneath the east, a piece of the west policed by the east, a piece of the west connected to the other pieces by an underground train that ran north to south. What confused everything was the appropriation of compass points by ideologies, the conflation of metaphorical directions with real ones. In reality parts of West Berlin lay on a more easterly longitude than parts of East Berlin. And vice versa. The Berlin Wall was not a vertical line, but a circular blob, haphazard and higgledy-piggledy like the wanderings of a drunk, like a cell under the microscope.

Carrying its cargo of westerners and advertisements, the yellow train left Friedrichstrasse at 12.23. The plastic seats were all taken. Astrid and I had to stand up, clinging to metal overhead while the train rocked through the tunnel. A woman with dyed blonde hair wore a tight white T-shirt that said LOS ANGELES in red capitals. I went there once, I told Astrid, and a few heads turned. No one else was talking. The iron beat of wheels on track, the coupled carriages creaking like a chain-gang, the flutter of pages turning in newspapers and magazines, the muffled thud of bodies colliding, the whispered apologies, the gasps of the brakes, these were the only noises accompanying the train bound for Alt-Mariendorf.

Some of the passengers' faces were blushed from a day or a weekend spent on the beaches by the lakes. Others, pale from the nightshift, were travelling to work, to bars and bus depots, to offices that needed cleaning, dustbins that needed emptying, all-night peepshows that needed objects of desire.

The train slowed to about 10 m.p.h. as it passed through the ghost of the station that had once been Franzosische Strasse,

Gothic lettering on metal nameplates, black on white, still affixed to the station's walls. Appearing from the gloom, an East German border guard stood on the platform shaking the last drops of water from his blue-and-white mug. Satisfied his mug was clean and dry, he walked along the platform to resume his vigil inside the canvas hutch that served as lookout.

It had been many years since anyone tried to flee East Berlin by jumping on to a moving underground train and maybe the guard in his canvas watchtower sometimes wished this archaic mode of escape would come back into fashion. Firemen I had met in London sat around at night playing cards, cursing fire prevention officers and longing for a decent blaze. The tedium of the night-shift was international. Clattering past another closed-down station, another bored border guard, the train came wheezing to a halt at Kochstrasse, the nearest station to Checkpoint Charlie. The western train was now beneath western earth, the American Sector to be precise.

Nothing had been spoken between myself and Astrid since our brief exchange on the matter of Los Angeles. I was wondering how she felt about her first visit to East Berlin in ten years. Her face betrayed no sadness. Maybe the time spent in prison had taught her to be unsentimental.

She had been in Prague when the Red Army invaded. When she went back to Weimar in East Germany all the students were being forced to sign a declaration supporting the occupation. Astrid refused. In that moment of refusal she knew she was chucking away her future in East Germany. She had planned to become an art teacher, but her refusal meant that even if she was able to continue her studies she would never get a job afterwards. She knew she would escape, knew she would probably get caught and imprisoned, but knew she would end up in the west. Bought out of jail after a two-year sentence, she went first to a refugee camp called Gieben in West Berlin. Her clearest memory of Gieben was being taken in by the door-to-door salesmen who toured the camp selling book subscriptions and life insurance to the newly arrived immigrants. Astrid bought all manner of things she did not want. The west was a mystery. Door-to-door salesmen, she thought, were key players in this mystery. Surely they had some

kind of official function? In due course she would unravel the
puzzle, she figured. Buying things she did not need would appear
less strange. Meanwhile, she signed on the dotted line. After a few
months in Gieben she went to stay with a cousin in Hamburg.
While she was there she received a telephone call from someone
she had known in the GDR. He told her that dozens of people she
knew from the old days were living in West Berlin, she should
come to join them. And she did. The young emigrés shared
apartments, hung out together, had affairs with each other, told
jokes about their childhoods no westerners could understand,
exchanged prison stories and shared anecdotes about the funny
ways of the west. It was years before Astrid got round to
cancelling her book subscriptions and life-insurance policies.

Standing now in the crowded underground car, she looked
every inch the chic West Berliner: razored red hair, black leather
boots, a white-faced woman with a fuck-you gaze calculated to
repel the predatory eyes that swarmed in the U-Bahn. Astrid had
broken with the circle of eastern exiles, that extended family of
immigrants, and many of the people she saw socially these days
knew nothing of her past. She was a cinema usherette who
wanted to be a photographer. She was in her early thirties, she
was childless, she wore black clothes and she went dancing in
nightclubs. What else did anyone need to know? I happened to
know that she and Johnny had been lovers when they were both
students at Weimar. Astrid had been in her first year, Johnny in
his third. How many lovers had there been since? Twenty? Two
hundred? Who cared? It was another accident of history that we
had known too many bodies and shared too many secrets.

'Let's go to the Djungel,' she said as the train drew into
Hallesches Tor station.

I started to protest that I was too tired, but Astrid slapped me
playfully, like a mother chiding a child, and hustled me out of the
door. We changed to Line 1 and travelled five stops to Wittenbergplatz.

'Sunday night's the best night at the Djungel,' she said,
mounting the escalator to the street. This received wisdom, like
other tenets of the nightclub folklore, had a thin rationale, it
being generally held that tourists and West Germans and people

with steady jobs did not go to the Djungel on Sundays. Astrid had said nothing about the excursion into her past. Whatever was running through her mind she had evidently decided she did not want to pursue those thoughts alone in her flat in Charlottenburg. She wanted to go to the Djungel to get the east out of her system.

Hunching our shoulders against the rain, we walked quickly down the street towards the pink Mercedes star revolving on top of the Europa Centre, a complex of shops and cafés housed within concrete for tourists. The pink star dominated the neon skyline of West Berlin, presiding over the blaze of electric light that rose up from all the bars and restaurants and clubs and peepshows congregated in the triangle between Wittenbergplatz, Savignyplatz and Zoo Station. KLM and Cinzano, ITT and Burger King, the fluorescent typographies all joined together in one riotous assembly, projecting their neon message to the sky, to the passengers at the aeroplane windows who addressed their fingers at the glow: the west! The border was a sodium halo ringing the gigantic advertisement that was West Berlin. Outside the halo there was only darkness: the east! Down in the neon furnace the rain trickled down the nape of my neck.

Yellow Mercedes taxis ferried the nighthawks hither and thither. One-man-operated cream double-deckers deposited their loads. Headlights, tail-lights, traffic lights and neon contrived familiar shimmering effects in the bright rain, the druggy swirl of city life on busy wet nights, the mood frozen in a million wide-angled art shots for the tourist brochures, the photographs captioned with humanising metaphors. The city that never sleeps! The pulse! The heartbeat!

'The weather was better under communism,' I said to Astrid as we reached the door to the Djungel. She rang the bell.

The same woman had been on the door at the Djungel since 1979. She wore a black leather mini-skirt. She opened the door just wide enough to get a decent view of prospective customers. Faced with strangers, she looked them up and down expressionlessly for a few seconds before making her decision. It was like facing the guards at the border except that here the dress code was stricter. To those that the girl in black leather deemed too old, too unfashionable, too poor or too fat, she shook her head and said *private* or *full*.

Anyone who looked as though he might belong to the British or American army was also banned. A few years ago the club had been wrecked in a battle between some squaddies and GIs, a bitter encounter which had been broken up finally by the Military Police, Allied soldiers being outside the jurisdiction of ordinary cops. Some squaddies still managed to fool the face-check girl by dressing up like David Bowie in the nearest public toilet to their barracks, taking care to remove their eye make-up before returning to base. French soldiers did not need to resort to such extreme measures. Because they tended to be conscripts, and also because they dressed stylishly and didn't cause trouble, they were more welcome in the nightclubs. West Berlin was sympathetic to conscripts. The city was adopted home for many thousands who had come here in the first place to avoid being drafted into the West German army. Citizens of West Berlin were ineligible for the draft. Uniformed members of the West German army were still banned from the streets, a constitutional hangover from intentions ratified at the 1945 Potsdam conference. Germany would be de-Nazified and disarmed. Berlin would be a de-militarised free city.

Outside the Djungel stood a small group of West German teenagers in rain-sodden pastel casuals. They had been refused admission.

Acknowledging Astrid with a miniscule movement of the eyebrows, the face-check girl opened the door and a flood of noise poured out.

'Every time I come here I swear I'll never come again,' Astrid said, picking her way through the crush till she was able to place one hand on the chrome rail of the bar. 'But where else is there to go?'

She ordered two beers from the skinhead barmaid, who looked about forty and wore a black vest. The harsh-lit bar was long and narrow and led to a small dark dancefloor. Next to a fountain was a circular steel staircase, permanently clogged with people like bits of cork in a corkscrew. The staircase connected to a champagne bar where the richer clientèle sat at white tablecloths and peered down through chrome railings to the throng below.

I met some familiar faces at the bar. A 29-year-old American called Dan briefly interrupted his conversation with the lead singer of Einstürzende Neubauten to say how you doing? Dan had come to Berlin on holiday four years ago and never gone home. He was working as a window-cleaner and still hoping to become a pop star. The lead singer of Neubauten wore a clerical collar and black coat and had a hairstyle like a palm tree. Another Sunday night regular, he was telling Dan about a forthcoming tour of Britain. Neubauten had been popular for some time in both East and West Berlin and were now beginning to attract a following among the disaffected avant garde of other cities. The band made music with industrial tools, pneumatic drills for example.

Neubauten were one of a few dozen West Berlin bands producing a form of alienated white noise known locally as Mauersound, Wallsound, the soundtrack composed in the shadow of a cliché. Mauersound was a homegrown reaction to the syncopated rhythms overlaid by Anglo-American lyrics that provided the background to public life all over West Berlin, the pop music singles flaunting cultural supremacy in a love song. The Internationale lasted three minutes and had a catchy chorus.

A dark-haired girl of about seventeen strode towards the dancefloor wearing a T-shirt that said, after the style of merchandise sold by pop groups on tour, ADOLF HITLER, EUROPEAN TOUR 1939. The list of countries which followed (Austria, Czechoslovakia, Poland, etc.) was written in black and red on white, the colours of the first German flag. The DJ followed up fifteen minutes of disco-funk with the Velvet Underground. *I'm waiting for my man, Twenty-six dollars in my hand.* The price of self-destruction had risen since then. West Berlin was the heroin capital of Europe. A lot of the stuff came into the city from Turkey via Schönefeld airport in East Berlin. GDR customs officials did not possess the drug-detecting dogs of their western equivalents and, in any case, were not overly concerned with heroin being smuggled to the west.

Astrid was on the dancefloor. I stood at the bar talking about nothing in particular to the window-cleaner who wanted to be a pop star. 'Waiting For My Man' was succeeded on the turntable by 'Suffragette City'. Its author, David Bowie, a man with a green and a blue eye, had sought refuge in this town between 1976 and 1978, a period of residence which had breathed new life into the notion of decadent Berlin. Marlene Dietrich, Checkpoint Charlie, David Bowie, the jumbled-up names somehow summarised the city for the millions abroad who vaguely supposed modern Berlin was *Cabaret* plus fifty years, *Cabaret* redesigned against the glamorous backdrop of the Wall. I had watched the film with a Jewish girl who later married a Tel Aviv cop. It made her cry.

At 3.30 Astrid decided to call it a night. She had danced and drunk sufficient. She could now fall straight asleep and resume her western life around lunchtime tomorrow with a café breakfast. Most of the cafés served breakfast up to 6 p.m.

Hustling cigarettes and deutschmarks were three women in their early twenties. Two of them had shaved heads tattooed with spider's webs. The third was a dwarf. The dwarf was the leader. Her voice was gruff, sexless, a woman's voice roughened by tobacco, a boy's voice about to break. She spat out lit cigarettes, bubbled wine all down her front and jumped up and down screaming at the lounge lizards: 'You're all mad. Fucking *mad*!'

Recovering their cool, the Djungel regulars shut their ears to the ranting dwarf. Her two friends enjoyed this phase of the performance, too. The face-check girl had committed a serious error in opening the door of the Djungel to this trio. The management would have words to say on the matter. The dwarf and her sidekicks belonged to the group of outcasts sometimes called City Indians in magazine photo-features. Living in Kreuzberg squats or sleeping rough on the streets, many of them were refugees from West Germany who had no legal status in West Berlin and who therefore lived by stealing and hustling the money required for their smack, their tobacco, their alcohol, their solvents. They made their mute statements by shaving their skulls, slotting metal studs through the holes drilled in their ear lobes, tattooing their faces, slouching the streets with bloody murder in their eyes. They were not peculiar to Berlin – self-mutilated chic had made its mark all over the west – but they seemed peculiarly at home in this theatre, Berlin, Babylon under occupation.

Having tired of her sport, the dwarf led her friends out of the nightclub and ran screaming down Nürnbergerstrasse in the rain.

All the lights were switched on at four. Electric bulbs gloated upon grey faces wincing in the glare. Panda eyes were smudged and showing red. Hair gel had lost its sheen. Lipstick had faded. Dirt had found its home in the cuticles of manicured nails. Fingers sparkled with shards of nicotine. Clothes were stained with drink and sweat.

Wearing the penalties of pleasure, the customers dispersed from the Djungel. Some would continue their search for sex, slake their thirst, dance in darkness, whatever was the reason, at the Cri du Chat, a club that was always more or less empty till 4 a.m. but became busy after five and stayed open till ten. Others walked east down Kleiststrasse for a nightcap at the Café Central. Recently renamed Café Swing, it was still known as the Café Central. It never closed. Its jukebox was oblivious to the passage of nights into days. Its window-display showed tailor's dummies constrained in red and black vinyl.

Usually I had a black coffee and Weinbrand in there on my way home to Kreuzberg, but tonight I wasn't in the mood. Some nights it seemed heroic, the celebration of emptiness that was the *raison d'être* of the Djungel, the Cri du Chat, Café Central and all the other dark and noisy refuges, but tonight it seemed shabby, desperate, like Christmas in prison. Opposite the Café Central, in a scrubby patch of green beneath the iron S-Bahn, a wino was snoring under the slatted shelter of a park bench. It was still raining. I hurried on past an ashen grey confection of Moorish towers that had seen service as a theatre and cinema and was now a concert-hall and discothèque called Metropol. I waited in the bus shelter for the number 19.

The shelter on Nollendorfplatz was spattered with the names of political and pop groups, with the Greens and the Psychedelic Furs, with slogans concluding in exclamations: YANKS OUT! FUCK THE DEVIL! TURKS OUT! It was 5 a.m. and the black was turning to grey. The pink Mercedes star above the Europa Centre was like a memory of another dawn. The Red Army

Fraction star on the bus shelter had almost faded into the brickwork. Taxi drivers slowed down and steered temptingly towards the bus stop. Usually I would have succumbed, but again not tonight. Waiting for the 19 in the rain was my penance.

Watching two Alsatians looting the gutters and litter bins, I tried to remember who told me there were more dogs than people in West Berlin? It was a tough fact to verify, but there were almost four pages of dog classifieds in the yellow pages of the telephone directory: dog-breeders, dog-doctors, dog-food specialists, dog salons for bathing and crimping and manicure. The city was overrun with dogs, with Alsatians to be specific, other breeds being comparatively few and far between. Statistics were unavailable on the relative dog populations of East and West Berlin. Alsatians were valued companions both sides of the border, but by my reckoning capitalist dogs outnumbered communist dogs by at least six to one. The evidence lay stinking on the pavements. Walking round West Berlin everyone kept half an eye open for dogshit. Strangers and tourists had to learn from their errors.

And where was the fucking bus? The number 19 in West Berlin was no more reliable than the number 19 in London on which I travelled from Rosebery Avenue to Cambridge Circus. Having worked as a bus conductor for six months, however, I had always refused to join in those choruses of condemnation that rose habitually from the bus stops. I had been on the receiving end. I had been on the other side.

Lit up like an ocean-liner, the bus swept through the rain. MEHRINGDAMM, it said on its destination board. Walter Mehring was a poet popular in the 1920s which was when Berlin, naughtiest city of the naughty decade, acquired its reputation for the thing called decadence, a euphemism wrapped in silk stockings and reeking of sex. The glass never empty! The night never done! I sat by the window on the upper deck among the sullen congregation of homeward-bound nightclubbers, workers on the nightshift, others whose dress afforded no clue to their reason for the journey. Decadence itself had been corrupted. Once it had meant a *falling away*, but language was corruption in perpetual motion. Words guessed at meanings like the blind imagine the layout of things from a tapping white stick. Seeking solace in dictionaries, people looked words up to divine their meanings. All they got was another word. Words and meanings, faithless lovers, embraced each other swiftly and stole away. Words were like colours. My blue was his grey was someone else's green. I once read in a colour supplement that on Chinese traffic lights red meant go. In western colour-code red meant danger and grey meant uniformity, the colour of the east, the shade of the enemy. No one colour was attached to the west. What was posited against the grey was the profusion of colour. Grey had no place in the rainbow. The cream bus cruised east, the driver speaking the names of streets into a steel microphone. His voice crackled from the PA.

'Potsdamerstrasse.'

Lounging against a lamp-post, a teenage prostitute summoned up a winsome smile for the potential customer in each passing car.

Potsdamerstrasse was another casualty. Before the war it had been a fashionable boulevard. Dressed in Berlin's finest, so the old people said, handsome couples had promenaded along a street livid with cafés and waltzed under crystal chandeliers in the ballrooms of Potsdamerplatz. These days Potsdamerstrasse was a litter-strewn red-light zone, its peepshows, squats and low-rent bars straggling north towards the border, towards the wasteland that had once been Potsdamerplatz. Only one dancehall there had survived the bombs and the bulldozers. It stood empty, facing a line of kiosks that sold knick-knacks to tourists, postcards of the Wall which had the various seats of Nazi command arrowed anachronistically above the East Berlin skyline. Tourists went to Potsdamerplatz to stand on the viewing platforms overlooking the Wall. Roughly fashioned from wood and scaffolding, like tree-houses made by children, these viewing platforms had served another purpose during the twenty-eight months after 13 August 1961 when West Berliners had been unable to visit their relatives in East Berlin. At pre-arranged times newly-weds would mount the platforms and their relatives would wave flowers and greetings from the other side. New-born babies, too, would be held aloft on the platforms. The parents would cup their hands round their mouths and shout out the names of their babies to the grandparents who would shout the names back and smile and weep and sometimes try and take photographs with a telefoto lens. Now the platforms were mounted daily by tourists armed with Japanese cameras taking shots of the Wall to pass around the neighbours in Phoenix or Florence, Nantes or Nagasaki. Peepshows and viewing platforms. A city purpose-built for voyeurs. The bus swung left into Yorckstrasse.

A bouncer dressed in British army beret and battle fatigues marked with East German insignia stood at the door of a bar called Risiko. The tentacles of a dead neon sign hung down over the smashed-up and boarded-up façade. By day Risiko looked as derelict as the rest of the shopfronts on the redbrick block. It opened around 2 a.m. and shut whenever. A snatch of music, an electronic screech like a jet out of control, forced its way through the perspex window as the number 19 drove past Risoko and down the hill to the rusting, dripping, S-Bahn bridges that straddled Yorckstrasse. The street was named after Yorck von Wartenburg, the Prussian general, and not after another famous Yorck von Wartenburg who was hung from a butcher's hook for his part in the conspiracy to assassinate Hitler.

Beyond the bridges Yorckstrasse became a tree-lined boulevard, a dual carriageway separated by a thin line of grass and shrubbery which looked undernourished in the pale grey light. The grey tenements facing the street had once been considered elegant. Mostly they had fallen into disrepair, but here and there stood brightly-painted and refurbished blocks, sleek potted plants in the windows of the flats occupied by another generation who thought it chic to live in Kreuzberg. Certain streets, like certain cars and clothes and foreign seaside resorts, went in and out of fashion. Some neighbourhoods died quietly while others were reborn. Property values rose and fell like civilisations. For postal purposes Kreuzberg was divided in two: Kreuzberg 16 and Kreuzberg 36. The former had recently experienced a small influx of wholefood shops and smart cafés. The latter was a ghetto that clung to the irregular meanderings of the Wall. The paupers, the winos, the teenage runaways, the guestworkers, they had all somehow ended up in Kreuzberg 36. West Berlin had swept its undesirables to the very edge of the city.

The bus driver said nothing more and nothing less than the names of the streets marking bus stops. Was he never tempted to tell a few jokes into the microphone, invent street-names that didn't exist or at least pronounce the names with some comic inflexion? I had never heard a Berlin bus driver improvising thus, but maybe I had just been unlucky and in any case impromptu cabaret would have been ill-received by this 5 a.m. cargo of the half-dead. Past an amusement arcade, El Dorado, past a massage parlour and the Kreuzberg headquarters of the SPD, past a white-coated boy sweeping the floor of a Lebanese takeaway called Falafel Station, the number 19 reached its destination and spilled its load at the junction of Yorckstrasse and Mehringdamm. To the north of the crossroads was the Tele-Tower, hanging in the sky like a bright bomb.

Only fifteen hours ago I had walked past that tower in the sunshine. It seemed like days. The silver globe brooded over Kreuzberg. It was topped by a red-and-white candy-striped spear reaching up into the gloom. For the many thousands of West Berlin residents who had never been to East Berlin the Tele-Tower was somehow unthinkable. Like a drunk lying comatose in the street, it was noted in the corner of the eye and discreetly avoided. Just three nights previously in the Cri du Chat I had met a dope dealer who boasted he had never been across the border. He drove a BMW. He said there was no reason for him to go to the east. Why should he make himself unnecessarily depressed? He could tune into a GDR television station if he wanted to know about the east. He himself was an exile from West Germany. He had come to West Berlin to escape history, not confront it. His only contact with the other Germany had been driving along the transit roads that connect West Berlin to West Germany. He had been to Athens and London and New York and Paris but he had never set foot in East Berlin and he was proud of it. His bored arrogance depressed me beyond belief. At least it had stopped raining, I thought, walking down another street named after a Prussian general: Gneisenaustrasse. Almost home.

By the entrance to Gneisenaustrasse underground, on the strip of concrete and greenery separating the four lanes of traffic, the first Monday morning customers were propped up against the bar of the orange kiosk adjoining the station. The Imbiss sold beer, various wursts, chips with either mayonnaise or ketchup. It was a popular hangout for middle-aged men who occupied some twilight zone between respectability and destitution. None were homeless and some had a job but all had seen better days. Periodically they flung chips and scraps of sausage to their mangy Alsatians, who prowled the fifty-foot-wide traffic island like animals in a zoo. Pigeons perched patient on the roof of the Imbiss, waiting for a lapse of concentration on the part of the dogs.

Dogs barked, men cursed, cars roared. Nothing much ever changed at the Gneisenaustrasse Imbiss. I dined there quite regularly myself. I toyed with the notion of a cup of coffee, the house where I lived on Mittenwalderstrasse was usually lacking at least one of the coffee ingredients, especially since the three punks from Copenhagen had taken up temporary residence, but I decided sleep was the more delicious prospect.

The cobblestones were still shiny from the rain. Walking past the Afro-German Shop on the street corner, which sold alcohol and newspapers and nothing at all in the way of African products, I pondered once again the mystery of its name. Ulrike, a founding member of the household, had said the shop was run by an African prince. She hadn't specified which nation or which tribe. Ulrike never got bogged down in detail. If a shopkeeper told her he was an African prince, that was that. Who cared by what route he had come to Kreuzberg or for what reason? She always got irritated by my tendency to worry away at her pronouncements with needless questions. There were as many reasons for running away as there were exiles in West Berlin, she said. Why bother hounding people's past? It was by chance I had met Ulrike in 1979 and by chance I met her again two years later, standing at the same spot in the Djungel where she had stood in 1979. Now I stood outside this grey stucco tenement which had become my temporary home. Next door was a Turkish nightclub called Karibik.

I knew only one houseful of stories, there were about twenty other flats in the same block. This place was like a transit camp. I pushed open the door that was never locked.

The flat was in the Hinterhof, the backyard. Most apartment blocks were divided into front ahd rear sections. Flats facing the street had grander entrances and staircases and were roomier and dearer than those at the back. Some of the tenements had been built in one long series of Hinterhofs with ever smaller court-yards, the rents becoming cheaper in this architectural progression from light towards darkness. Most people I knew lived in a Hinterhof. I knew no one who had any desire to own a house or take out a mortgage on a flat, West Berlin was more or less immune to this affliction. Only eight per cent of its population were home-owners. It was a city of tenants.

Sitting on the floor, for the main room in the flat was completely without furniture, were the three Copenhagen punks (two gay men and one heterosexual woman) drinking a bottle of bourbon they had purchased in Friedrichstrasse. It was around 5.30. They were discussing whether or not to go to the Cri du Chat. I took one slug from the bottle and went straight to my room, collapsing on the polystyrene board which for some reason Ulrike thought was good for the back. She and her baby and sister, Charlotte and Uschi, were all sleeping in one bed in a room shared with George, the Tamil from Sri Lanka. I lay on my bed looking at a picture on the wall, a splashy grey cross, two black suggestions of eyes, a half-moon that wanted to be a mouth, the whole thing done swiftly on rough grey paper, mounted on white and framed in black, hanging on this lumpy white wall. The painting was done by a Swiss artist who was a former lover of Ulrike's. She said he was quite big in Switzerland. Another of his paintings was on the facing wall, above my head. This one was black and grey with smudges of purple and pink, like a dull landscape briefly enlivened by dawn. I heard the door slam as the Danes left the house for the Cri du Chat. There was a black cat in my room, I was suddenly aware, a black cat I had never seen before. Lucky or unlucky? Mittenwalderstrasse: middle-of-the-forest-street. I imagined sleeping for weeks in the long grass of a kind city.

2 The German Sisters

There was only one clock in the house. It belonged to Ulrike and was passed around the various bedrooms depending on who had to get up for what. Ulrike and her sister Uschi were from Heidelberg. They shared the flat with three other exiles from West Germany (a taxi driver, an actor and a graphic designer), a Sri Lankan, a Peruvian and myself plus a constant stream of visitors from Denmark, France and Spain and anywhere else Ulrike and Uschi had happened to make friends. An unemployed guestworker who lived near by with his mother spent most of his time in the household too, arriving every afternoon with two bottles of Buzbag, a strong Turkish wine the colour of black-currant juice. His name was Murat, it meant peace in Turkish. He was in love with Ulrike. She was still in love with the father of her small daughter, Charlotte. The last time Ulrike had seen Charlotte's father was by chance seven weeks ago on the U-Bahn.

When I woke up I still felt wrecked so I suppose I had slept for five or six hours rather than eight or nine. I had dreamt about pearl fishermen who went diving with their dogs. I was living in a house with a sea-view and, in the biography re-made in my dream, I had lived in a similar house when I was a child. The pearl fishing village was off the coast of East Germany. Johnny and his parents were also living there. His father had said that the young people found it hard adjusting to village life after the diversions of the city. There was a reason everyone had fled to this coastal village, but I couldn't remember what it was.

En route to the bathroom, I wondered if anyone had considered compiling a comparative study of dreams dreamt in East
and West Berlin. What was the political economy of dreaming?

Andreas, the graphic designer, was sitting on the toilet reading
a book.

'Morning,' he said, briefly averting his eyes from the page.

I had lived in the house long enough to be unembarrassed
about such things. With ten people sharing one bathroom there
was no room for prudery. I splashed water on my face and
scrubbed the film from my teeth.

'You have some interesting books in your room,' said Andreas,
holding up one of the books in question, *From Red to Green,
Interviews with Rudolf Bahro*. Andreas must have selected this
volume for his toilet reading while I was still asleep.

Yeah, I said, trying to avoid my red-eyed 32-year-old face in the
bathroom mirror. Five years ago I had been to see Rudolf Bahro
give the Isaac Deutscher Memorial Lecture at the London School
of Economics. Short and square-faced, he had worn heavy
spectacles, slicked-back hair and an open-neck shirt with large
floppy collars worn outside his leather jacket. He had looked like
the East German factory manager he had once been. Jailed for
writing a Marxist critique of the communist states that was
published in the west, Bahro was released in 1979. He came to the
west and swiftly became a leading spokesman for the Greens.

Five years ago the black rings beneath my eyes had been fainter,
the skin tauter. I had listened eagerly to Bahro, believing that wise
words *would* change things, it was only a matter of time. The new
threats of nuclear war and eco-catastrophe had made old dogmas
redundant, Bahro said. The proletariat was no longer, if it ever
had been, a universal class whose interests coincided with the
exploited everywhere. The basic contradiction in the world was
now between the northern countries and the southern countries,
between what he called the metropolis and the periphery. East
and west were just different methods of organising death-by-
industrialisation. As the time went by Bahro drifted further from
Marx and closer to God. Rejecting the communist idea of the
development of the forces of production, rejecting too the
capitalist celebration of the joys conferred by the market, Bahro

began to see in God a kind of alter ego representing more noble aspirations. Forward development, he wrote, should be an inward journey rather than an outward expression. Recently there had been photographs in *Stern* magazine showing Bahro in orange shorts. He had joined Bhagwan.

'From red to green to orange,' I said to Andreas.

Frowning, Andreas replied that he respected the Bhagwan philosophy. He had once been a member of the German Communist Party, the pro-Soviet KPD, he had been to East Berlin with fraternal delegations, but these days communists and capitalists made him equally angry. Andreas had been to the Bhagwan disco and wholefood restaurant at the western end of the Kurfürstendamm. He had been impressed.

'They give people what they want, at a price they can afford. And they don't do any preaching,' he said, wiping his bum.

'Isn't that what successful businessmen have always done?' I said. 'Why get excited about another hustler in tune with the times?'

Andreas shrugged. This shrug said he was not excited. The whole point was his absence of excitement: if people generally were less excited about their beliefs and ambitions then perhaps life would be a mite less miserable. Andreas left *From Red to Green* in the bathroom. He was already late for work. The only member of the household who had a full-time job, Andreas worked in a studio producing artwork for press advertisements. He ran out the house and drove to the studio in his blue Polo.

The white telephone rang. Though the bill had not been paid in months, the telephone still received incoming calls. To make outgoing calls everyone had to use the public kiosks next door to the Imbiss at Gneisenaustrasse U-Bahn station. The telephone at Mittenwalderstrasse was in a state of limbo, suspended between legality and illegality, neither totally cut off nor properly connected. Out of its earpiece came the rasping voice of Pint.

'Ian? Up already? What's wrong?'

'A mistake. Aren't enough clocks to go round.'

'What about tonight?'

'Tonight's all right.'

'Okay. See you at ten at the café-with-no-name.'

He replaced the receiver. The café-with-no-name was in fact Café Lenz, an establishment opened up by some friends of Pint some months ago. It had no sign displaying the name and had never advertised its existence in any way. It had been a huge success. Pint liked the place because of the total absence of chic decor and music. I sat on the living-room floor looking dumbly at the telephone. All my calls would have to wait.

An open-tread staircase led from the furnitureless living-room to the basement, where Ulrike stood in the kitchen heating up some milk for her two-year-old daughter. The Hitachi radio-and-cassette-recorder was tuned to Armed Forces Network: 'All the hot hits on AFN'.

Ulrike was recovering from the trauma of a job interview to which she had been sent by the unemployment office. She had been on the dole for, oh, three maybe four years, she couldn't exactly remember. When I first met her she had been a secretary, rosy-cheeked and long-haired, but in the course of the last five years she had become thoroughly Berlinised, her blonde hair now short and bobbed, her green eyes more suspicious, her clothes mostly black. The interview that morning had been at a country and western restaurant called Nashville. Ulrike had no intention of waitressing in such a place, but her unemployment benefit would have been cut off had she not attended the interview.

'I took Charlotte with me and borrowed some sixties sun-glasses which I intended wearing throughout,' she said, smiling. 'And I plastered my hair with gel. I considered going in there chewing gum, but I thought that might backfire. A country and western restaurant, whatever *that* is, might like the idea of gum-chewing waitresses. To be on the safe side I was half an hour late.'

'And?' I said.

'It worked out okay. The guy had given the jobs to two other girls by the time I arrived.'

Having sucked the teat of the bottle to make sure the milk was the right temperature, Ulrike gave it to Charlotte who drank noisily. Charlotte was thus named, Ulrike said, because she had been made in Charlottenburg, in an apartment on Kaiserdamm that she and her sister had shared with a psychiatrist and a dentist. The father of Charlotte was a third-year philosophy

student who spent most of his time and money in the nightclubs.
When the baby was first born this philosophy student had
demonstrated some fatherly feeling, taking Ulrike and Charlotte
to meet his parents in West Germany for example, but after a year
or so his interest had dried up and Ulrike's only contact with him
now, apart from the occasional chance meeting in an underground train, was the DM 200 he sent every month in the post.

'It's about time I made him pay properly for his daughter,' she
said, carrying a tray full of breakfast things out into the garden
which gave on to the kitchen. 'Us girls, we must either work or we
must find a rich boyfriend. But if we have a rich boyfriend, that's
hard work too.'

She poured out the coffee then rolled her first spliff of the day.
Charlotte was getting dirty in the sandpit that was still damp
from last night's rain. Puddles exposed the warps on the table-
tennis table. The threadbare lawn was muddied, seeds planted
last spring had only taken here and there. Ulrike thought it was
probably due to the lack of sun, the garden being enclosed by a
fifteen-foot-high fire-wall.

Beyond the fire-wall was a bomb-site that was now a car park.
The other side of the car park was a redbrick factory, perpen-
dicular iron bars over its tall windows. Figures in overalls were
sometimes visible from the garden, standing at those barred
windows.

The next-door neighbour, dismissively referred to as *the hippie*
by Ulrike, had built a wooden catwalk from his basement up to
the massive oak which kept his garden permanently in the shade.
The black cat in my room last night probably belonged to the
colony of cats next door, Ulrike said. The hippie had a dozen or so
cats.

It was early afternoon. Apart from the hours between noon and
three, sunlight was blocked from our garden by the fire-wall. I
guessed it was about two. Like most fire-walls in Berlin it was
pitted with bullet holes and shrapnel blasts. I speculated out loud
whether the wall was most damaged during the Spartacist revolt
of 1919, during the street-battle in the twenties between the
communists and Nazis or, most likely, during the Battle for Berlin
in 1945.

'Your imagination will be your downfall,' said Ulrike, proffering the smouldering depressant.

I took a quick drag, to be sociable, then handed it back. I had always preferred alcohol.

'Did you know that sales of peroxide soared under Nazi rule?' I said. 'Also, your haircut, the bob, was considered un-German.'

She laughed and shook her head, then closed her eyes to feel the sun on her face. 'Do You Really Want to Hurt Me', the Culture Club single, was playing on AFN.

'What did they teach you in school about the Nazis?' I persisted.

'Nothing at all,' Ulrike said, her eyes still closed. 'There was just an embarrassed silence about the whole period. At my school in Heidelberg history ended in 1933.'

'What about your parents?'

'Yeah, they talked about it sometimes. My father was very embarrassed that my grandmother had kept a picture of him as a little boy, all dressed up in some Nazi uniform and doing the *Sieg Heil* salute. My grandmother's the worst. She still believes Auschwitz and Belsen were propaganda stunts dreamed up by the enemies of Germany.'

Ulrike's father was a stonemason, a gentle man, she said, kind and unambitious. Her mother didn't work. She had been very beautiful when she was young, was still beautiful now, Ulrike added, perhaps thinking her own 26-year-old beauty would also mellow into something more careworn. Ulrike had returned prematurely from a visit to her parents in order to attend the interview at the country and western restaurant. Right from the start her parents had accepted with good grace the fact of Ulrike's pregnancy, Ulrike said. They were sweet liberals, she said, a rarity among the middle-aged of Heidelberg. They doted on Charlotte.

'Last week they taught her a new word,' Ulrike said, lifting her daughter from the sandpit and flicking the dirt from her clothes. '*Arbeit*. From her mother she has learned how to say shit, from her grandparents, work.'

She repeated this new word to Charlotte. *Arbeit*. The daughter had copied her mother's smile, a fulsome smile, eyes and mouth stretched wide, the head slightly on one side, a crowd-pleasing smile.

'Her father may be a bastard, but at least he's a handsome and intelligent bastard,' Ulrike said. 'In that sense I chose well.' A down-to-earth hustler one moment, Ulrike was a whimsical mystic the next. She dabbled in occultism and had once had an affair with a voodoo. She believed in tarot cards, astrological signs, a whole suitcase of ancient mythologies. She never read newspapers, apart from the occasional copy of *Taz*, the left-wing daily, and although she smoked hash and lived in a house that some might call a commune she reserved her most bitter vitriol for hippies. Sometimes it seemed as if the whole house existed in a kind of philosophical chaos.

Uschi, Ulrike's sister, was still asleep. She had apparently accompanied the Danish punks on their dawn excursion to the Cri du Chat. Unlike Ulrike, Uschi was a genuine dreamer. She never spoke unless she had something to say and she looked somehow Egyptian, proud-nosed and sloe-eyed. Uschi had missed a period and felt sure she was pregnant, though she had as yet avoided going to the clinic to get her suspicion confirmed. She lived a wild life and she never used contraception, apart from some version of the rhythm method that was based on a rough calculation of lunar cycles. It therefore came as no great surprise that Uschi might be pregnant. Like Ulrike, she had had two abortions. She had decided that if she was pregnant she would have the child. Her baby would grow up alongside Charlotte. Things could be worse.

Ulrike took Charlotte for a walk round the neighbourhood, came back and made further cups of coffee and three-paper joints. The ashtray on the garden table piled higher as the afternoon wore on. A black DJ dropped by for a shower. His father was some ambassador, Ulrike said. A dancer turned up for a chat and also to ask Ulrike when the house next wanted its aerobics class. For a short time there was a thin young man with wispy hair playing classical guitar in the garden. Charlotte was delighted by the arrival of a Saint Bernard dog, which to her must have looked big as a horse. People and dogs came and went. Ulrike loved holding court in the garden, charming the men with the smile that Charlotte had copied so effectively, chattering to the women and quite often making bitchy remarks about them when they had left. She was a kind of society hostess for the bored and the dissolute. Two or three nights a weeks she dressed up and went down to the Djungel where she met many of the people who drifted in and out of the garden. Sometimes rich men took her to expensive restaurants, too. The Paris Bar was her favourite. She said it had been founded by former members of the French resistance.

Sometime after three, when the sun had disappeared beneath the fire-wall, Uschi emerged tousle-haired from her sleep. There had been a raid last night at the Cri du Chat, she said. The cops had cleared out all the girls from the club and strip-searched all the men. Uschi wasn't sure if the police had been looking for drugs or weapons, but she had heard a rumour it was political extremists they were after. In any case she thought it was absurd that the police suspected only the men.

'Haven't they ever heard of Ulrike Meinhof?' she said languidly, sipping her coffee.

Ulrike Meinhof had been a writer and maybe that was why she had managed to script her life like a thriller: SUCCESSFUL JOURNALIST TIRES OF TRYING TO CHANGE THINGS BY WRITING, TAKES UP GUN INSTEAD! Born in 1934, she grew up in Jena, east of Weimar, the daughter of two free-thinkers belonging to the only church which had not fallen under Nazi control. She had a sister three years older. Her father, the director of Jena museum, died when she was six. After the war her mother drove her two daughters in a truck from the Russian zone to Oldenburg in British-occupied Germany. Her mother died when Ulrike Meinhof was fifteen. She was adopted by her mother's best friend.

Sometimes I called Ulrike and Uschi The German Sisters, after the title of a film by Margaret von Trotha about the Red Army Fraction. In retaliation Ulrike called me The English Boy.

Sitting in the languorous garden with the sisters from Heidelberg, I wondered if Berlin had somehow contributed to the lethal rage of Ulrike Meinhof. She came to West Berlin with her twin daughters in the Christmas of 1967, having decided to divorce her husband, Klaus Rainer Röhl, the publisher of *Konkret*, the Hamburg-based magazine in which she had made her reputation.

She found a small flat in Dahlem, later moving to Kufsteiner-strasse, nearer the centre. Her face became known to the public through her work on television. She hung out at the Republican Club on Wielandstrasse where the radicals paid for their food and drink by chucking money into a bottle on the bar.

'Everyone here is so loving,' she wrote in a letter to a friend.

When she took the irrevocable decision, she had just finished writing a television play called *Bambule*, based on her research at the Eichenhof orphanage for girls in West Berlin. One of the girls she befriended there, Irene Goergens, the illegitimate daughter of an American soldier, became an accomplice, a teenage member of the RAF. *Bambule* was scheduled for transmission on 24 May 1970 at the peak time of 8.15 p.m. It was never shown. Ten days earlier Ulrike Meinhof and Irene Goergens, wearing wigs and carrying guns in their briefcases, had with three others freed Andreas Baader from the German Institute for Social Questions in Dahlem. WRITER TURNS OUTLAW!

Convicted for setting fire to a Munich department store in 1968, Baader had been released pending appeal after fourteen months and had fled to Paris and Zurich whence he returned to Berlin. He had been re-arrested after an abortive search for weapons which he thought were buried in a cemetery in Rudow close to the Berlin Wall. Locked up in Tegel prison, he had been given permission by the prison authorities to research a book at the German Institute for Social Questions. In the getaway car, a silver Alfa Romeo, police found a tear-gas pistol and a copy of *Introduction to Capital* by Marx.

Ulrike Meinhof went to Jordan for arms training, returning in August to West Berlin where a few weeks later three banks were robbed on the same day by different units of the RAF. SHE CARRIES A 9MM FIREBIRD PISTOL IN HER HANDBAG! The television face was now up on wanted posters all over West Germany. After a spate of bombs at US Army headquarters in Frankfurt and Heidelberg in early May 1972, Ulrike Meinhof masterminded the bombing of the Springer press building in Hamburg. Arrested a month later, she was sentenced in November 1974 to eight years' imprisonment for her part in the freeing of Andreas Baader. The authorities at Stammheim maximum-security jail alleged she committed suicide by hanging herself on 9 May 1976. She was buried in the Protestant cemetery of the Church of the Holy Trinity in Mariendorf, West Berlin. Four thousand mourners attended her funeral.

'Smalltown Boy' by Bronski Beat was playing on AFN, which had apparently been Ulrike Meinhof's favourite radio station. She was a child of her time, same as everyone else. After Uschi's description of the raid at the Cri du Chat, she said nothing else for about an hour, then went into the living room to paint. Flinging red, black, white and orange paint on grey paper, she scraped it furiously with a knife till it looked like a city in flames.

Sprawled on the floor over her livid abstraction she paused now and again to peer out the latticed window, examining the sky for signs of rain. Uschi had a job waitressing at a steak restaurant in Charlottenburg, but she only worked if the restaurant could open up its garden to customers. She was due to start tonight at seven o'clock. She was always praying for rain.

The Danish punks were still sleeping. George, the Sri Lankan expatriate, was at one of the political meetings which took up so much of his time. Posters proclaiming the just war of the Tamil liberation army, the Tigers, were stuck to the wall of the bedroom he shared with Ulrike, Charlotte and Uschi. An illegal immigrant, George was confined to West Berlin and had to report to the police station once a week. It was partly for this reason he had decided to go to Nicaragua with the Berlin Brigade of volunteers, one of whom was a boy from East Berlin who had been in the west only four months. Though George shared nothing in the way of ideology with Ulrike and Uschi they both loved him and were worried about what might happen to him in Nicaragua. Out in the garden Ulrike was again expressing her concern.

'He's told me all the brigades get arms training,' she said. 'And I think that's one of the reasons he's going. Charlotte loves him too, you know. These Sri Lankan boys, they aren't scared by children like the Germans.'

Her idea of hell was being married to a Bavarian who drank beer and ate sausage and subscribed to the casual bigotry that Ulrike held to be typical of her race. *Very German* was a pejorative she applied most days to people and characteristics she detested. *Very German* was the ghost of the enemy she had left behind in Heidelberg, for 17 Mittenwalderstrasse was a no-go area for anything or anyone that Ulrike deemed *very German.*

'What's she like, this English girlfriend of yours?' Ulrike said. I never knew what to say. It was hard describing someone you loved. Everything about them was tainted by your love. You couldn't fix someone you loved with a cold eye.

'She's young,' I said, 'artistic, moody, a bit vague, though she has a very practical side, much more so than me. She can wire plugs and mend things when they go wrong. She knows how to use a Black and Decker high-speed drill. She maintains her own car.'

'Good looking?' Ulrike said.

'Beautiful,' I said, having self-consciously avoided this adjective in my initial description. In the past people had criticised me for overusing that word in respect of Laura, as if everything else about her was subsidiary. But she was unarguably beautiful and however hard I tried to dress up the relationship in respectable-sounding words (mutual, compatible, shared this and that) her beauty was a central fact of my love. She was vivacious and shy at turns, dancing in the air and screaming at the top of her voice one minute, peeping coy at people through her hair the next. She nibbled her nails and had an exaggerated way of frowning, as if she carried some sadness she could never talk about. I never really discovered the source of her sadness, although I had various theories.

'Beautiful,' repeated Ulrike. 'And how much younger than you?'

'Nine years,' I confessed. I hated the fact Laura was nine years younger. People always leapt to conclusions. Always in the past I had been out with women my own age (I often said that to people to let them know that I knew what they were thinking) and I was uncomfortable with this clichéd sociology of my relation to Laura: older, richer. She came from a rich family, I said, but she didn't have much money of her own.

'Does she have a job?' Ulrike said.

'Oh, she's done the usual things, waitressing jobs, cooking jobs. She sold double-glazing door-to-door for a while. She's a good photographer and sometimes she likes to paint. She's good at making things, repairing and doing up the stuff she buys at junk shops.'

'Does she have one of those horrible high-pitched voices, like most English girls?'

I smiled, said I wasn't sure, her voice sounded okay to me. The subject was dropped for the time being.

'It's about time you had your hair cut,' Ulrike announced, jumping up from her chair. 'You're starting to look like a West German rock fan. I'll do it for you now.'

She led me into the bathroom, ordered me to undress, sat me in a chair and cut off my hair with nail scissors, the same scissors with which I had seen Uschi trimming the grass three days previously. Ana, Andreas's friend from Peru, opened the door, said sorry and shut it again. She was the only person in the house who ever locked the bathroom door.

'That girl!' said Ulrike, sighing theatrically. 'When will Andreas learn? He's too good for this world.'

Andreas had had a tough childhood. Growing up in an orphanage, he knew what it was like to be treated like dirt. It was accordingly an article of faith with him that everyone should be given a chance, helped, assumed innocent until proven guilty. Ana had stretched his tolerance very thin, but still he got angry when his flatmates suggested Ana had outstayed her welcome.

'She contributes nothing to the house,' Ulrike continued, snipping away with the rusty blades. 'Nothing at all. All she does is lounge around in Andreas's bedroom. She never does the shopping, never goes out, never talks to anyone except Andreas. I don't think she even knows herself why she came to Berlin.'

Ana spent her days combing her henna-red hair, applying thick blue eye-shadow and crimson lipstick, lying on the bed and listening to the BBC World Service, waiting for Andreas to come home. She had left Lima, her home town, because she believed she was being pursued by magicians. They sent her letters which arrived every morning, she had once told me, *but not with the postman.* Every night they rang her up and played a tape-recorded message containing sinister threats. Ana reported the magicians to the police, fled Lima and went to live in the countryside for some months, but when she returned her tormentors were still at large. She decided to leave for Germany. Someone she had met in a bar had told her Germany was a peaceful place where no one went out very much.

She went first to Munich for two months, then telephoned Andreas (whom she had met four years previously in Peru). She had gained West Berlin citizenship by marrying a punk rocker from East Berlin, who spent two years in prison before coming to the west. She had paid him DM 2000. Every now and again he came round the house to sort out various legal affairs. Accompanied by a friendly mongrel on a leash, he always wore a torn leather jacket and decayed Levis. He seemed very shy, but that may have been a consequence of his mercenary marriage to Ana. He knew everyone in the house knew the whole story.

Having run outstretched fingers through my hair to check the cut was even, Ulrike placed arms akimbo to consider her handiwork.

'So,' she said. 'Now you need have no fears about the face-check girl at the Djungel.'

'What about the face-check man at Friedrichstrasse?'

'That's your problem,' she said. 'You shouldn't spend so much time in the east. It makes you too agitated, English Boy, thinking about all these things. The Wall will still be there when you've finished writing about it.'

'No empire lasts for ever,' I said, dusting the hair from my body.

'You're a typical Leo,' she said with deliberate provocation.

Our differences on the matter had been well rehearsed. I would say astrology was another form of fatalism, another excuse. If life was predetermined by particular constellations of stars, why bother actually doing anything? Ulrike would smile, cup her face in one palm and lean her head to one side. *Of course*, her eyes would say, *action changes nothing*.

Arguing with someone who believed only in mystery, destiny and pleasure was a dispiriting and unsettling business. On this occasion, therefore, I registered my disagreement with a grunt, stepped inside the shower and shouted through the din of the teeming jets, 'Why don't you come to East Berlin with me on May Day?'

'Politics, Shmolitics,' she yelled back.

'But you'd love it. Everyone gets dressed up in fancy uniforms and goes marching and dancing and waving flags. It's really wild.'

I heard her laugh and shut the door.

Ulrike had been once to East Berlin. Three years ago I had taken her on a brief tour and then we had gone to visit Tommy and Vera at their flat on Kollwitzstrasse. As always, Tommy had cooked. Ulrike had been friendly, effervescent even, but the evening had been tense somehow and afterwards I felt I had made a mistake in bringing Ulrike with me. No bridges had been built. Ulrike had not returned to East Berlin. Tommy and Vera had not inquired after Ulrike. And whatever impression the east had made on Ulrike, she kept it to herself. She had never talked about that night at Kollwitzstrasse. In the past I had invented reasons for her silence. People had built walls in their minds, that was the traditional Berlin lament, a nebulous truth worn out by repetition. For me, the outsider, Berlin was a city of opposing halves, a hall of mirrors, a symbolic contest. For Ulrike West Berlin was a haven and the rest of the city was a foreign country.

The truth was, East Berlin bored her. East Berliners exiled in West Berlin were a different matter. Once they were within her reach, potential recruits to her scene, she was intrigued by them. They have something different, something *special*, she would say, after a visit from Pint or Astrid. She would tell me I must invite them round more often.

From inside the shower I could just make out the sad deep voice of Zara Leander, a sleazy surrender to the hopelessness of love. It was Uschi's favourite tape cassette. It hadn't yet rained and therefore Uschi would have to go to the steak restaurant to smile and be nice to people she detested. Waitresses were chameleonic as journalists or double-agents. Which reminded me: I had to call the number Wolfgang had given me, leave a message I was coming over for May Day.

I closed my eyes to feel the hot water jets massaging my newly shorn head. Zara Leander gave way to the Style Council. The Johnson's Baby Shampoo shone like honey in my palm. I washed my hair and then shaved with a blue disposable razor, a Gillette with two parallel blades and a non-flexible head, another of my

brand-loyalties along with Heinz ketchup, Frank Cooper's
marmalade, Branston pickle, McVitie's digestive biscuits, J&B
whisky, Marks and Spencer underpants, Fred Perry tennis shirts,
Dr Marten's shoes, Bic pens, Oral-B toothbrushes and Wright's
Coal Tar soap. Products had personalities, I had been solemnly
assured by people who worked in advertising agencies. Con-
sumers assembled their identity and established their uniqueness
by particular combinations of brand-names. The west had
become unimaginable without advertisements. *Company logos
were wounds worn like medals.* And here I stood naked, another
identikit personality, a son of the west, a sum of my parts.
Perhaps, after all, it was not simply the case that Ulrike was bored
by East Berlin. Perhaps Ulrike and Uschi and the nameless
thousands of their ilk felt hostile to East Berlin because it
somehow reminded them of the contingent character of their own
personalities. How might they have turned out if they had been
born in Dresden rather than Heidelberg? I cleaned my teeth
again. With toothpaste as with flags I had no particular loyalties.

It was eight o'clock. There were still two hours to go before
meeting Pint at the café-with-no-name. I decided to go into town,
mooch around for a while.

Walking out the house, I bumped into Murat bearing his two
bottles of Buzbag. Doffing his cloth cap, he bowed ostentatiously
and said he was born alcoholic because his father drank too
much. He opened his mouth in a broad smile, wiped his
moustaches like a music-hall comedian and proceeded into the
shady garden, probably to tell the same joke to Ulrike. Like most
jesters, Murat tried too hard to please. He lived in a small
basement flat with his mother, who had brought him from
Ankara to West Berlin when he was thirteen years old. There had
been no spare seats on the train and Murat had sat on a suitcase
for most of the three-day journey. His mother had been a teacher
in Turkey; she was a cleaner in Germany. Murat was unemployed; he was the same age as me.

Girls in red dresses ran up and down Mittenwalderstrasse.
Younger boys played football and older ones sat astride BMX
bikes, teasing girls who pretended not to notice. Turkish mothers
wrapped in purplish silks stood chatting on the street and

occasionally told the children to behave themselves. Bicycles rattled as their wheels bumped along the cobblestones. Cyclists who avoided the cobblestones by riding on the pavement earned the wrath of the mothers.

From the open windows and doors, radios and televisions and record players contrived a crackling symphony of violins and love songs in English, echoes of gunshot and wailing zithers, canned laughter and German news bulletins, car chases and electric guitars. Faces old enough to have lived through the war leaned out of the tenement windows and looked up and down for potentially newsworthy items, for an argument or a stranger, a police car or a removal van. One of the spectators, his elbows propped on cushions at his habitual ground-floor vantage point, dropped a lit cigarette. A small boy picked it up for him and the old man smiled in gratitude. Maybe he intended turning the incident into a parable, a story at odds with all the gloomy newspaper reports about youth, drugs and violence? Some old people liked those kinds of parables.

I walked down past the Karibik nightclub and Video Ahmad, past a flower shop called Salon Rossband, and entered a small bar at the corner of Mittenwalderstrasse and Fürbringerstrasse. It was empty apart from the Turkish woman dressed in black who was the owner. Her Alsatian was desultorily watching a western on the black-and-white portable. She served me the packet of cigarettes without taking her eyes from the television. I left the right money on the counter.

Up at the entrance to Gneisenaustrasse U-Bahn, by the usual crowd of men and dogs hanging around the Imbiss, I waited twenty minutes for one of the three telephone kiosks to fall vacant (three others had been vandalised) and then made two calls to East Berlin. Having rung the number Wolfgang had given me, I heard a woman's voice tell me that Wolfgang had left town and would not be back in time for May Day. Next I rang Johnny at his parents' house in Grünau. He was out, but his mother, Florence, invited me over for afternoon tea next week. I still had an hour or so to kill before meeting Pint.

I took the underground to Zoo Station, then walked through the red-and-white plastic tassels hanging across the doorway of a place called SEX SHOP. It sold the usual range of magazines and sex aids. It also had one corridor full of video cabins equipped with paper towels in orange dispensers. The videos were activated by coin slots. For one deutschmark punters received one minute of whichever video they desired, TEENAGE SEX or HOT DREAMS or MAN BUMST SICH DURCH. The video cabins stank of stale sex.

Cream plastic vibrators, twelve unrealistic inches long, cost DM 49.50. An item called Miss Cassie had a price tag of DM 149.50. I took a closer look. *Miss Cassie was nothing but a mouth.* There were two versions of the Miss World Specials: the white doll cost DM 79, the black doll DM 77. Had the black doll been reduced because it was selling more slowly than the white doll? Did Sex Shop habitués find it less pleasurable making love to black dolls than white dolls? I saw hundreds of black Miss Worlds remaindered in the autumn sale, hundreds of sad rag dolls built with soft apertures for West Berlin romantics. In the film taking shape in my mind I saw the sex toys rising up to enslave their masters, who would be too ashamed ever to confess their subjugation. It became an international insurrection. From the Philippines to Thailand, from South Korea to the Ivory Coast, the sex slaves captured the sex tourists and put them to work converting massage parlours into workshops, brothels into apartments, peepshows into cinemas. *Sex toys of the world unite!* In one ending the Marines were sent in to save the sex tourists from communism. In another, the revolt of the sex toys led indirectly to a nuclear war that destroyed black and white Miss Worlds alike. I stepped out on to Joachimstalerstrasse and spent ten fruitless minutes trying to identify potential Miss Cassie fuckers from the sets of eyes walking in and out of Sex Shop.

I felt thirsty as a wooden god. My mother used to say that before putting the kettle on. Dodging along the crowded street, past the Kaiser Wilhelm Memory Church that had been left in bombed ruins as a reminder of the sins of the past, I walked down to the Europa Centre. There was scaffolding up on the Memory Church.

Inside the Europa Centre grim steel lilies stood in the ground floor water display, guarding the coins chucked in there for good luck. A red plastic barrel, the Watney's logo, hung outside the fake-beamed English Pub where a fugitive from the 19th hole of some Home Counties suburb was trying to engage the barman in conversation.

'Fantastic place,' he said. 'Disneyland. Absolutely fantastic.'

'You've been there,' replied the barman, mopping up spilled bitter in mechanical clockwise strokes.

'Yes,' said the Englishman, and he gave the date. 'It's like an amusement factory. Humans entertained with computers. Really amazing.'

The barman said he had been to the USA, but not to Disneyland. The Englishman said, truly, he should have gone. Tight-lipped, the barman nodded, concluding the exchange.

I responded to the barman's rolled eyes with a sympathetic shrug.

The notion that travel broadens the mind had become the worst kind of official optimism. Westerners gave stars to countries the way gastronomers did to restaurants. Politeness of the natives, relative absence of other tourists (plus the nationality and class of same), cheapness of the liquor and whores, edibility of the cuisine, opportunities for historical or cultural enrichment, standards of hygiene, these were some of the pertinent items on the checklist. Armed with only a passport and a credit card the consumer was able to wander in this supermarket of countries, collecting beaches and mountains like furniture, taking photographs to prove it was all true. You should have been there. You must go. In the society of choosers the supermarket was *the* metaphor in which we struggled to be free and unique. I chose Berlin. He chose Disneyland. I took the lift to the top of the Europa Centre. Close up, the Mercedes star was a grubby blue-and-white plastic wheel, like a piece of fairground machinery that had seen better days.

Groups of tourists strolled around the viewing platform that was caged to prevent suicides. Through the convex bars there were open vistas on three sides of the square roof: to the west, the north and south. The Tele-Tower, the Opera House, Humboldt University, the museums on the island adjoining the Palasthotel, all these landmarks of East Berlin were eliminated from the panorama, denied by a slab of concrete. Doubtless this structure had some technical function, and there were air-vents to prove it, but it remained a laughably childish thing. The skyline had been censored.

Tommy and Johnny would both enjoy this story of the censored skyline, I thought, the enforced blindness of the western tourists. I stared down towards the Kurfürstendamm. In the fading light the four rows of trees alongside the dual carriageway still retained enough of their colour to cut dullish green paths through the jumble of neon. Up here the drone of the cars was so soft it seemed almost silent.

Most of Berlin's beautiful buildings were in the eastern zone. The memorial tea-towels draped over the counter of the roof-top Souvenir Shop exhibited the paucity of architectural treasure on the western side: the Reichstag, the Freedom Bell in Schöneberg Town Hall, the Memory Church, the Congress Centre, the TV Transmitter, the Europa Centre. These tea-towels cost DM 14.50. Did people buy them to hang on walls or to dry dishes? Or was this dilemma circumvented by giving them away as presents? It was a dangerous train of thought. I turned my attention instead to the high-tech building that rose up from the Tiergarten like a blue Michelin man with pink arms sticking out. Closer to the border was the chessboard façade of the Intercontinental, a hotel much favoured by visiting pop groups on account of its manager's music industry connections and its windows on the Wall.

For me the black-and-white check of the Intercontinental always summoned up the life within sixty-four squares, the hundreds of hours spent poring over chess moves, dreaming of them too, the peaceful escape into abstract possibilities. Purest and most chanceless of war games, chess was like a drug. Maybe this was why the Weimar Republic had introduced mass chess instruction for the poor in the Tiergarten. So far in Berlin I had not partaken of chess, only considered the manner in which it had been tainted, the grandmasters who competed with their miniature paper flags facing each other across the time-clocks, the fact that Stalin had made chess compulsory in Russian schools to demonstrate the intellectual superiority of the communist system.

It had worked. Since Bobby Fischer went mad the Americans had more or less evacuated this particular battlefield. Of the two best players in the world, both Russians, Kasparov was more popular in the west than Karpov, the latter being a Party member. Kasparov was Jewish, his real name was Weinstein, but he had been encouraged to take his mother's name when it became apparent he was going to become famous. He had an agent working out of Chicago who struck a hard bargain with would-be profile writers from the west, myself included. Chess was an international language, big business. Books by grandmasters way outsold the best poets of the day. The computer companies were also making a pretty killing, computer chess having eliminated the necessity for friendship or association which previously had been a precondition of being able to play. Now chess could be lonely as writing. The world championship of chess computers was fervently contested by all the high-tech multinationals. Maybe in the end people will not play at all. They will drive their computers to the tournaments and the winners will accept silver cups on behalf of their charges, like breeders at a dog show. Karpov and Kasparov will become a quaint memory. *Human* chess. *Those* were the days. THE TWO K'S. This was the *Daily Express* headline remembered over a front page showing Kennedy and Khrushchev nose-to-nose in the Cuban crisis of my child-hood, my parents suddenly concluding their conversation when, dirty from football, I entered the living room with the strange knowledge that as a result of Americans and Russians arguing about Cuba, wherever that was, bombs might also fall on Swindon and we might all die, this at a time when death was incomprehensible as infinity. In those days I thought John Kennedy was a hero. Later I found out about the Bay of Pigs and Marilyn Monroe. Later still I found out about the US naval base in Guantanamo Bay, Cuba. Its continued existence mocked the convenient theory of the superpower balance, the equality of imperialisms. Such political mathematics fell foul of Guanta-namo Bay. To balance the equation would require a Russian naval base in Turkey or South Korea. As the British army officer stationed in Spandau would later tell me, *there is only one superpower.*

Meanwhile, I stood on the roof-top of the Europa Centre. Under cover of darkness the Mercedes star had recaptured some of its glamour.

Waiting for the lift back down to the street, the gloomy thought occurred that, much as I detested the prospect of computer chess, I would probably end up buying a set. This was the way things went. No escaping the supermarket.

A few will always think for themselves, even among the guardians of the multitude. So wrote Kant. Along the street named after him, I walked west, beneath an iron bridge engraved with further histories of romance and struggle. Past the multi-coloured tassels hanging over the doorway of the peepshow called Lifeshow, past a closed Shell garage, I paused outside the gleaming windows of the Paris Bar. Founded by members of the French resistance, Ulrike had said. These days it was patronised by collaborators who affected designer clothes and risqué haircuts and a casual pride in their hard-won position under the umbrella afforded by the title, The Creative Professions. Welders of slogans, polishers of prejudices, mechanics of noise and form, caretakers of fashion, these guardians of the multitude were clustered round the white linen tablecloths, forking flesh into their mouths. They drank cognac with their espresso, smoked American cigarettes and paid their bills with credit cards. On a building site across the street yellow cranes stood idle like giant question marks.

Clad in long white aprons tied tight at the waist, their short dark hair swept back and shiny with oil, the waiters performed like stand-up comics, their eyebrows moving in effortless parabolas from concern to horror, from surprise to gratitude.

Watching this mechanical cabaret through the window, through the distracting shimmer of my own reflection, I confessed again my complicity. I was no saint. In the west careerism was the most effective form of censorship. Knowing this had not prevented me from knocking on the right doors at the right time and penetrating deep into the mansion where, of course, I learned to heed the warnings of the policemen in my own mind. I became a dab hand with the self-mutilating blue pencil. *Yes sir!* Once I had found someone a flat to live in as a result of an article I wrote on homelessness. This was the only practical benefit that had accrued from anything I had ever written. One flat in eight years. A poor score, I thought, continuing along Kantstrasse.

I had dined twice in the Paris Bar, for my sins, but I had not paid with a credit card. A letter received some years earlier from solicitors acting for Access had demanded I cut my plastic in two, place the pieces in an envelope and send them back to an address in Southend. Probably now I was blacklisted. A credit rating of zero. Cheered slightly by this, I quickened my stride. Blue pencils, brown envelopes with windows showing red ink, the ringing threats of unanswered telephones, the endless conversations about mortgages and careers and the bloody news, I had dumped all that in London. Here in Berlin I had no more excuses.

From the open door of a narrow bar lit by art-deco lamps shaped like cocktail glasses came the slow chorus of a drug song: 'If you want to ride, ride the white pony'.

Its sinister bass and snarling vocal contrived to ape the Doors, whose reputation had been considerably enhanced by the suicide of its lead singer, Jim Morrison, in a Paris hotel room. But the song was a pale imitation, manufactured in some lowland country that was also under cultural occupation, Belgium maybe. I slouched towards the café-with-no-name, Pint's favourite, the steel half-moons on the heels of my brown suede brogues clicking like castanets.

3 Cross-country runner

Pint had once been the fastest sixteen-year-old in East Berlin. More precisely, in 1966 he had been the best cross-country runner in his age group. Much had happened since then, but he still had the lean hollow-cheeked face that seems characteristic of the endurance events. His small bright eyes ran quickly to bloodshot. His shoulders were hunched, unrelaxed. Even sitting alone in the café-with-no-name, reading a newspaper, he still looked somehow wired.

He wore faded Levis, training shoes and a second-hand jacket of the kind worn by workers on Saturday nights in the sixties: three-buttoned, thin-lapelléd, sky-blue polyester. He claimed to smoke only one pack of Camel per day. He was the fastest talker I had ever met. His sentences were short and precise. Like this. He had spent most of the day in an isolation tank, he announced, a coffin-cum-bath in which he had lain on water that was buoyant as the Dead Sea. The tank admitted no light or sound.

'Like a sensory deprivation unit,' I said.

He nodded and gestured to the barman for more beer. The café-with-no-name served draught beer properly poured, which meant it took about five minutes for each glass.

'*But*,' he said, holding his right index finger perfectly erect. 'It's different if you decide to go in there yourself.'

'A prison is still a prison, even if you walk through the gates voluntarily,' I said, immediately regretting the pompous tone.

'A prison can look like anything at all. It matters only that you cannot leave it when you want to,' he said, beating time with the manic finger.

His opinions on this subject carried more weight than my own. He had been jailed in both East Germany and Rumania. He had swum across the Danube at night. He had been pursued by the police through the streets of Budapest. He had waved the Czech flag at Russian tanks in Prague. He had been heavily interrogated. Throughout the two years he had spent in various prisons in Eastern Europe he had continued to describe himself as a Marxist. These days his politics had found temporary lodgings somewhere between anarchism and nihilism, between the joke and the gun. *Better to be in the east with two legs than in the west with one!*

His mock-heroic oratorical style was another joke that had stuck, like his nickname. He wrote under the name Wolfgang Spielhagen, but was known to all and sundry as Pint, to rhyme with mint and not to be confused with the imperial unit. He intended writing up his experiences in the isolation tank for the German edition of *Playboy*.

'All there is to do in there is think,' he said. 'You realise that you are not very free. You want to stop thinking, but you cannot. You try and relax but your mind still races away. It is like a man who has been running twenty miles. He stops by a tree to take a rest, but still his legs are pumping up and down. We can't stop thinking. It's a real problem.'

'This is the beauty of television.'

I said this merely because it was about time I said something. Talking was another compulsion. Mouths were working hard round every wooden table.

'No,' Pint was saying. 'Not television. Not the Coca-Cola culture. But there *are* cultures where people know how to stop thinking, how to empty their minds. One point I reached in the tank, it was quite interesting, I was scared, on the verge of panic, my brain was bursting. Then suddenly, *whoosh*, I went through it. I went through the wall and then I felt okay. Exhilarated. Look at my arms. I got goosepimples just thinking about it.'

His choice of image was quite deliberate. *I went through the wall.* He was self-conscious of his own history, proud of his enforced schizophrenia. Sanity was another illusion. A beady-eyed witness to the madness flourishing both sides of the track, Pint wore his eastern ID in the west like a badge, a sneer. Since living in the west he had travelled to Athens, London, Los Angeles, New York, Paris, the usual places, but he had never managed to escape Berlin and he no longer wanted to. Once he had tried. With another exile from East Berlin he had bought a cottage in Cyprus. (At the time he said he had this fatal attraction for divided countries.) Their intention had been to take up permanent residence in the village, Pint working on his screenplays while his friend made stained-glass windows. The friend, who closely resembled Alain Delon, had actually been born in Shanghai, the son of a German father and an English mother who were assisting the Chinese revolution. The Alain Delon lookalike was still in Cyprus, though he had moved from the village to Nicosia. Pint had returned to West Berlin after less than a year. He said it was because he fell in love with Sonia, the woman with whom he now shared a flat in Charlottenburg, but I had always chosen to believe that it was the city itself he was in love with.

He had introduced me to the city and taught me how to love it. He had held open the curtain and shoved my face against the window. I had screamed in delight and gasped in horror. He enjoyed watching my reactions. Good actors, we brought out the best and worst in each other. Telling each other truths and lies, we confessed and competed, the usual dialectic of the soft and the hard, the kind and the cruel. So we took ourselves too seriously, we joked and jeered, boasted and debated, but somehow we never forgot that our meetings constituted a drama of our own invention: THE ENGLANDER AND THE KRAUT IN THE BERLIN PLAYHOUSE.

Casualties of history, they egged each other on. They never admitted of fear or tiredness. (There was always more pleasure and meaning to be squeezed out of the night. Sleep meant defeat. They waged war against boredom and the more pedestrian realities of their own lives.) It was a progressive buddy-buddy film, or so they liked to think, a kind of Anglo-German Thunderbolt and Lightfoot. They wrote the dialogue and chose the locations as they went along. They never admitted it, but they believed someone might be watching. They had never written to each other or telephoned from another country, but whenever they met they were bringers of news: bulletins on the latest state of their consciousness and lovelives, messages from island Britain and occupied Germany. They were free to say all the things they couldn't say to people who knew them better. An odd friendship, it probably would not have survived more routine exposure. It was too self-consciously decorated with significance, too good to be true. Every time they met they had to contrive some new episode in their occasional series: THE ENGLANDER AND THE KRAUT RIDE AGAIN! Both obsessed by the war which had betrayed their fathers, they often felt as if they were consorting with the enemy after the event. They played like children, willing accomplices in each other's fantasies, and they were sufficiently narcissistic to think their adventures meant something, that they spoke for someone. They were after all more or less the same age and class. They shared similar personal and political ambitions. They both possessed the ability to see themselves like this, in the third person.

'The profound things are not so very difficult. It merely requires the courage to state them,' Pint said, as we left the café-with-no-name.

Mumbling assent, I wondered again at Pint's knack of sounding wise. We boarded the U-Bahn at Kaiserdamm. I had done my best to thwart the categories, but *suffer*, as Pint had? I had suffered only fools. Alongside him, in the rocking yellow train, I felt like a pimp.

Walking north past the dossers and whores that habitually hung out around Nollendorfplatz, we made our way to a cabaret on Winterfeldplatz starring a transsexual called Sugarmoon. She was a beautiful six-foot blonde in a tight scarlet dress slit to the thigh. I had seen her once before, being chatted up by a GI in the Cri du Chat. She sang songs by Zara Leander and Gloria Gaynor. *I am what I am.* Having undressed down to her black suspender belt, black silk stockings, black brassière and black high heels, she sang, 'I am just a sweet transvestite'.

Pint knew the song from the *Rocky Horror Picture Show*, which he had seen on stage in London. I had never bothered to go.

From what I had heard of the show, it fed drab clichés about the pop underworld in the same way that this camp cabaret rehearsed clichés about sin city. It catered mostly for bourgeois tourists who were distinctly ill-at-ease with Sugarmoon's sexuality, but who needed an anecdote about a Berlin cabaret to take home with their duty-frees. Accordingly, they sat tight and stared at the tablecloth. Sugarmoon enjoyed their discomfiture.

Next she gave the tourists a song from *The Threepenny Opera* about a ship with eight sails. One day it will sail away with her, but first she will kill all the men in Berlin. Pint hummed along with the tune.

'It's a song about freedom or something,' he said, downing his Schultheiss and suggesting another change of scene. We left Sugarmoon doing her Grace Jones impersonation.

Pint had never been to the Metropol cafe on Nollendorfplatz. It was not really his kind of place. 'Triangle people,' he said, drawing this shape swiftly with the manic finger.

All the black plastic chairs had been turned round to face the ten-foot-square moving picture of Them performing 'Here Comes the Night', a clip from *Ready Steady Go!* Many of the Metropol spectators were clad in the mod garb of the studio audience that had danced twenty years ago for the TV cameras, short-haired men wearing dark suits and thin ties, girls in PVC skirts and op-art dresses.

'Triangle people?' I said.

This phrase, Pint delighted in informing me, described a class of West Berlin consumer attracted to triangular manifestations of imagined good taste. They wore triangular earrings, hats and handbags. They frequented bars furnished with (art-deco) triangular light fittings and serving alcohol in glass triangles. At home they drank tea and coffee from cups that had triangular handles. They also read magazines that explored the typographical possibilities of the triangle (in particular *The Face*, from London, which had reworked the A of its title into a solid red triangle). Often their fringes were cut in an irregular triangle obscuring one eye.

In the same way that Calvinists required capital to demonstrate their suitability for heaven, triangle people required success to vindicate their style. For such people, continued Pint, politics was a hippie illusion. Art was acceptable, as was a passing knowledge of avant-garde critics like, say, Foucault, but the only things that really *counted* were money, sex and fame, the holy trinity of glamour. Them were followed on the monochrome screen by the Pretty Things and then by the Zombies, whose one hit I knew by heart.

Black girl, black girl, tell me no lies,
Where did you sleep last night?
In the pines, in the pines where the sun never shines,
Shivers the whole day through.
They found her body all crushed and torn under the twisted steel.

Pint knew the words to the *Threepenny Opera* songs. I had memorised my words from *The Battle of the Giants* on Radio Luxembourg.

'In those days,' I said, 'square was the geometrical pejorative. Straight people were square.'

'But hip people weren't bent or round?'

'There *was* a circular quality to their philosophy,' I said, laughing, my fingers touching in the professorial prayer. 'You're either part of the problem or part of the solution.'

'Yeah. And Eldridge Cleaver ends up as the owner of a trouser factory.'

'Which later went bankrupt,' I added, this being true. 'But on the subject of the new non-squares, the triangle people, I think the plague of chic conservatism is more virulent in London. Here, nihilism is still the nightclub consensus.'

'On the subject of trousers,' replied Pint. 'I think Die Toten Hosen are the best band in West Berlin.'

'You know they did a gig in East Berlin earlier this year? They went through Friedrichstrasse wearing crimplene suits they got at a Turkish tailor's. A friend of mine called Mark organised it. He dresses like a Nazi, a bit off-putting when you first meet him, but he's a nice bloke. He's got lots of friends in the east. He's from Manchester. Anyway, the gig was apparently an absolute road-block. They went wild.'

'I must meet this Mark,' said Pint, half an eye on Manfred Mann singing doo-wah-diddy diddy-dum-diddy-dooh.

Manfred Mann, it had never occurred to me before, was a German name. West German groups of the same era bore names like The Rattles, The Scorpions, the City Preachers. They all sang in English, too, a form of cultural collaboration the musicians tried to justify by saying that the German language was just not built for rock and roll.

'Maybe if Hitler had won the war the Beatles would have sung in German,' I said.

'And a soap opera called *Düsseldorf* would have conquered the world.'

And so on through the drunken hypothesis, funny at the time, while the sixties revivalists expressionlessly watched the Small Faces sing 'Itchycoo Park', the nickname for Victoria Park in the East End of London, the venue for the first major Rock Against Racism carnival, starring the Clash, an event I reported for a magazine named *The Leveller* in honour of the radical wing of Cromwell's army. The first magazine Pint had worked for when he came to the west was *The Hobo*, also now defunct. Later he helped found *Zitty*, which was still alive. Little magazines were another link in our chain, but now I wrote for *The Observer* and he contributed to the German edition of *Playboy*. Both of us knew which way the wind was blowing.

Pint was looking tired. His last Camel had burned right down to its speckled filter without his noticing. His eyes were small maps with all the highways drawn in red. I felt like death, too, and had avoided the mirrors in the Gents. I knew if Pint had not come out with me this night he would have stayed at home working on his screenplay. A modern story of star-crossed lovers, its hero was Herr Proll, a masochistic worker, a member of an evangelical sect named the Bottle Baptists, recognisable by the initiation scars on their face. Herr Proll was brought together with his lover by three tramps who had all had the same dream. The three tramps possessed extraordinary powers. One could become iron, one could become a fly on the wall and one could blow himself up into a balloon and fly. But the price of exercising these powers was death, mandatory suicide. After Herr Proll was jailed some people tried to rescue him, but Proll told them to go away. He was happy the way he was, the scarred Bottle Baptist in his prison cell.

The previous screenplay Pint had written, still waiting to become a film, was based on a true story about a boy from East Berlin who had spent most of his life in institutions: orphanages, mental hospitals, prisons. He came to West Berlin and after six months was behind bars again after being caught trying to blow up a warehouse.

Like the West German history teachers who drew a polite veil across Nazism, Pint had remained silent about his own most traumatic period, his own time in jail. Finally, tonight, I wanted to screw up courage to ask him again. *Courage? You don't know the meaning of the word lad.* This was the voice of my father. He had volunteered to fight the Nazis when he was eighteen. He had survived U-boat attacks on convoys in the North Sea. Meeting a Russian sailor at a re-fuelling port in the Baltic, my father had exchanged his red jumper for a bottle of vodka. I had always loved that story. Many years later Reg Walker confessed that the bottle contained only water. He had been double-crossed.

He had voted Labour all his life. He had never believed in God. He had a routine dislike of the rich, a distrust of the powerful. He was a decent man and had it come to it he would have killed Pint's father, believing this to be necessary. At the time he had believed in all the futuristic stories about democracy. His last illusion had gone down with the *Belgrano*. I had come to Berlin to free myself from the bullshit, to avenge the sullied honour of my father and all the other millions of nameless heroes who knew the difference between right and wrong.

'You can't betray an idea, only people,' Pint said firmly. 'I meant to talk to my father properly and record everything he said, everything that happened. But unfortunately he died.'

'I won't make the same mistake,' I said, taking deep breaths and scrunching up one side of my face with violent fingers till, sweet mercy, I was rescued by Billy J. Kramer and the Dakotas. *Me and your sister we're going steady. But how can I kiss her when I'm ready too. With little children like you. Around. I wonder what I can do.* We laughed, offering up thanks to life for spewing out so much daft detail. Like a death in the family or a broken heart, it restored perspective, the smiling face of Billy J. Kramer in close-up, his hair glossy with the Brylcreem used by every Elvis impersonator in England.

'Here's to the Dakotas,' I said, raising my glass.

'Named after the north and the south. Destined to die unknown,' added Pint, making the sign of the cross.

'To all the backing bands! To the Miracles and the Tremeloes! To the Hermits and the Wailers! To the Big Sound! To the accumulated noise of the unknown musician!'

'To all those who still sing in the bath!'

'Tuneless multitudes!'

'Unsung heroes!'

Heads turned. Eyebrows made question marks. We didn't care. (Cool is fear turned into fashion.) We were drunk in the Metropol, drunk in the centre of the world, the old world of books and trains, the mighty metropolis that had simply run out of ideas and therefore intended to incinerate itself, to burn everything, to cheat the future, to remove the possibility of worlds which would shame this world, to pre-empt the time the world map would be published upside down with the south on top and the north below. Like spoiled children, the guardians of the past stared down the future with their sulky bombs. *Turn this map upside down and we rip up the map! Into a thousand pieces!* Never before did anyone have the chance to do this, to just tear up the map.

We knew this. We were not fooled, as our fathers had been. We were not scared of the Wall. We were fascinated by the border. What else kept us here? The Wall was epic, beautiful in its way, the white concrete, the metal crosses, the watchtowers standing like toy soldiers. We had loved that snowy night when we scaled the wooden watchtower in Spandau. We wanted to go there again, *now*, but we had no car and in any case it was usually unwise to try and re-live the past, to return to the scene of a holiday romance. Instead, we had one last drink in the Metropol and I tried once more to ask the question that had been sidetracked before by my father's voice.

'You never told me what happened to you in jail. Not the jokes. The tough stuff.'

'You want to make money out of me?' he said, examining my eyes. 'Okay. Why not? We all need the money. The day after tomorrow. Let's go cycling. To Wannsee.'

I caught the number 19 home. The Afro-German Shop was shut. Further along the empty street the yellow oblong of flashing light enclosing the sign for the Karibik, the Turkish nightclub next door, was still winking its invitation. I had never seen anyone either entering or leaving the club. Maybe it was a front for something else, drug trafficking, Turkish militants in exile, some secret service. I picked my way through the cycles and motorbikes and trash in the dark courtyard, pushed open the door (that was never locked) and found a small congregation down in the kitchen basement. Ulrike was holding forth on the subject of voodoo. Her knowledge of the phenomenon was based on an affair she once had with someone she met in Morocco. Listening to her exposition and periodically proffering their opinions were her sister, Uschi, the Danish punks and Murat, still wearing the flat tweed cap that always reminded me of depression photos from the thirties. Four empty bottles of Buzbag stood above the rest of the clutter on the wooden table. The radio was tuned to Armed Forces Network.

'It's one of those nights. You can't sleep. You're thousands of miles from home and you're wondering exactly what it is you're doing here in Berlin,' crooned the downhome voice, placing north American emphasis on the burr of *Ber*lin. 'But I want to tell you. Your folks back home are real proud of you. Your President thinks you're doing a real important job. You got that pay check coming and then you got that leave due. You can go visit that girl back home. Do you feel better now? Sure you do.'

'These Americans,' sighed Uschi. 'Really, they're too much.'

En route to my bedroom I noticed a scrap of lined paper on the floor. It contained three messages. Johnny had rung to say hello. Laura had called to say she would be joining me as planned in seven days' time. And the British Army PRO wanted to know if I was still interested in writing something about the Brits in Berlin. No way of telling how old the messages were. I collapsed on my polystyrene bed and awoke around noon with the taste of war in my mouth. Once I had drunk coffee from a broken Thermos and somehow in my dreams this bitter taste of glass and plastic, mingled with imaginary dust, had come to mean war. East and west, governments had become dream dictators, hell-fire gods. They could turn on the rain and re-paint the sky.

4 Dangerous Moonlight

In the sky behind the tramp was the Tele-Tower. It resembled a revolving crystal globe in the lobby of an expensive hotel, but he was oblivious of the photogenic possibilities through which he was walking. Slowly, stooped, eyes fastened on the pavement, he shuffled along Mehringdamm. I was sitting beneath a red Cinzano umbrella on the street, drinking Berliner Kindl. Inside the café were four one-armed bandits, three pool tables and about forty customers, mostly tattooed young men with long hair but also some older women with dyed hair and bright lipstick.

Walking past the café, the tramp suddenly stopped in his tracks to watch a pigeon, its purple breast heaving as it scurried in quick circles on the paving stones. The tramp just stood there watching and slowly his dirty face widened into a smile that meant a nice thought, an *idea!* He plucked a half-eaten loaf of bread from the plastic bag in which he carried his belongings. With some difficulty, the bread being so hard and stale, he tore the loaf into pieces, tossed three handfuls on to the street and waited expectantly for the pigeon to gobble the first piece. Nothing happened. The tramp continued to stand and watch hopefully, but still the pigeon spurned his gift. The tramp's smile faded. He turned heel and continued on his way, wherever that was. Five minutes later pigeons were simply raining down on the street, fighting for the scraps of stale white bread. Such is life.

Such was the commotion of pigeons outside the café it attracted the attention of another benefactor, a thin old woman who cast more bread to the flock. The pigeons dined greedily, there was plenty for all, but as soon as one pigeon abandoned the feast all the others followed suit, fickle as lounge lizards. Some twenty pigeons flew away together, causing pedestrians to duck their heads, and presently the birds were so distant they looked like a trail of smoke in the Kreuzberg sky.

I stayed outside the café watching a taxi driver feed ice cream to his black poodle, who sat on the passenger seat of the yellow taxi. A middle-aged woman whose face had never known malice dropped a leaflet on my table which announced an evening of gospel music. I thanked her and she gave me the sweetest of smiles.

Back at the house I asked Uschi if she knew what day it was. She gave the matter some consideration, then plumped for Friday. In Ulrike's opinion it was Wednesday. As usual, the two sisters between them had contrived some approximation of the truth. It was Thursday.

'I can't walk past a bed without falling into it,' croaked Ulrike, wiping the sleep from her eyes.

It was three in the afternoon. Uschi decided to go to the clinic to get the results of her pregnancy test.

'But first I have to get stoned,' she said, walking into the bedroom to collect the relevant materials. Her reaction to her suspected pregnancy was somewhere between panic and resignation: anger at the tricks a woman's biology can play and a kind of stoic acceptance that you had to take things as they come. She felt sure the trip to the clinic would be a formality.

Two nights before Uschi told Ulrike that she thought she was pregnant, Ulrike had a dream. Ulrike was carrying Charlotte in her arms, but in the mirror it was another child, a child with darker hair. For Ulrike there was no mystery about such dreams.

'That was how I first received the news of Uschi's pregnancy,' she said matter-of-factly, adding that she was going to the bathroom and could I take care of Charlotte for a few minutes? 'She likes it when you sing those dumb English songs.'

I complied, gathering up Charlotte and placing her on my shoulders. Her legs dangled like white sausages. In addition to work, shit and car in German she already knew how to say goodbye in English. What would she remember of these days in later life? A blur of strange faces and a babble of foreign tongues? I held her fragile hands and sang I'll-sing-you-one-oh-green-grow-the-rushes-oh, bouncing up and down in time, careering round the room and taking care not to tread on Uschi's half-finished paintings.

One is one and all alone and ever more shall be so.

Uschi sat on the floor, mournfully smoking her spliff. Four nights ago I had walked with her past a shop selling bridal gowns on Kleiststrasse. It was sometime between dark and dawn. 'Do shops like that still exist?' Uschi had asked. 'Do they still make money?'

Ulrike had finished her toilet. She asked me when Pint was next coming round. I said I was seeing him tomorrow.

'His laugh was made in bedlam,' she said, wiping Charlotte's face with a wet flannel.

Down in the basement George was cleaning up in the kitchen: 'Because if I don't no one else will.'

This was not, strictly speaking, true, but the kitchen was a mess, the remains of last night's spaghetti stuck like limpets to plates and pans, fag-ends in wine glasses. Feeling guilty, I gave George a hand. We talked, as we invariably did, of the twin struggles: politics and love. On this latter question, George was again lamenting the fact West Berlin girls seemed so unromantic.

'They only want you for your body?' I said, only half-joking for George was six-foot, slim-hipped, broad-shouldered. He moved languid as a dancer. One of his teeth, on the upper row, was missing and the gap showed whenever he smiled. His smile was so ingenuous you wondered if that made him vulnerable in a city where smiling was so often a matter of tactics. His face was the colour of coffee made with cream. His black hair was kept nice and short by Ulrike.

'The moment you get depressed, they don't want to know,' George said, standing over the sink. 'They say, oh, I can't handle this. Not my problem.'

He wanted companionship, comradeship. He needed someone who shared some of his ideas, recognised his loneliness. He had slept with twenty-one women in the two years he had been in

West Berlin, he continued. *Twenty-one!* Ten women less than the years he possessed. In his own country men slept only with their wives. George's politics had led to forms of architecture and life that once had seemed remote as the planets, to the thin bit of America and the small bit of the west in East Germany, to twenty-one fucks with Berlin strangers.

He wore black jeans, no socks, tattered plimsolls and a white cricket shirt, the sleeves rolled up to his muscular biceps. I knew he had worn that shirt on cricket fields in Sri Lanka which I imagined to be brown, sun-baked, with pitches made of jute that lent themselves to spin. We had talked in general about cricket, but I always avoided asking him specific questions about his past, about the home he left in a hurry in 1980. He had tried in vain to track down the four brothers and five sisters who were scattered somewhere in the world. He didn't even know if they were all still alive. There was no one he could write to in Sri Lanka. His parents were dead. His friends and possibly some of his brothers and sisters were underground, fighting with the Tigers. In these circumstances cricket had faded in importance, though he still followed Test Matches on the BBC World Service.

He had surrendered his passport to the local police station, where he had to report once a week. He was stateless. He could not claim unemployment benefit, he lived on food stamps and whatever money he could bum off Andreas. Unable to leave West Berlin, he could go neither to the east nor to West Germany. He had once tried to travel to Hamburg with a friend of his called Peter. He was detained at the West German border for three hours till finally one of the border guards flagged down some guy in a BMW and pointing at George like he was an unwanted parcel, said, 'Take him back to West Berlin.'

George's friend, Peter, had been in West Berlin only one month at the time. He was a toolmaker from Jena in the GDR.

In a week's time George and Peter and the rest of the Berlin Brigade would be flying to Nicaragua, to build houses for peasants' families in a village sixty kilometres north of the Costa Rican border. Peter was going for three months, George for the duration. As long as it took. Nicaragua, he thought, was going to be the final showdown between the forces of light and darkness: our Spain.

George was washing up, I was drying. Intrigued that I spent so much time in East Berlin, he was always asking questions I found hard to answer.

'Is there less racism in the east?'

'Yeah, but there are fewer races too. There are no guest-workers, no Turks or Yugoslavs, apart from those who go over on day-trips like myself. I think de-Nazification was taken more seriously in East Germany, but on the other hand I know Johnny's father had a number of problems throughout his career which, in the end, he was forced to put down to anti-semitism. So. I don't know . . .'

'But everyone has a job, right?'

'In theory, yes. In practice there are some people who don't work, you know, some of those punks I told you about . . .'

'But you told me there were no tramps and junkies. What about whores?'

'There are a few working out of the Palasthotel, earning hard currency, but in general, no. Compared to West Berlin, prostitution is more or less non-existent.'

'And no advertising?'

'No. Not really.'

George's full lips stretched to reveal the gap-toothed smile. He liked the idea of East Berlin and I could understand why. For him the enemy was Yankee imperialism. In Africa, America and Asia the Soviet Union was supporting those liberation struggles which the USA was trying to defeat by bombing El Salvador and Guatemala, financing counter-revolutions in Angola and Nicaragua, propping up military dictatorships in Paraguay and Chile, collaborating with apartheid in South Africa, maintaining tyrannies in Thailand, the Philippines and South Korea, not to mention suppressing its own descendants from slaves, the millions of black Americans who lived in ghettoes where people died from heroin and bullet wounds. This was George's view of the world. He was genuinely baffled why most West European leftists were so militantly anti-Soviet.

'Because they feel the revolution was betrayed,' I said. 'Because the Red Army has become identified in people's minds with repression, not liberation. Because of the invasions, inter-

ventions, whatever you call them, in Hungary and Czechoslovakia and Poland. Because of Afghanistan too.'

'But there was a socialist revolution in Afghanistan. And the
rebels in Afghanistan do the same things as the Contras in
Nicaragua, blowing up schools and clinics, assassinating
civilians. They just want to return society to the ninth century or
something. They're the same fanatic mullahs the Yankees hate so
much in Iran.'

'I know,' I said, trying to remember where the glasses and cups
were kept, then remembering that there was no system, no
ideology, only a vague commitment to unlocked doors and
existential opposition, a general feeling that order was at one end
of the continuum that led via uniforms and more laws to the Nazi
state. Accordingly, I stacked the dry cups and glasses in places of
my choosing. Swastika, I thought, was a word stolen from
Sanskrit, an emblem dating from the first millennium BC, a
problem for Hindu brides arriving at Heathrow Airport with
Nazi crosses inscribed on their faces and hands.

'The thing is,' I continued, 'that national self-determination is
everyone's inalienable right and, therefore, whatever you think
about the Afghan rebels it's something for Afghanistan to deal
with, not Russia.'

'But the Afghan rebels are financed by the CIA, the same
people who put the Shah of Iran on the throne, who destabilised
Chile and Jamaica, who arm and train the mercenaries in
Nicaragua . . .'

'That's true and, I agree, what the west calls Soviet imperialism
is not really comparable to US imperialism. But as long as
everyone accepts that the world is like some city run by two
warring gangs then there isn't much chance the city can ever live
in peace.'

The kitchen was beginning to look more decent. Plates were
clean for the next heaps of pasta, glasses dry for the next bottles of
red and white, ashtrays empty for the next mountains of cigarette
butts, the wooden table scrubbed for the next collection of voices,
the whole kitchen prepared like a theatre for the next torrent of
night words.

Uschi returned from the clinic wearing a wan smile that said, yes, Charlotte will have a brother or sister. She went into her bedroom and, for once, shut the door.

'No one knows how strong she is,' Ulrike said, before going to join her.

I didn't really know what to say. *I hope everything will be all right?*

George shook his head and murmured he found it hard to understand what had happened to make people live this way in the west, to conceive so casually with no fathers in sight, to wander from one love to another without ever believing . . .

'But how many,' I interrupted. 'How many of your twenty-one did you ask about contraception before you become lovers? How do you know you aren't already a father? Maybe she didn't bother telling you.'

He nodded slowly, frowning, a massive sadness that pitted his forehead and cheeks, pouting his lips like the coming agony. Extreme as his smile, his frown was often preceded by a pummelling of his face with his big brown fist. Ulrike had sometimes seen him crying alone in his room.

George felt sad about Uschi, he loved the German Sisters, but he was also like those who cry for themselves at the funerals of their loved ones. In this house, this city, he was half-drowned in nihilism and struggling to keep his head above the poisoned waves, fighting to remember what it was he believed in: most people he knew in West Berlin had succumbed to the present state of things because they could not imagine how things could be any better. He had to keep repeating his faith, he had to think his life was worth living. He cried for himself.

Andreas came home from his design studio at six, received the news about Uschi and then suggested a quick bite to eat round the corner at the Turkish Imbiss. George started to say with face and hands that he was broke. But Andreas replied wordlessly, slapping a palm on the stitched back pocket of the faded Wranglers where he kept his paper money. Andreas, remember, was an orphan. He had a heart of gold. He led the way down the street, past the Afro-German Shop, across Gneisenaustrasse where some old Turks sat on benches fiddling with worry beads. We ran across the second section of the dual carriageway while the red man said *no*, stay there, and we strode the final twenty yards up Zossenerstrasse towards the wailing sound of the zithers.

The tiny café had ceramic plates hanging from one wall and a vast poster of the Golden Gate suspension bridge framed in gold plastic on another, a history of civilisation on two facing walls. One of the two fruit machines was being played, a continuous blur of oranges and lemons and bananas from hot countries, apples and pears from cold ones too, the crank of the steel arm every ten seconds and the stuttering of the machine as the last fruits clicked into place, the flashing of the red and yellow HOLD buttons, the periodic ejaculation of tokens, usually accompanied by grunts of human satisfaction and often by shouted remarks in Turkish from the proprietor and his two cronies who sat drinking on high stools behind the bar, which was right next to the open door, affording a view of the street and the occasional wonders and beauties thereon. We ordered humus, green salad, lamb kebabs, a bottle of Buzbag. George ate more hungrily than Andreas and myself.

George felt at home with the Turks, he was saying, between mouthfuls. They suffered the same averted gazes and sidelong glances, the same whispers, the same shake of the head at certain nightclubs, the same miserable condescension meted out to black and brown immigrants everywhere in the west, the functional hate for the foreign poor that was laughably wrapped up in the English phrase, racial prejudice, as if there would be no problem if only people would start being nice to the darkies. We drank sweet black coffee in small white cups.

Nescafé or Maxwell House, espresso or cappucino, au lait or Turkish, every cup of coffee we had ever drunk was composed of hand-picked berries, George said. People who died young in Africa and America took pains to pick the red berries and leave the green ones to ripen further in the sun.

'How many people know this?' he said, angrily. 'How many cups of coffee and tea have you drunk and how often have you thought about where it comes from, who picked it, who set the price for the labour? Yes, I know, you've both thought about such things, but how many people have?'

Andreas replied that things were slowly changing and he added an optimistic homily on the theme of the rise of the Greens in West Germany but especially in West Berlin and especially here in this neighbourhood where bright green metal domes on street corners were dutifully filled each day with thousands of glass bottles by the collective ecological conscience of Kreuzberg 16.

Andreas asked for the bill. Someone came into the café trying to sell a pink hair-drier.

Art-for-art's sake was the next subject under discussion. Andreas was for, George against. Where did I stand? The taste of coffee, like the beauty of cathedrals, was disfigured by knowledge of their manufacture, thinking barefoot children in plantations, wondering how many died working round the clock to raise those great stone dreams to the sky. Our small white cups now ran with brown tears that had dried and caked like paint, tears that would be removed with steel wool in hot water by invisible female hands.

'This one's for Berlin and England and Germany and everyone else affected,' the singer said in English between numbers.

She stood on stage at the Loft, the low-ceilinged concert-hall at the top of the Metropol in Nollendorfplatz whence I had come to escape the art-for-art's-sake debate. Her head was half-shaved, the remaining hair dyed blonde and wet with gel. Her eyes were black with mascara and late nights. Honest Levis displayed her thick thighs and ample arse. Her brown leather jacket was of the kind worn by airmen in the last war. Probably in her late twenties, she had a premature double chin. Her name was Anne Clark. I had never heard of her, though I had known other Anne Clarks.

'We had faith like a cross, we had trust like a flag,' she sang, her eyes liquid with the usual combination of indignation, sadness, rage, a face which declared that it is after all the world which breaks our fucking hearts.

On the screen behind her a black-and-white tableau unfolded through the six-minute song. Auschwitz, Belsen, Bikini, Dachau, Dresden, Hiroshima, Nagasaki, Vietnam, the images clicked quickly past, thin figures with shaved heads, barbed wire and smoke, portly men in uniform, the first bomb falling on an island whose name became identified with a two-piece swimsuit, the next bombs rendering cities into simmering deserts, the last bombs making children catch fire. The song was called 'Killing Time' and there were legions of critics prepared to announce that the whole song was a thinly disguised scream, that its anger had overpowered its art, that its title was the clumsiest of puns, that Anne Clark's voice would never charm the birds from the trees and that, frankly, who *needs* this kind of stuff? Rock and roll was founded on the dance ethic baby don't give me any of that protest poetry shit.

By the time Anne Clark finished 'Killing Time' she was plainly crying. In a broken voice she recited a poem: 'Without Sex'. Faces aged between fifteen and forty were uplifted to the stage in attitudes of meditative cool and lip-pursed reflection, like believers before the Sunday sermon, except this preacher spoke in a tongue that probably was understood by only a fifth of the congregation.

'This is a new one,' she said, nodding her head in recognition of the sincere applause for the poem about bad sex and celibacy. 'It's called "Nothing At All".'

'Typical bloody miserable Mancunian,' said Mark Reeder, the doorman at the Loft, who had himself grown up in that city famous for rain and cotton and Manchester United. Aged twenty-five, he had been a resident of West Berlin, Kreuzberg to be precise, for five years.

He was the Factory Records representative in Berlin and also played in a band with another friend of mine called Al, a former northern soul fan from Middlesbrough. Previously they were known as Die Unbekennten (The Unknown), but this year they had changed their name to Shark Vegas, which Mark said he liked because it meant nothing at all beyond reminding him vaguely of *The Thunderbirds*, the science-fiction TV series, although to me Shark Vegas sounded like the conflation of two Hunter S. Thompson titles, a connotative disadvantage which Al had acknowledged. Their last single, only available in the twelve-inch version, was called 'Dangerous Moonlight', part of a genre that Al described as *depro-disco*, depressive disco.

Mark couldn't really play any instruments and when Die Unbekennten were on tour with New Order he had taped different colours to the synthesizer so he knew which keys to press. Unashamed of this lack of musicianship, Mark always recounted with great glee his stories about on-stage panic and confusion. From the Monkees to Frankie Goes To Hollywood there was a long tradition of pop stars who couldn't play a note. Pop music was a joke that sometimes made money. The greatest sin was to take things seriously.

Anne Clark was now performing 'Sleeper in the Metropolis' in which she pronounced the city to be either a waking disease or a walking disease, I couldn't quite make out the words.

'She was a hero of the student revolution in the sixties,' Mark said, pointing to a woman in a black mini-skirt drinking champagne from the bottle. From a distance this woman could have been a teenager. Close up she looked fifty. She was the manager of the Loft.

Standing next to Mark I was, as always, conscious of his clothes, conscious of the looks flung in his direction whenever he was in public. Mark dressed like a Nazi and sometimes I felt tainted by association. At least he wasn't wearing one of his uniforms tonight, I thought. He was in civvies: a thirties-style double-breasted grey suit, white shirt with detachable starched collar, a black tie, highly polished black shoes which I imagined had metal toe-caps. His naturally blond hair was short and side-parted, lightly oiled. His eyes were blue as a tropical sea.

Mark Reeder had first run away from Manchester because his mother wanted to get him certified insane. At an age when other boys were out playing football, cadging cigarettes, making mischief, asking girls if they would like to go to the pictures, Mark was still at home making model aeroplanes. He had also joined the ATC and, a couple of times, had managed to get taken up in the air. His mother could not understand what she had done to deserve a seventeen-year-old son who dressed like a Nazi, read war comics, collected war memorabilia from Manchester junk shops and, if he had any ambition at all, it was to be a fighter pilot. Mark fled to Germany. He found a job working in the kitchen of a youth hostel near a castle somewhere in Bavaria, making a bit on the side doing English breakfasts freelance. Two years later he came to Berlin. He had no intention of ever again living in England.

He had a fascination with East Berlin and went there as often as his finances would allow. He had helped organise a gig with Die Toten Hosen (Dead Trousers) in the same Lutheran churchyard in Rummelsburg where I had seen Kotzbrocken (Bit Of Puke) and Klassenkrampf (Class Cramp) in the summer of '83. Dead trousers, in Berlin slang, meant really bad taste. Die Toten Hosen were Liverpool FC supporters who sang contemporary drinking songs with much gusto. The East Berlin punks had loved them. Mark said it was the most moving night of his life.

He had also researched and presented a Channel 4 programme on Berlin. He had agreed to collaborate with the television people on three conditions. 1: that the show would not be propaganda; 2: that it would not mention Marlene Dietrich; 3: that it would not mention David Bowie. I never saw the edition of the Tube that Mark presented, but I knew one girl in London who had fallen in love with his television face.

Mark had rung me in London immediately he saw the feature I wrote on East Berlin punks. He had introduced himself, babbled breathlessly about the music scene in Berlin and said he knew one of the blokes who had appeared on the cover of the *Observer* magazine. That was how we knew each other.

But of all the people who had become friends as a result of my cushy job, Mark was maybe the weirdest. I liked and respected him, but *why* did he dress like a Nazi? What had happened in his life to feed the obsession? On a number of occasions he had told me his father had been in Manhattan that day in 1938 when an aeroplane crashed into the Empire State Building. Was that somehow a significant detail? In the war his father had been in the merchant navy. He had shot down a Messerschmidt and had a medal to prove it. Mark was very proud of his father, who after the war had worked for Manchester Liners till the firm closed down. Was Mark gaining some sort of revenge for his father? Or did he just enjoy consorting with the enemy after the event? The strands of style leading from the Third Reich wove a complex web. Factory Records, from whom Mark received a pittance if anything, had gained notoriety as a Mancunian outpost of Nazi graphics, its most popular band metamorphosing, via the suicide-by-hanging of a lead singer, from one Nazi name to another: Joy Division to New Order.

Yet Mark was only at the extreme edge of the general militarist tendency packed tight inside the claustrophobic Loft, the shaved heads, the black clothes and polished army boots. In the continent of fashion, the society of appearances, he was a cartoon version of the post-war flirtation with the Nazi aesthetic. Leni Riefenstahl films were in permanent circulation on metropolitan art-house circuits. War films in England were still guaranteed large Sunday afternoon television audiences. Swastikas on paper-backs at railway station bookstalls still commanded commercial appeal. Billy Butlin had bought Ribbentrop's desk at an auction to entertain the holiday-makers at Pwllheli camp. Volkswagen Beetles were still popular examples of Nazi minimalism. Architec-tural journals acknowledged the monumental contribution of Albert Speer. People in England still made concentration-camp jokes.

Still, I was never quite sure exactly where Mark belonged in this mess of fashion and fascism. The few times I had quizzed him he had got upset. His cheeks would flush and he would start jabbering that of course it was just a hobby and anyone who thought he was a Nazi was off their fucking rocker. He'd been to Belsen, he would say, and it had disgusted him the way it disgusts everyone else. Yes, he had always liked uniforms, but it wasn't just Nazi uniforms, one of his most prized possessions was a GDR field officer's uniform. He had worn it beneath his normal clothes one time when he came back to West Berlin through Friedrich-strasse checkpoint. He had First World War uniforms too and, as a matter of fact, the uniform he most coveted in the whole world was the really beautiful one worn by Red Army tank com-manders. It was just a hangover from a childhood thing, he supposed. It gave him harmless amusement and, anyway, the war had still been a big deal when he was a boy. *My father shot down a Messerschmidt and he's got the medal to prove it.* Everyone read *Eagle* comics and bought Airfix kits in those days. Everyone played the tommies against the Nazis in the streets. It was just that Mark had decided to delve deeper into it all, he said, to find out more about the history of Nazism, the cut of the uniforms, the light-spectaculars stage-managed by Speer, the china and the cutlery and the everyday objects of Nazi design. He had a propaganda record made by Goebbels's Ministry of Propaganda consisting of Cole Porter songs re-recorded with anti-semitic and anti-British lyrics. Shit, he hadn't been to university, he said, unlike me and many others he knew these days, but he had managed to educate himself through his interest in these things. He spoke fluent German. He had travelled the two Germanies and spent holidays in Prague. The justification would pour forth like a river in flood and then he would stop and maybe tell one of his sad stories. For example: once he was picked up by the police in downtown East Berlin. It was a hot summer's day and Mark was wearing his Rommel desert-rat ensemble: knee-length socks, khaki Bermudas and matching shirt. He was taken to a police-station and interrogated.

'Why are you dressed like a militarist and a fascist?'

Mark tried to explain he didn't see it that way, it was just a hobby, he hated all the western cold war propaganda about the east, he liked East Berlin and had plenty of friends there. The policeman let Mark go, telling him that next time he came to East Berlin he should show more respect for the anti-fascist German state. Subsequently Mark had worn civilian clothes whenever he travelled through Friedrichstrasse.

Anne Clark finished her set and the crowd roared for more.

'Oh dear,' she said. 'Are you really that unhappy in Berlin?'

5 Song of the shirt

'There are no Xerox machines in the GDR. *None*,' said Pint,
bringing down his hand in a slow karate chop on the chrome
handlebars. Weather conditions were against cycling all the way
to Wannsee. Instead, we had settled on a more leisurely ride to the
Grunewald. It was a grey day forever on the edge of rain.

The absence of Xerox machines in East Berlin was the critical
detail, the start of the story that would embrace the quality of the
cuisine in Rumanian prisons, the intoxicating possibilities of
dandruff remover, the writing of poems on shirts. We were
cycling double-breasted along the Kurfürstendamm, uphill,
against the wind.

'The only duplicating machines in the GDR are those old-
fashioned ones that use photographic paper,' he continued. 'To
get access to one of these you need to fill out five or six forms and
then get them counter-signed and *then* you get given a key. There
is no way that duplicating machines can be used for anti-state
purposes in the GDR.'

I was struggling to keep up. Uschi's bicycle, which I had
borrowed, had a sticking back wheel and no gears. It was Uschi's
bicycle in the sense that she was its current user. In all the time she
had lived in West Berlin she had never bought a bicycle. Bicycles
just materialised and then disappeared, she said. What this meant
was that her friends stole bicycles which later were stolen by other
people's friends. Bicycles were in permanent circulation among
friendly thieves. Pint made a disparaging gesture at the BMW

showrooms which had attracted the usual clutch of window-dreamers. He had never owned a car.

Pedalling past the Bhagwan Far Out disco at the top end of the Kudamm, Pint said everything began after he returned to East Berlin from Prague. I knew this part of the story.

He went to Prague with a contingent from East Berlin to support the movement of spring 1968. He was eighteen. When the Red Army invaded he threw stones at the tanks and ran the streets flying the Czech flag. Returning to East Berlin, he was sickened by reports in *Neues Deutschland* about the Red Army lending assistance to Czech socialists in their heroic fight against petty bourgeois and CIA-backed counter-revolutionaries. Pint and a friend of his called Bootsman (who I was to meet some ten years later in the flat off the Old Kent Road) decided to produce some propaganda of their own. With two typewriters and six carbons they sat up all night writing leaflets. In the morning they dropped them on the S-Bahn trains and in the afternoon Bootsman was arrested. In the evening the Staasis came for Pint.

'I remember, I was in love at the time,' he said, pelting no-hands down Koenigs Allee, past the first lakes on the edge of the Grunewald. 'I'd been to the cinema and taken my girlfriend back to her parents. Outside her front door there had been a good deal of kissing and cuddling. By the time I got home it was quite late, but I was walking with a spring in my step. I saw a guy standing on the street and then another one sitting in a car. The red lights flashed in my brain. I walked past them as calm as I could. I remember thinking at the time: *at this stage they don't know what I look like*. Which would maybe give me ten minutes' grace. As soon as I was out of their sight I tore up the stairs to my parents' apartment and started to gather up all the leaflets from the previous night, all the newspapers and stuff I had got in Prague, different letters, all this shit. I lit a fire in the corner of my bedroom and burned as much as I could. But I was stupid. I hid some of the papers under the carpet. And when they came in it was like an atom bomb. The flat was destroyed. There was no way something hidden under the carpet would remain undiscovered. No chance.'

Pint was shouting his story against the roar of the wind and the traffic. Certain details were lost in the noise, sabotaged by cars and trucks that came too close. When the police came to his house he lay on his bed and shut his eyes.

'*I thought it might help,*' he yelled, laughing.

As he was being escorted from the apartment by the Staasis, his father gave Pint the lunchbox he had intended taking to work.

'Just in case it takes a little longer,' his father said.

Having been driven from Köpenick to the police station on the Alexanderplatz, Pint was interrogated for fifteen hours, with a few breaks of fifteen minutes designed to give him time to brood, to get scared, to betray his friends. He walked the tightrope: he confessed enough, but concealed more. He tried to give his interrogators the impression they had achieved some success, while protecting the identity of his accomplices. Held in custody for three months, he was questioned a few times each week. Finally he was charged with conspiracy and sentenced to eighteen months imprisonment.

'Luckily, one month later, there was a general amnesty for young prisoners. They just let us free, on two years' probation. They didn't tell us in advance we were going to be released. They told us just one hour before to get our things together. They don't want to give you the satisfaction of a whole night thinking about imminent freedom,' he said, turning off the main road into the network of mud tracks that wound around the lakes and threaded the woods.

Pint knew the Grunewald like the back of his hand. In good weather its tranquillity was despoiled by screaming children and transistor radios. Pint came here on sunless days for the peace and quiet that was harder to find in West Berlin than it had been in the east. These days, he was fond of saying, he had to organise his loneliness.

After cycling through the forest for twenty minutes we reached his chosen spot, a wooden bench on a sandy slope. The wind had dropped, the lake was still as a mirror. On the far shore was a green-and-white telephone kiosk marked POLIZEI. Pint liked the view. He thought it would make a nice painting, he said, watching a middle-aged couple plunge naked into the lake. 'They live here all the year round.'

'Immured in the phony countryside?'

'There *are* worse lives,' he said.

Before he was jailed Pint had secured a place to study medicine at university. Such places are few and far between. He had worked hard at school because from childhood it had been his ambition to be a doctor. Instead, after his release from prison, Pint was set to work as a male nurse. He was told that if he was diligent, kept his nose clean, he would eventually be able to study medicine. For two years Pint obeyed this instruction, he never missed a day's work. Finally, he went to see the admissions tutor at the medical school. Laughing, the admissions tutor said Pint would never be a doctor. He would work in production.

'It was then I thought, okay. Now I have to escape. If they had let me study medicine I would by now be a doctor in the GDR. So in a way I am grateful to Bootsman for giving away my name. Just one little word he spoke, Spielhagen, it changed my life. For the better, I think,' he said, still staring at the nude couple splashing in the lake.

Having decided to flee, his problem was twofold: which method and which companion? In those days, early in 1971, only ten years after the construction of the Wall, escaping was more difficult. The car boot method of escape only became possible after 3 September 1971, when the ambassadors of the four occupying powers initialled the Four Power Agreement, making it easier for West Germans to travel along the transit roads to West Berlin. For his fellow escapist Pint chose an old school-friend.

'More of an acquaintance really. He is also in West Berlin now,' Pint said. 'But I was looking for the best person to escape with, not the best friend. He was the best friend for this, a little tougher than the others, and also he had less imagination than others. To get really scared you need a good imagination.'

Their plan was to travel down to Yugoslavia, from which point it is relatively easy to cross the border into Italy. Pint had found two helpers in West Berlin, who were to drive them through the countries, the helpers crossing the borders legally in the car while Pint and his friend of little imagination crawled under the barbed wire at places Pint had chosen on maps bought in East Berlin.

Pick-up points and signals were arranged. Unlike the junkies employed by gangsters to drive would-be immigrants to the west in car boots, which later became a familiar feature of the escape industry, Pint's helpers were leftist students who sought to aid a comrade from the east.

Sworn to secrecy, Pint could tell nobody of his plans, not even his loved ones. It was hard not being able to say goodbye properly, but his father's eyes told Pint that the story about the vacation had not cut much ice. The father knew he would not see the son for quite some time. They shook hands and wished each other luck. In the VW Beetle the West Berlin communists had brought respectable clothes, canned food, torches, water bottles, knives, everything they thought the escapists would need. They drove south to Czechoslovakia and celebrated their successful negotiation of the first border with lavish dinner at a Prague hotel.

After spending a pleasant couple of days in Prague they set out for the Danube, which divides Czechoslovakia from Hungary. The Beetle dropped them by the river at three in the morning. They saw the beam of a patrol boat. It was too late to risk crossing, they decided. All they could do was hide in the bushes and wait till night fell again. In the morning at around ten a family arrived and started picnicking close by. The children played hide-and-seek.

'*I thought, oh my God. Play where you want, my children, but not near us.*'

As soon as it was dark, Pint and his partner made a reconnoitre along the river. On an island about 100 yards from the bank they heard voices and saw a boat of some kind. Later a fire was lit on the island. Pint wasn't sure if the people on the island were soldiers or civilians, but he had decided it was the only chance, swimming to the island and stealing the boat. Pint had always felt that crossing the Danube would be the most difficult sequence of the whole escape. They stripped down to their shirts and underpants. Their passports were in the Beetle.

At 9.30 they started swimming, as slowly and silently as they could. The current wasn't too bad, Pint remembered, it took about twenty minutes to reach the island. They crawled ashore and hid once more. Pint was relieved to hear that the voices around the fire were jovial and drunken. When the hubbub died down after midnight the two East Germans set about trying to find the boat. Instead, they stumbled across the ridge-tent in which the merry-makers were sleeping. Pint almost tripped over another of the campers, who was outside the tent in a sleeping bag.

'Then we saw the boat. A canoe. Beautiful.'

But there was no paddle in the canoe. Thinking it might have been left by the camp, they returned to the danger zone. After fifteen minutes' fruitless searching Pint found a stout branch, trimmed it with his knife and tied his shirt to it like a lacrosse stick. Using this as a paddle, they laboriously made their way across the remaining 400 yards of the Danube. Under a full moon they beat the glittering water with the makeshift paddle for almost an hour before reaching the Hungarian side of the river, where they concealed the canoe behind some shrubs.

Partly to release the tension, to return himself from the Danube to the Grunewald, Pint chuckled again at the plight of the stranded revellers. 'No boat? Impossible!' he exclaimed, eyeing the nude bathers as they ran shivering from the lake. 'They really must have thought they drank too much the night before.'

His smile vanished. His head nodding, his eyes unfocused, he continued his account of the night he still dreamt about often.

Walking away from the Danube, they soon came to a railway viaduct. Beneath the railway track was a small village built either side of one long street. It was one or two in the morning. Jumping from shadow to shadow in the moonlight, the two men, half-naked and passportless, made their way along the main street. They were searching for their helpers, the West Berlin communists who had agreed to patrol the village at regular intervals, driving slowly, turning the headlights on and off. But having walked the three kilometres from one end of the village to the other, all they had seen was a milkman's cart. Hungry and thirsty, they stole two bottles of milk each from adjacent doorsteps and sat behind some bushes to drink it. While they were both midway through the second bottle, the Beetle passed by, its headlights flashing on and off. The two barefoot men chased after the car, but they couldn't shout or scream. Pint later calculated that he was running at twenty kilometres per hour, while the car was doing twenty-two. Slowly it pulled away from him and disappeared into the night.

Pint and his former schoolfriend walked for another ten kilometres. Sometimes police patrols came past on bicycles and cars, but it was easy enough to hide. Then in the distance, shining with electric light, they saw a huge industrial complex working on the nightshift. Pint's friend said there was no way he was going any further. Pint said it was pointless staying where they were because soon it would be daylight. They had a fierce argument which ended with Pint leaving and his friend staying behind. Wearing only his underpants, Pint walked alone towards the bright lights.

There were factories both sides of the street, convoys of lorries coming and going. There was nowhere to hide so Pint simply strolled, calm as he was able, straight through the centre of all the commotion. Nobody bothered him. Two kilometres beyond the industrial complex he found the Beetle. His friend was already inside the car, which had driven back into the village. He was wearing one of the suits the helpers had brought with them from the west. Pint changed into a suit too. They ate cheese and chocolate then slept for the remainder of the journey to Budapest, where they had breakfast at a first-class hotel. The western suits distracted attention from their bruised and cut faces and hands.

They spent one night in Budapest, staying with friends, and the next night were dropped by some cornfields 8 km from the Rumanian border. It was a spot Pint had chosen from the maps, but he had been able to buy only tourist maps in East Berlin and these had no information about border posts. While they were walking through the cornfields they heard oohs and aahs from the grass and thought maybe it was the soldier on border patrol making love to his girlfriend.

The border was marked only by barbed wire, electrified at certain points and armed with a device which automatically fired signal rockets when the wire was breached. There were also big wooden watchtowers, about twenty metres high. Pint said they were quite impressive, the biggest watchtowers he had ever seen, much higher than the one we had climbed together in Spandau. Having located an unelectrified section of the border, they lifted up the barbed wire and crawled from Hungary into Rumania.

'We were walking quite a while. We knew that at some point we had to cross a river to get to the road where our helpers would be waiting. But, you know, they have elderly people in these villages whose job is to watch the fields for fires and suchlike. One of these old men was sitting half-asleep outside a hut. He didn't see us, but his dog did. The dog ran after us, barking, and the old man followed, shouting. I confess I tried to kill the dog,' Pint said, his smile acknowledging the far-off barking of two dogs the other side of the lake.

'I approached him slowly with my knife, but every time I was within one and a half metres the dog jumped back three metres. There was no way I was going to get him. The dog knew what I wanted.'

I had returned Pint to the landscape of his nightmare, I thought, writing as fast as I could in the black-and-red notebook, wondering if I could ever pay him back.

'We had to run,' he was saying. 'It was the only way. We saw the river and the bridge at the same time. We should never have headed for the bridge. It is the unwritten rule: *avoid bridges*. But we were panicking. As we stepped on to this wooden bridge, a guard came out. He had a beautiful Kalashnikov. Our friends had been waiting just 600 metres from the bridge. They saw what was happening and drove away. It was the best thing they could do.'

The guard looked about eighteen. He was very nervous, sweating. Pint had dropped his knife in the flight from the dog, otherwise he might have tried to kill the guard. As it was, a bribe was Pint's last chance. He still had six East German 100 mark bills in his back trouser pocket. Slowly, he lowered one hand, pulled out the money and held it up. The guard shook his head.

'I should have known. I should have brought dollars,' Pint said.

The guard tried to fire his flare-gun, but it wouldn't work. Pint and his friend started laughing crazily, theatrically, trying to panic the guard with this hollow laughter that is the speciality of cruel children.

Eventually, a yellow flare was shot to the sky. Within five

minutes seven Rumanian soldiers arrived on the bridge. They roughed up the Germans, trod on their fingers, kicked them, bound their wrists tightly with rope and marched them for two hours across the grasslands, jabbing them with bayonets, till they reached a wooden hut which served as the local border station.

Interrogated by a captain who spoke only Rumanian, Pint and his friend tried to say they were westerners who had lost their passports. Pint tried speaking some Russian, then remembered that Rumanians hate Russians. The rope still tied around his hands had blocked his circulation and Pint fainted. His hands were untied, his face mopped with a wet cloth. He was brought a meal of salad, bread and fetta cheese. In the morning the two prisoners were driven to the nearest town in an army jeep.

The next interrogator spoke good German. Pint and his friend stuck to the story that they were West German tourists doing a trip to the Black Sea and back. Asked in separate interviews whether they were on the way to the Black Sea or coming home, Pint said they were on their way there and his friend said the opposite. In the evening they were taken to a small jail in a Rumanian border town. The cell had a tiny barred window, two beds and two other prisoners. They had to sleep two in a bed. There was no pot to piss in, the prisoners had to do their toilet at allotted times. In the toilet itself there was no paper and Pint prevailed upon a cleaner to give him a plastic bag. For the ten days he was locked up in that prison he wiped his arse with this plastic bag.

They were moved to await trial in another prison, which dated from the Austro-Hungarian Empire, but at least every cell had wooden pots which were emptied every morning. In other respects, however, their situation was worse. They didn't know exactly where they were, nor how long they would be held. They kept demanding to speak to the GDR ambassador, to the consul, anyone. Every time they banged on their cell door, yelling they had some rights, guards came to beat them up. After some weeks Pint was separated from his friend.

'If it's yourself being beaten up it's bad enough, but in a sense you are quite busy. When you're listening to your friend being beaten up next door, then it's really bad,' Pint said solemnly, as a lone jogger clumped past, a fortyish man presumably worried about his body's decline. 'Then it's bad. Then you have time to think: they will beat him for five minutes more and then they will come for me. Okay. A little psycho-terror. Beautiful.'

He clenched his teeth in a mean grin. I managed a cackle. I hadn't spoken in over an hour. Still sitting on the wooden bench with the view of the lake and the police box, Pint was leaning forward, his elbows propped on his thighs, his fists supporting his chin. Glinty-eyed and hollow-cheeked, the former long-distance runner still looked as if he could keep running a long while.

After two months in the old Austro-Hungarian prison Pint and his friend were taken with fifteen others to court, which was a wooden hut with barefoot spectators and children running around. The prosecuting lawyer puffed his chest out. The way he was talking, Pint thought he would get sentenced to death. He still didn't understand much Rumanian and his defence lawyer spoke no German. Pint and his friend each received an eighteen-month sentence.

Most of the other accused men were black marketeers, who got between six and ten years. All the other countries in the eastern bloc sent East German prisoners home, but Rumania had poor relations with the GDR. Pint had not even been able to send a message to his father that he was still alive.

He travelled from the court to his next jail in a train. The journey took three nights and four days. There was no room to sit down. All the carriages were jam-packed with standing prisoners, with hash dealers and gold smugglers, art thieves and gun runners, all sorts. In the jail he befriended a small Chinese murderer called Lim. Each cell was shared by twenty men, two to a bed. At the time it surprised Pint that none of the men in his cell had formed a sexual relationship. Pint himself had a platonic romance with one of the Arab prisoners.

The prison food was cornbread and very thin soup. Bread and cigarettes were the main currencies. In those days Pint was less dependent upon tobacco and he swapped cigarettes for bread. Together with a West Berliner called Herbert, serving a long sentence for smuggling Marlboro and Winston cigarettes into Rumania, Pint also patented a method of getting drunk. The dandruff-remover dispensed free at the prison clinic contained 99.5 per cent alcohol, he discovered.

'The night me and Herbert first tried it all the other prisoners gathered round,' Pint remembered. 'Some of them thought these mad Germans would immediately go blind or die or something. I poured some into a little bit of cold coffee, took my first sip, everyone's eyes on me. It was okay. Nothing happened. I drank some more and got drunk. I had a slight headache the next day, but I was happy to have figured out a way of getting drunk. It continued for a few months till everyone started complaining of dandruff and the screws finally cottoned on. The other thing we used to do was get hold of pain-relievers and sleeping pills and grind them down to a powder. Mixed in with tobacco it was quite okay. If you wanted to have a blue hour, smoke two aspirin and forget about it.'

The rain pattered on the trees and dappled the lake. It had been drizzling for some minutes, but Pint had either not noticed or didn't care. His blue eyes were glazed. There had been hundreds of blue hours both before and after his imprisonment and these days the pain-relievers were books, beer, wine, hash, films, music, sex with someone he half loved, holidays in hot countries, etc., but those blue remembered hours in the jail haunted him like a broken heart. He had gambled and lost, run away and been caught. Sitting on the damp bench, he looked totally drained. I felt like I'd just taken a lot of money from a friend at cards.

His father had travelled across Hungary in a fruitless search for his son whom he had presumed dead, until he received a telephone call from West Germany saying Pint was safe. This message, smuggled out of jail in the rectum of a friendly Pole, had been sent to one of his father's former lovers (a woman whom Pint had been brought up to call aunty) because Pint did not want his father, or anyone else in the GDR, to know he was in prison in Rumania. He thought a worse fate might await him in East Germany. The poems Pint wrote in jail he transcribed on to a shirt which was sewn into the lining of his jacket by a prisoner who used to be a tailor.

Towards the end of his eighteen-month sentence Pint began to suspect that, instead of being released in Rumania or taken to the west, he would be transported to prison in the GDR. He decided he would try and escape at some point in the expected transit between the two countries' jails. To this end, he started training hard in the prison gym. He did not know how or when he would make good his escape, but he thought he had nothing to lose. He felt sure he would be locked up for another five years in East Germany.

The day came, they told him he was to be freed. Everything is okay, they said. They put him in the back of a car, a guard on either side, and drove to Bucharest.

One of these guards had a yellowish complexion which Pint hoped was the result of a liver complaint. As he was being escorted through Bucharest, Pint elbowed this guard hard as he could in his liver. The guard doubled up in pain and Pint ran off. The other guard took pursuit, shouting, 'Stop! Stop him! He's a rapist! Rapist!'

His second attempted escape, so much more desperate and unplanned than the first, ended after a ten-minute chase through the city streets. Pint was set upon by a crowd of men and had to be rescued from their righteous wrath by the prison guard with the sound liver, who thanked the citizens for helping to apprehend the rapist then took Pint to a nearby passport office where he beat him about the face with his steel helmet. Pint was driven back to the special security wing of the prison in which he had spent eighteen months. He was clapped in leg-irons and handcuffed. Before leaving him alone the guards said they were going to come back and thrash him to within an inch of his life. Pint was so scared that for the first time in his life he prayed to God for mercy. The next morning he was taken to the airport and flown to East Berlin.

'Home sweet home. When we reached Schönefeld it was snowing. I was wearing the same light clothes I'd been wearing when I left two summers before. A guy wearing a buttoned-up trench coat and a brown Derby hat met me. He said, "Follow me and don't make any trouble." I couldn't believe it. It was just like some corny film. The snow, this idiot in a trench coat, shit,' Pint said, shaking his head.

'I was taken to the jail in Pankow. It's a secret service jail full of attempted escapees and a lot of stupid unpolitical people who'd been identified as a threat by someone or other. Here and there was a Nazi. Here and there a genuine socialist. Throughout all this I described myself as a Marxist, which is rather funny in a way.'

Pint rose from the bench blinking like a man coming out of a trance or a hungover sleep and tartly announced we had better go elsewhere. What was he doing sitting in the rain telling his life story to an Englishman? he said, wiping his bicycle seat dry with the sleeve of his second-hand jacket. He led the way out of the woods to the metalled cycle-lane that ran from the Grunewald down the hill, past the barracks of the F.40th Berlin Brigade, US Army. A road sign said TANK! Pint turned round and grinned. He was back in the here and now. The Berlin Brigade troops lived with their families in functional post-war apartment blocks, generously surrounded by trees and lawns, quite similar to some blocks of flats in East Berlin. Walking along the boulevard was a black GI in camouflage battledress. He had the spring-heeled rolling gait, short-stepped and cocky, that was the badge of the streetwise in every black neighbourhood from Harlem to Watts. He carried a stone in his hand which he suddenly threw full-pelt at a chicken-wire fence. Homesick, lovesick, armysick, or just practising his baseball throw, we didn't stay to find out, continuing on through the university quarter of Dahlem where Pint had spent four years studying German literature and Russian before abandoning academic life in favour of journalism. Here in Dahlem, at the Institute for German Questions, Ulrike Meinhof had carried out the action which translated her from a journalist to an outlaw. Rudi Dutschke was buried in a nearby graveyard. I knew people who made regular pilgrimages to his plot.

Another generation of students was standing on the steps of a faculty building holding placards, but it was a small unserious gathering. The students were chatting and laughing, enjoying their protest. There wasn't a cop in sight. We didn't bother stopping to ascertain the reason for the assembly. The rain ceased and a weak April sun made one glimmering circle in the bland sky. At some traffic lights we drew up alongside a red Ford pick-up, Boy George on AFN blaring out of the open window.

'I studied Russian for eleven years in school in the east and four years at university in the west, but I can hardly speak it at all,' Pint said, one foot on the ground, the other poised on the pedal. The Ford pick-up tore off, tyres squealing, when the lights turned green. 'No chance to practise.'

'Cowboys galore in West Berlin, but no cossacks in the eastern sector,' I said. 'The Russians never stood a chance in the glamour war.'

From his days at the Free University of West Berlin Pint remembered a café where he had passed many agreeable hours discussing with other students why studying should be taking place at all. The café, as it happened, was still locked at that time, sixties and seventies singles on the jukebox, long-haired topers at stripped-pine tables and an artificial bush with gold paper leaves establishing this mood of the permanent autumn.

We ordered sugared coffee and Weinbrand, sweet and sour. We drank in our circumstances. The Rolling Stones were succeeded on the jukebox by Simon and Garfunkel. '*All gone to look for America . . .*' Both of us knew the words.

'What cigarettes are we going to smoke when the Yankee empire finally crumbles?' I said.

'The Cubans make good cigarettes,' Pint said.

He had grown up in the shadow of a different empire. He had not, like me, pleaded with his parents to let him stay up and watch *Rawhide* and *Cheyenne*. He had never followed *The Fugitive* and *The Flintstones*. He learned Russian at school. While I was hitch-hiking around France in the spring of 1971, Pint was making his perilous attempt to reach the Italian border. While I was fooling around at university, Pint was locked up in Rumania. In the winter of 1973 I was sailing to Crete and Pint was in motionless transit between the Germanies at Pankow, a name later adopted by one of the East Berlin punk rock groups. By 1974 I was a bus conductor and he was a student. Three years later we finally contrived to be doing similar things at the same time in different cities. I was working on *The Leveller* and he was at *Zitty*. In 1979 we met at Johnny's flat in south London. As all the best gamblers know, chance boils down to percentages. I made a mental note to make this point to Ulrike the next time she embarked upon one of her paeans to the beauty of chance, mystery, destiny and related modes of mystic surrender. Meanwhile, the cheap cognac was doing its work and Pint had still not finished his story. Outside it was getting dark. Pint's eyes again began to glaze. I took out my notebook. The pages were still slightly damp from the rain and the pen tore some holes in the paper.

When his father came to visit in Pankow jail Pint handed him the jacket which contained the poems written on the shirt. His father knew the score, he had spent four years in a Russian jail. He took the jacket quickly and without saying a word popped it into his bag. Pint was detained in Pankow for four months without trial, listening to the midnight ravings of Nazis and forming some friendships with others of his own kind.

'The day I was released, it was the same as before,' he said. 'They just told me to collect my things. They said transport was available. I only had two hours' notice. You could be going anywhere, you don't know. I was flown to Heisen in West Germany, a camp for freed prisoners from Poland, Russia and other eastern countries. It still exists. From Heisen I called my father's lover and the next day she was there. She's great. She'd tried to get me out of Pankow earlier by offering to marry me, but it wasn't possible. I knew her from the time my father was having the affair with her. She used to spend a lot of time in East Berlin.'

Pint had been bought from the GDR for DM 40,000. Other people he knew fetched more. The going rate for doctors and university professors in those days was around DM 80,000. Like all such purchases from the East German jails, Pint was treated like a minor VIP in his new home. He moved from Heisen to West Berlin, where he was given a flat, a government grant and a place at the Free University. He was de-briefed by the West German intelligence services and by the CIA. He told them nothing. He had learned the art of saying nothing during his interrogations by eastern agents.

'Eight Days a Week' was playing on the jukebox. I asked for the bill.

'My grandmother was eighty years old when she died,' Pint said, taking another Camel from his package. 'She could never remember anything from the last forty years, but she could remember things from when she was young very well. Maybe when I'm eighty I will remember that period best of all and will have forgotten most of my time in the west.'

While we were cycling back to Pint's apartment in Charlottenburg, he told me about a friend of his named Gavroche who escaped to West Berlin but didn't like it and returned to the east next day. Gavroche was now back in West Berlin, living in Kreuzberg.

'He's a gangster,' Pint said approvingly, haring up Bismarckallee.

I remembered him saying some years ago that he liked gangsters because they caused mayhem and lived outside the law but made no pretence about doing anything for the people. His mood in those days was darker, however. His heart had been broken by Tutu, a beautiful woman who had messed up a number of lives through no particular fault of her own. Originally from East Berlin, she had also spent two years in jail. After being released to West Berlin she arranged a rendezvous with her two-year-old son at Checkpoint Charlie. He had been staying with Tutu's mother in the east. Tutu's son pedalled across the border on his tricycle. Lugubrious Tommy, who hated the west for depriving him of most of his friends, he had been in love with Tutu as well. She had wreaked havoc in both Berlins. I saw her occasionally at the Djungel and the Paris Bar. She now had a boyfriend twelve years her junior and was carving out a career as a fashion designer. Somehow she reminded me of Laura. She had the same childlike selfishness, the same dangerous innocence. Around the time Pint had loved and lost Tutu I had met him in a high-tech café called Mitropa that was fashionable for a while. Mitropa was the brand-name for the chain of maroon dining cars and railway cafés owned by the East German railway company, Deutsche Reichsbahn. Mitropa, everyone had agreed, was a deliciously decadent name for a West Berlin café. Pint had been at the bar applauding the recent assassination attempt on the Pope. Since then litigation by the Deutsche Reichsbahn had compelled Mitropa to change its name and it was now known simply as M. For his part, Pint was now happily settled in Charlottenburg with Sonia. Born in East Berlin, she was the daughter of a rags-to-riches shoe salesman who lived in a chateau in northern France.

Sonia had moved to the west as a young girl, before the Wall was built. She had a son by a Turkish bartender. For the first time Pint was leading the life of a family man. If not cosy, it was comfortable. It meant gregarious breakfasts, secure bedtime smells, half-asleep embraces, the half-trusting eyes of a child. He had slowed down. Less given to violent outbursts, his hate had lost its edge. But he still had his dark side. He was an immigrant who had no desire to assimilate.

This year, 1984, for the first time since he was released from Pankow jail, he had been granted permission to return to East Berlin and visit his brother and sister, see the nephews and nieces he had never known. When he first received the news he could go back . . . *home?* . . . the knife turned in his stomach. He felt a panic that was gut-wrenching as sexual jealousy. When he eventually passed through Friedrichstrasse checkpoint to stand in the queue for S-Bahn tickets at the iron alcove opposite the dingy Mitropa, he said it was familiar as a half-forgotten dream. He stood on the street trying to isolate the chemical components of the sentimental sensation. A scientist as well as a poet, he decided it was the different petrol burned in the communist cars. Maybe the east smelled different because the oil was from Russia. The sweet carbon odour unlocked his past, too much too quick, a jailbreak of memories. Walking with his father through the dreamy wasteland of downtown East Berlin in the late fifties. Crying confessions to his mother who died too young. Playing on summer afternoons in the children's park called Pioneer's Republic. Running on cinder tracks. The heart-busting crack of the starting pistol and the sea of strange faces at the finishing line.

Pint spent hours talking to his brother and sister. He brought gifts for their children. He wanted a catharsis, a homecoming, but it ended up as a pedestrian afternoon spent in the company of people with whom he had little or nothing in common. He found their lives boring. He kept returning, however, and by now had visited five times, but it was always the same, hours of chat that failed to ignite a single spark. He had promised to take me with him on one of his trips across the border. Meanwhile, we were nearing his domestic circumstances on Bregenzerstrasse.

Half-drunk, fighting to keep up with him on the gearless bike

Uschi had acquired from friendly thieves, vaguely worried about its lack of lights, I was watchful for police cars in the whirl of mechanical noise and colour that always attended the Kurfür-stendamm at night, the familiar fairground of weeping silver and screaming crimson, the neon lights that used to be called sky signs.

'*The song of the shirt*,' I yelled to my friend. 'That was the title of an English lament about the sweatshops.'

'Sweatshops?' he shouted back.

'Yes. Your story about the poems and the shirt. Sweatshops are places where people make clothes in slave conditions.'

'Yeah. We have them here too.'

'Could I see the poems sometime?'

'Maybe.'

But he had told me too much. I would never see the songs he wrote on the shirt.

Outside the Zoo-Palast Hotel a busker was playing a Spanish guitar. Farther along a girl of about nineteen with bright black hair knelt on the pavement over her half-complete chalk picture that would be washed away by tomorrow's rain. The street artists were the respectable beggars, the hard-up students whose place in the official gaiety of city life was enshrined in the glossy brochures. The other beggars, the raggedy men who shuffled along the street with slurred requests and cupped palms, they advertised the fate that befell the drunk and the idle, the dumb and despairing. *Beware! It can happen to anyone!* Hell was just a stone's throw from heaven.

The moneyed promenaders, alert eyes everywhere, moved slowly past the permanent displays of jewels, watches and electronic toys shining in lit glass cases on the paving stones worn smooth by the endless procession. Teenage tarts sought hungry eyes in the crowd. Men with wives and girlfriends pretended not to notice. Tourists sat beneath flapping canopies drinking beer made pink by raspberry juice, the Berliner Weisse that their guidebooks had told them was the traditional tipple of the city. I had never seen it drunk anywhere but the Kurfürstendamm.

We turned off the main drag at Olivaerplatz by a place that had been a hash café in the October snow of 1979, a dark refuge that had played loud reggae and was frequented by the kind of people who claimed to know someone who had once been in the Red Army Fraction. The café had since been given a black-and-chrome facelift and now served gaudy cocktails in triangular glasses. The night we scaled the wooden watchtower in Spandau had begun on those premises. The West Berliner who had driven us to the edge of the city in the white Ford spoke English like a north American. His name was Oliver. Only a small coincidence, I had thought at the time, meeting a boy called Oliver in Olivaerplatz, but it had helped me remember his name.

'What happened to Oliver?'

'Last time I met him he was working for the Legalise Marijuana Campaign. But now?' Pint shrugged. People had a habit of disappearing .

Pint's third-floor apartment was also in the furthest block from the street, the Hinterhof, a grey six-storey tenement built around a paved courtyard, thirty feet square, in which one tree led a cramped and solitary existence.

The apartment had a bath in the middle of the kitchen. Sonia was in the living room examining her day's work, the latest in a series of photomontages built around the hot-dog motif. The other six were already framed on the wall. To me they were a pointless exercise in porno Lichtenstein, but Pint looked at the seventh in the series and made encouraging noises, the way lovers do.

Sonia's son, Anatol, had a new toy: a clockwork plastic helicopter, red with yellow blades. He wound it up and launched it in the air with both hands, like someone setting free a bird, and watched it crash miserably on the carpet. The sequence was repeated five times. Pint lent technical assistance but still the thing refused to fly. Anatol was twelve, too old I thought to be preoccupied with a malfunctioning toy helicopter. He was dyslexic and Pint had been trying to encourage him to read more. One of Pint's techniques had been to introduce him to the lonely hearts classifieds in *Zitty*. Apparently Anatol had pored for hours over the ads requesting blonde film lovers, well-built sports enthusiasts, single anti-nuclear campaigners, leather fetishists, bisexual socialists, non-cruising gays, preferably slim nonsmokers, etc., but it was still too early to tell whether he had profited much from the exercise.

Anatol had seen his mother's lovers come and go. He spent the weekends with his Turkish father. The lonely hearts columns probably confirmed what he had already gleaned about the nature of adult romance. He was a typical enough child of West Berlin.

I left Uschi's bicycle in the shed and caught a Mercedes taxi back to my own makeshift home. Anatol was still trying to make the red helicopter fly.

6 May Day

Down in Gneisenaustrasse U-Bahn station the platform was deserted except for a derelict fast asleep on the bench with his Alsatian. It was half ten in the morning, according to the station clock, 1 May 1984. The Alsatian slept more fitfully than his master. For the sake of variety I had decided to take the U-Bahn to Kochstrasse and cross the border at Checkpoint Charlie.

The other side of the tracks was a billboard for a pink-and-red cylindrical lolly shot through with ice cream and called Twister. *Frucht am Stiel – total verdreht*, it said across this giant colour photo of a teenage couple licking lollies and looking lustfully at each other. In further hoardings for cigarettes and clothes other models with glossy hair and even teeth patrolled the length of the platform, their only human imperfections a consequence of the slight distortion achieved by the concave wall of the green-tiled tunnel. The yellow train entered the station and blocked out the bottom half of the billboards. I wrenched open the doors.

I travelled one stop and changed trains at Mehringdamm. I sat alongside a young family who were also bound for the eastern zone, though they would be travelling one stop further, to the Friedrichstrasse checkpoint. Checkpoint Charlie was exclusively for use of foreigners. The mother and father were in their late twenties or early thirties and, guessing, could have been teachers or librarians. They were studious-looking, financially secure, their clothes neat and conventional, their spectacles plain, but today unlike most days they were showing their colours. The father had a red carnation in the buttonhole of his cotton jacket. The mother's red carnation (from the same plant in their window box?) was threaded through the straw basket in which she carried the day's provisions. Their small daughter held a red flag and her hair was tied in red ribbons. Their baby son was in a blue-and-white pushchair also decorated with red bunting.

Their presence in the carriage was evidently unsettling various burghers aged between fifty and seventy, some of whom were also going to Friedrichstrasse, but not for the May Day parade, perish the thought. Some intended to buy coffee, cigarettes and brandy at the Intershop. Others carried bags loaded with the kind of food and drink it was hard for their relatives in the east to find. Before the Wall was built the traffic in commodities was the other way round. Who would sell bread, milk, eggs and potatoes in the east when they were worth four times as much in western deutschmarks? It was cheaper to live in the east, but more profitable to sell in the west. A famous cabaret creation in East Berlin at the time was this complete Berliner, the Gesamtberliner, who lived in the east and worked in the west. Johnny had told me about the Gesamtberliners.

As the train left Hallesches Tor, glares that said *traitors!* were still being flung in the direction of the young family wearing red. The parents adopted the kind of self-consciously expressionless gaze best suited to underground-train hostility. Their little girl was energetically waving the tiny red flag. Her easy innocence eventually softened the stares. Can't blame the children after all, muttered the burghers. Children will wave any old flag. I think I waved a Union Jack once when I was about six and Prince Philip came to Swindon in a helicopter. One can't blame the children. These days I avoided even sartorial combinations of red, white and blue. I possessed a discreet red medal star which I had considered wearing in my lapel today to curry favour with the border guards and to blend in with the crowds and also because I think May Day is something worth commemorating, but I somehow couldn't bring myself to wear a red star in the east. I had worn it in West Berlin and, as a result, had narrowly avoided a fight with a bearded American one night at the Djungel. *Brit commie* he sneered, fingering the star I wore in the buttonhole of a grey box jacket spotted with miniscule green squares, a jacket that had been much coveted in its day and was only slightly spoiled by the ink stain on the breast pcoket, a stain dating from the drunken replacement of a Pentel on my second visit to Berlin in 1981. The bearded American's main criticism of East Berlin, which he had visited once, was that no one was hanging out on the street. The streets were fucking empty, man, everyone scared in their fucking apartments. He said he wasn't the typical narrow-minded Yank and then he tried to hit me.

The selective wearing of the red star reflected the simple fact that it is more fun to offend than to conform. Sometimes revolutionaries find it traumatic when their revolutions turn into governments. Castro comes down from the mountains. Mugabe starts wearing suits. No such problem of romantic disillusionment existed in East Berlin, there having been no revolution in the German Democratic Republic. At a meeting of the four Allied powers in London on 12 September 1944 Germany was passed round the room like a bag of sweets, one-for-you-one-for-me, and divided into zones of occupation. The London Protocol, as the shareout became known, was still valid now, almost forty years later.

At Checkpoint Charlie the Union Jack and the Tricolour flew from one corrugated cream hut, the Stars and Stripes from another. The British and French military police had one window each, the US hut had three windows. I tapped on the British window and a Scottish MP reluctantly got up from his seat. The two other MPs looked up briefly then resumed their conversation. I gave the Scot my spiel. Journalist. Book about Berlin. Blah-blah.

'Does it get boring in here sitting around all day doing fuck-all?' I said, often having wondered what the MPs in the corrugated boxes actually did, if anything. I had never seen anyone being stopped and asked to produce their papers on the western side.

'Aye, it does a bit,' said the Scot, smiling.

At this point one of the other MPs came to the window. He spoke in a London accent. 'How can it be boring to serve your Queen?' he said, fixing me firmly in the eye.

I said I couldn't imagine, but I could take a hint. As I walked

away from the kiosk I heard the Londoner reprimanding the Scot:
'Don't *ever* talk to the press. Believe me. Fucking journalists.'

Tourists were trickling in and out of the privately owned Wall
Museum whose star exhibit was an Insetta bubble-car in two-
tone blue which had been redesigned to accommodate two (or
even three?) escapists. Other attractions included a home-made
submarine, a fake Red Army uniform and a female dummy inside
two leather suitcases. I bought a Coca-Cola and hot dog at the
Checkpoint Charlie Imbiss and walked round the back to sit
down with my breakfast on one of the iron benches strewn about
on the sand fifteen yards from the Wall. The printshop of *Neue
Zeit* (New Times!) rose up above the Wall on the other side, steel
bars on its windows. One of the nine daily newspapers in East
Berlin, *Neue Zeit* was the organ of the Christian-Democrat
Union, one of four parties of token opposition. I ate the hot dog
with my neck stuck right out so that falling ketchup and mustard
would land on the sand, saving on dry-cleaning bills. Pigeons
were wandering among the usual mess of Fanta cans, pink plastic
straws, ring-pulls and stained napkins. It was like an English
beach the day after August Bank Holiday.

A black American couple were arguing because the husband
refused to take the wife's picture against the Wall. He said the
light wasn't good enough, the picture wouldn't come out, it was a
waste of money. It was another grey and windy day.

'Michael. *Please*. Take my picture.'

She kept half-posing hopefully then breaking her stance to
scream blue murder again. Michael! Please! But Michael was
stubborn.

Seven French soldiers, in those hats that look like cake-boxes
with peaks, mounted the steps of the viewing platform. Their blue
trousers had a thick black stripe down the side. All the soldiers
carried a camera and I began to wonder how many photographs
had been taken from the scaffolding at Checkpoint Charlie. Of
the four million visitors per year maybe half had a camera and of
those maybe another half, a conservative estimate, would take
pictures on the scaffold. One million cameras a year, therefore,
each taking about six standard shots.

1. The wide-angle taking in a section of the Wall, graffiti-

spattered in many languages on the western side, and showing the blue-and-white apartment blocks built high on the other side to block out the view of the west.

2. The close-up of the East German guard behind glass in the broad concrete tower that looks like the bridge of a ship. (Often the guard will be training his binoculars right back at the lens, adding an appropriately threatening ambience to the composition.)

3. The art-shot of the *Neue Zeit* sign, faded black on an oblong of sludgy green, with a barred window up above. Best in colour.

4. The landscape-shot north along the Wall to the West Berlin HQ of the Axel Springer newspaper empire, a high-rise coated in gold symbolising opulence. Also best in colour.

5. The upright-shot of the Kochstrasse street-scene: western flags, the sign for the Wall Museum, tourist coaches, men in white coats dispensing soft drinks under brightly-coloured canopies, the blue U-Bahn sign in the distance.

6. The head-shot of one's loved one or relative or oneself (if travelling alone one can usually prevail upon a sympathetic fellow tourist to take this) sometimes smiling but often staring moodily against the background of candy-striped road barriers and GDR flags.

Assuming an average of six shots per camera meant six million photographs a year for the last twenty-three years, making 138 million Checkpoint Charlie scaffold pictures as the current rough world total. I finished my breakfast and chucked the can of Coke on the sand with the rest of the detritus.

Walking past the US military hut on my left, the scaffold on my right, I proceeded across the twenty-five yards of no-man's-land to the first metal door. When it buzzed I pushed it open and joined the queue behind five fashionable young men from Norway. It was not so much a queue, in fact, as a collection of eight people in an enclosed square space, the system at Checkpoint Charlie was quite different from Friedrichstrasse. All of us surrendered our passports at the same time to the woman's hand that appeared through the bars. The male half of an American couple tried to engage me in conversation on the architectural merit of Edinburrow in Scotland.

'This is deliberate harassment,' he said, after we had all been waiting ten minutes. 'And completely illegal under the terms of the Potsdam Agreement you know.'

Two minutes later all the passports came back except mine. The others proceeded into the next room. A guard came out holding my passport, but he didn't give it to me.

'So. You're a journalist,' he said, waving the passport which contained this information. If I hadn't got the passport in such a hurry one morning at Petty France I would have thought of something else to put opposite profession. In Pint's passport it said clerk. For the purpose of borders I had been a student till my old passport ran out two years ago.

'That's right,' I said.

'Which newspaper?'

I told him, adding that I was not here on any assignment: I was taking a holiday in West Berlin and wanted to see the May Day parade. He chewed this over for a while.

'Okay,' he said, handing me the passport. 'Just a tourist today, right?'

I nodded and was ushered into the next room where I had to fill in one of the forms stating how much money I had on my person. I paid the entrance fee, five deutschmarks, changed a further twenty into ostmarks and strolled down Friedrichstrasse vowing I would never again cross the border at Checkpoint fucking Charlie.

The flags were hung out but the streets were ghostly quiet, bereft of cars, bicycles, bodies, trams, as if the venue had been changed at the last minute. I remembered Johnny saying that because hundreds of thousands came to the capital from all over the republic on May Day, most East Berliners escaped to the beaches and lakes.

It started to rain as I walked up the Unter den Linden and saw what looked like a red armada sailing down Karl Marx Allee, red sails bent in the cool wind. I smelt again the different odour of the east. Was Pint right in saying this was a function of the Russian petrol burned here? Was it not also the different kind of bread, sausage, ice cream, beer, cigarettes, the absence of that perfumed sweetness which always mingled with the sweat of the crowds on the Kurfürstendamm? I heard a brass band playing diddlee-*yum*pahpah, from metal loudspeakers attached to the lamp-posts like open mouths.

The green-tiled ten-storey blocks overlooking the marching thousands were draped in red. For the inhabitants of those apartment blocks it was a serious disadvantage of an otherwise plum location, having to remember which flags to hang out on which days. Probably someone went round to remind them.

Young athletes in the parade were followed by older athletes, all wearing green, orange and white tracksuits and applauded loudly by the citizens of the sport-proud state who formed a human corridor all along Karl Marx Allee as far as the Alexanderplatz. People wore red plastic carnations in their buttonholes and some carried whole bouquets of phony flowers. Children, bright promise on their faces, held the hand of a grown-up and waited breathlessly for their mother or father to come marching past. Look there she is! Mama! Children waved the plastic flowers for all they were worth.

The blue shirts of the Free German Youth movement were succeeded by rows of grey suits pinned with medals, worn by men who would have been children in the last war. The medals were awarded to former members of the army and the militia. Current members, men and women, boots polished, clumped along in time. Those in the middle of the lines were shielded from the rain by the creaking banners and flags.

One punk marching on his own through the A-platz carried a home-made placard showing a mushroom cloud painted black.

The brassy music kept being snatched away by the wind then returning louder than ever. Searching for the brass band in the marching forest of red, I finally realised there was no brass band. The music was piped. When the Internationale was played at the end of the parade that was piped too, like in a western supermarket. Marxist muzak, I wrote in my notebook, believing this to be a usable phrase. Then I saw two men standing upright making the clenched fist salute, two men old enough to remember troops leaving in trains for Spain making clenched fist salutes out of the windows to loved ones on the platforms, two men old enough to remember the Reichstag fire and the days when this city was swathed in swastikas. These men wore dark double-breasted suits and grim determined smiles that said they had not lost faith. There are no Nazis now in East Berlin, their fists said. We are old communists and, okay, this society is some distance from the utopia once dreamt of, but it was some kind of achievement, the establishment of a system without private property and inherited privilege, their fists said, pointing to the grey sky as the Internationale was piped over the PA.

A rabble-rousing DJ chanted some slogans into the microphone, but there was scant response from the crowd. VIPs in the stand on the A-platz constructed specially for the occasion were photographed and filmed for the evening news then the celebrants were free to enjoy the candy floss, toffee apples, currywurst, sweet pancakes, draught beer, jazz, opera, acrobats, comedians, sound systems, souvenir stalls, there was something for everyone. The rain stopped and a weak sun took the edge off the chill wind.

Small children drew with crayons on the pavement like the street artists of the Kurfürstendamm. One little girl had drawn her impression of May Day: four umbrellas and one red flag in a straggly line. Parents standing behind their offspring looked at the pictures and tried to remember how it was they had once seen trees, sky, streets, people, cars, trains, houses, all the magic of everyday life. Children scribbled swiftly and parents lamented the passing of the years.

Other games for the children involved tests of memory and mathematics with cardboard puzzles and building blocks, wholesome games that smelled of wood and had no need of electricity. Small boys cut out the shapes of wings and tail-fins drawn on plain green card, affixed these shapes to the two-dimensional balsa-wood bodies and in no time at all were describing extravagant figure eights with their one-foot-long aeroplanes. *Whoosh!* The manic music of the video war-game arcades was a whole world away: two miles and four tube stops.

I wandered among a crush of blue-shirted Free German Youth, past souvenir shops selling revolutionary third-world posters, stoic queues for beer at 50 pfennigs a plastic glassful. Blue-shirted crowds danced alongside sound systems playing tape-recorded music from Britain, Jamaica and the USA. Walking through the Alexanderplatz, 'One Love' by Peter Tosh faded into 'Karma Chameleon' by Culture Club. 'Baby Come Back' by the Equals was slowly overpowered by the Talking Heads. Howard Jones mingled with Otis Redding. It was like strolling through a history of rock and roll thronged by youth in blue, an army of adolescents hell-bent on a good time, like the Bank Holiday invasions of English seaside resorts except here there was no violence, only drunkenness and lechery, eyes inflamed by the possible promise of pleasurable indiscretions on the homeward-bound charabancs. Slogans on red banners strung across every public building were concluded by exclamation marks. FRIEDEN IST DAS ERSTE MENSCHENRECHT! MIT ERFÜLLTEM PLAN ZUR WAHL! 1 MAI, DER KAMPFTAG DER INTERNATIONALEN-ARBEITERKLASSE!

One DJ was playing 'Relax' by Frankie Goes To Hollywood, the single banned by the BBC, the first banned single to be number one in Britain since the Sex Pistols released 'God Save the Queen' in Royal Jubilee week. A small crowd was clustered round the DJ. Some were dancing, others scrutinising the Hitachi hi-fi.

Later in the afternoon live bands occupied a stage set up before a gigantic billboard of a dove emerging from the flames or the sun, I wasn't sure which. A band of girl pipers and drummers wearing pearl-grey blazers and powder-blue rah-rah skirts kicked off proceedings with a version of 'Yellow Submarine', prompting shouted requests from the drunks down at the front of the stage.

'Can't buy me love!'

'I want to hold your hand!'

In 1965 Johnny had appeared on East German TV dressed as a Red Indian and performing Beatles covers. One of the reasons Johnny had been a pop star in the GDR was that he was one of the few people around who could sing convincingly in English.

Johnny didn't play the guitar anymore. In fact he hadn't really played since he came to the west. I went and joined one of the queues for beer. All of them were depressingly long. Some young but serious topers, I noticed, had instituted a system which involved a permanent presence in the queue and a plentiful supply of the cheap and delicious amber fluid. The girl pipers were

succeeded on stage by a jazz-rock five-piece who evidently had a
big local following: a rush towards the stage led by men in their
twenties wearing leather jackets had the beneficial effect of
depleting the beer queues. (Queueing is part of life in East Berlin
and the queue, particularly the *food queue*, is a recurrent theme of
cold-war imagery. I am therefore aware of the problems involved
in writing about beer queues. Access to everything in the west is
determined by money. In the east scarcer resources are more
equitably distributed but you have to wait a bit longer.)

I bought two glasses of beer with one shiny weightless ostmark
and made my way through the queues for pancakes and
doughnuts to the stalls selling knick-knacks for the day-trippers:
May Day 1984 tea towels, engraved spoons and ashtrays, brass
replicas of the Tele-Tower. The stall doing the busiest trade sold
only black-and-white postcards of pre-war Berlin, Friedrichstrasse and Königstrasse bustling with horse-drawn carriages,
crowded streets, stately Mercedes driven by uniformed chauf-
feurs, rich men in tall hats and slim women in long dresses gaily
swinging parasols. The older customers matched the postcards
against their recollections. I bought five postcards, including one
of the now restored cathedral going up in smoke during the war,
panicked people in the foreground fleeing towards the camera.

A kind-eyed woman placed the cards in a paper bag, graciously
accepting my two ostmarks. I went to watch the bicycle race on
Alexanderstrasse.

A soothing *swish* as a hundred or so perfectly-maintained
machines glided past in a pleasant blur of aluminium spokes and
white caps, all the cyclists together still on the first lap of sixty,
racing clockwise round the fenced-off streets. I stood behind a
family of three who all wore black vinyl jackets of the same design
in different sizes. The father was explaining the finer points of
cycling to his wife and son, meanwhile tapping his foot to the
chorus of 'Old Cotton Fields Back Home' that came from one of
the sound systems. It was five o'clock and people were folding up
their flags and banners, drifting across the great concrete plain of
the Alexanderplatz to the trains back home. To a disco version of
'Singing in the Rain' three women in blue chiffon danced in front
of the dove that flew from the flames or the sun.

It started raining again. Beneath an iron railway bridge by Alexanderplatz station a group forty-strong had gathered round an acoustic guitar. They sang 'Guantanamera'. Smooth clean faces sang with gusto. They wore the blue shirts of the Free German Youth Movement. White kerchiefs, slung carelessly round their necks in some vague approximation of a guerrilla army, had all been signed with the names of friends and acquaintances, kerchiefs which would probably be neatly folded in some drawer and brought out twenty years hence when old friends or strong drink, or both, stirred some longing for the lost days. Ah, May Day 1984. And what has come of all these names written on the kerchief? Twenty years prior to the sentimental reminiscence, they sang their hearts out under the railway bridge, 'Guantanamera', a romantic song that would stick in the craw of western youth, a song based on one of the simple verses of José Martí, a Cuban revolutionary hero. Guantanamera was a girl from Guantanamo, the coastal village where the US still maintained its military base on Cuba. Everyone in England knew the tune, fans on the football terraces adapted it to the names of their heroes, but few people knew the history of the song or its Spanish words. People in the east knew the Reagan administration had desecrated the memory of José Martí by naming a Miami-based radio station after him, a station broadcasting gringo propaganda to Cuba. I took the underground train back to Kreuzberg, a fifteen-minute journey across thirty years of youth culture, from the gangshow innocence of the Guatanamera singers to the electric hatred of the Mauersound, from blue shirts to black shirts.

7 The Candy Bomber

Propped up against the wall of the sunless courtyard was Mark Reeder's sit-up-and-beg bicycle which he had resprayed khaki and refitted with a polished leather seat and saddlebag he had found in one of Old Man Plotzki's junk shops. It was a well-maintained bicycle, well oiled and clean. Mark Reeder took good care of his things. He lived in a small first-floor flat in the Hinterhof of a pre-war tenement block on Nostitzstrasse. He shared a toilet and washbasin with an old couple across the landing who had lived in the same flat ever since they were married in 1940.

Knocking on the door, I heard the theme tune from *The Good, the Bad and the Ugly* playing at medium volume on his record player. Mark had the strangest collection of records, including a Czechoslovakian cover of 'You Make Me Feel Like Dancing', a Japanese version of 'Do You Really Want to Hurt Me?' plus Italian and German covers of 'Blue Monday', not to mention all the Nazi propaganda records.

He opened the door, grinned broadly and gestured he was on the telephone. I walked past the six military caps on the hat-stand by the door and sat in one of the 1930s wickerwork chairs. Down the telephone Mark was cursing Frankie Goes To Hollywood for doing a cover of the Edwin Starr number, 'War (What Is It Good For?)', an idea Mark had been toying with for quite some time. It was eight-thirty on Saturday morning, the thirty-fifth anniversary, as it happened, of the lifting of the Berlin Blockade. The past was recycled endlessly in parades and marches, monuments and anniversaries. Spring and summer in the occupied city were known to foreign soldiers as the marching seasons. Today, for example, there was some official ceremony at Luftbrücke Platz (Airlift Square) and afterwards the Americans were holding an open day at Tempelhof airport. I was due to attend these events in my professional capacity, that's why I was up so early, as I told Mark, vaguely hoping Mark had other plans. Anonymity was problematic in his company, even when he was only wearing his demob suit. No, he said. He was busy. Stuff to sort out for the band.

His bedsitting room was tiny and it was some miracle of organisation that Mark had managed to cram in here a three-piece suit, a foldaway bed, two walnut-fascia wirelesses, a pre-war black telephone that (like the radios) didn't work, an electric guitar, about 200 LPs, a huge stack of army magazines, mostly from East Germany, and a bookcase full of secondhand hard-backs. There was a GDR Army calendar on the wall and five Second World War aeroplanes on the mantelpiece above the fireplace. On a table by the sash window was his newly painted plastic model of a MiG fighter.

I never had the patience myself to construct and paint Airfix models, the Messerschmidts and Spitfires and Lancasters. I enjoyed sticking together the big bits of grey plastic, the wings and fuselage, and slotting home the perspex cockpit, but I could never be bothered with all the fiddly bits. I admired the finished product very much and always wondered why it was that others had the patience and I did not. I saw it as a sign of future failure. Probably I would fail the eleven-plus. Tanks and cars and field guns were also available in Airfix, but aeroplanes were always the most popular vehicles. You could never resist picking them up, wanging them through the air, making aeroplane whines as you made them cruise, swoop and attack, *rat-tat-tat*, and off and away again. Mark Reeder never lost the bug and it deeply worried his mother.

I was looking through Mark's collection of pre-war postcards: the Unter den Linden lined with gold eagles and swastika pennants, the Wehrmacht Orchestra at the Titania Palast, a family saluting Hitler as he accepted flowers from a child, a photograph of the Gestapo HQ with its Bauhaus arch on Stresemannstrasse, the Reichskanzlei where Hitler spent his last days, a monument designed by Albert Speer that once stood in Orianenburg.

'Part of that monument is now a cinema in Neukölln' said Mark, who had finished on the telephone. 'And they used part of the marble for the Soviet war memorial in Treptow, just outside East Berlin.' He went into the kitchen, which was really just a galley, and put some water on for coffee.

'A bloke was killed here, in this flat, during the Battle for Berlin. The old dear next door told me,' he shouted from the galley.

'Whose side was he on?'

'I think he was a Nazi, but a civilian, not a soldier. He was just the bloke who lived here.'

I picked up a copy of *Bravo*, the West German equivalent of *Smash Hits*, and leafed through the colour pictures. The view through the sash window was dominated by two walls: one made of yellowish brick, overhung with trees and vines, the other grey and pitted with bullet-holes. There was one small triangle of grey sky in the top right hand corner of the window. During the eleven days and nights of the Battle for Berlin all the residents of this tenement had been down in the cellar, children crying, dogs barking, the sound of fighting drawing nearer. Maybe the people had tried to raise their spirits by singing a few songs, or was that a peculiarly English response to a crisis?

Waiting for the water to boil, Mark played 'You're the Top' by Charlie and His Orchestra with vocals by Karl Schwedler. Recorded in Berlin in August 1942, it consisted of anti-semitic and anti-British re-workings of popular hits of the time. Poor Mr Postman became Poor Mr Churchill. On the cover of the LP it said: 'War makes rattling good history: but Peace is poor reading.'

Mark was like a museum caretaker who took pride in his work, in his intimate knowledge of every exhibit on show. He enjoyed giving visitors the benefit of his wisdom, watching the surprise on their faces. Walking back into the galley, he pulled on an oven glove to remove the pan from the flames.

'On those postcards they always lie about the dates,' he said, tipping the bubbling water over the heap of coffee into the filter paper resting on the white china V. 'That postcard of the Funktum, the radio tower, for example. On the back it's dated 1929, but I've worked out from the little birds on the tunics of them walking the streets in the foreground that the picture must have been taken in 1936 or thereabouts. You very rarely find a postcard here that'll own up to being taken after 1929. *I wonder why!*'

Giggling manically, he brought through the Third Reich coffee set on a metal tray. He had bought the cups and saucers, with the tell-tale green eagle markings, at Old Man Plotzki's, DM 6 for the whole set. Old Man Plotzki set things aside for Mark. He had two junk shops in Kreuzberg: one on Mehringdamm where things were dusty and cheap, another on Bergmannstrasse stocked with more expensive items for tourists. Most of Mark's treasure had come from the Mehringdamm shop. *I have something that might be of interest to you*, Plotzki would say whenever he had put something under the counter for Mark. He must have had a soft spot for the eccentric Mancunian who spent so much time rummaging through his shops. He wrote down each sale in a leather-bound notebook in immaculate longhand with a fountain pen. Plotzki wore horn-rimmed spectacles, baggy flannels, white shirts and buttoned cardigans. From his name and appearance, he could have been Jewish, but knowing his sympathy for Mark's hobby it seemed more likely he was a Polish gentile who took secret pleasure in his conspiracy with the Englishman who spoke fluent German.

A bit mad was Mark as he himself cheerfully acknowledged. In the conditions existent in Manchester, he would say, his mother was probably right to try and get him certified. But in Berlin Mark's irregularities went more or less unnoticed. He had started the group with Al as compensation for his thwarted ambitions to be a rock-climber or pilot.

'Even now I'd rather be climbing mountains or flying aeroplanes than playing in a pop group,' he said, between sips of coffee. 'But I don't have the money. Being in a band is the best substitute down here for being up there.'

He lifted a finger to the tobacco-coloured ceiling. I made light conversation on the theme of Anne Clark's lachrymose performance at the Metropol.

'Oh, that kind of thing goes down a fucking storm here,' he said, getting up from the wickerwork chair to place a record of Goering's speeches on the turntable.

'I never told you,' he continued. 'I met an old friend of mine from Manchester at the Café Central the other day. I hadn't seen her for years. She told me she was here to see her boyfriend. I said, oh yeah, who is he? She said, his name's Bobbi Baumann, maybe you've heard of him?'

'Bobbi Baumann. Former member of Red Army Fraction. Drifted into the armed struggle via romanticised experiences in the druggy pop underworld of West Berlin. Published his memoirs a few years ago. Called: *How It All Started*.'

'The self-same. The *terrorist*.' Mark's blue eyes gleamed. I could never decide whether he wore eye-liner or eye-shadow or whether nature itself had given him such hypnotic pupils. Sometimes his gaze was so intense you just had to look away. The whites of his eyes were smooth as stone and possessed none of those frayed streaks of red that betrayed appetites for alcohol and tobacco. Mark neither drank nor smoked. His one chemical indulgence was a kind of sleeping pill that could be bought across the counter at chemists in East Berlin. On each trip over the border he purchased dozens.

'World war has broken out in the finest sense of the word,' Goering screamed, the diamond stylus bobbing up and down in its stormy passage across the warped 78. 'A world war between the powers of construction and the powers of decay.'

What did the old couple next door make of Mark's taste in records? Mark claimed to be on good terms and I asked if maybe I could have a chat with them sometime. Mark said he'd pop next door and see. He was gone five minutes. I recited in my mind one of the songs sung in the playground because of the dirty words: *Hitler has only got one ball, Goering has one but very small. Himmler has something simmler, but poor old Goebbels has no balls at all.* Songs the tommies sang marching their sons but not daughters sang unknowing in those late fifties dinner-hours when they also played off-ground tig and kiss-chase and dreamed of being grown-up. When I was six or seven the war had been a far-off event in which my father had sailed in big ships against the Germans and my mother had been evacuated from Birmingham to Derby because of the bombs, but the older I got the nearer the war seemed. Years went by more quickly and the past edged closer, like gunmen in nightmares.

'Okay,' Mark said, standing by the door. 'Let's go and have a chat now.'

Frau Plenk's hair was white and permed, her suit blue and pressed. She wore a pink cardigan. She shook my hand and said it was a pleasure to meet me. She had kindly eyes. Herr Plenk was sitting at the table doing a crossword puzzle, ignoring the intrusion. He had bad teeth. His glasses were poised at the end of his nose. He was ill with bronchitis, you could hear him wheezing 100 yards away whenever his wife brought him back from a visit to the doctor's.

The three-piece suite was arranged around a Telefunken colour TV in a cabinet, dominating the room. Red plastic flowers stood in a vase on the table, where the husband was bent over his puzzle. We all sat down at the same table.

Frau Plenk was born in Westphalia. All her family were in East Germany. She came to Berlin as a teenager in 1925, she said. The city was so beautiful then, she said. All the cafés and nightclubs and parks. Leipzigstrasse, you wouldn't *believe* how it was, seeing how it is now. It was so beautiful. And the cabaret on Rosenthalplatz. She clasped her hands together. Everything's gone now, she said.

She met her husband one evening in 1938 at a café in Schönberg. In 1940 she married and moved into this flat, where she had been ever since. Before Hitler came to power, she said, she had one holiday in Prague and since the war she had been once to West Germany on holiday, to a spa town called Hessen. That was the extent of her travels. Her husband had also stayed in this flat throughout the war, she said, speaking for him. He worked at the same optics factory all his life. During the war it was turned over to military production.

Her brother and father were members of the Nazi Party. She

herself was apolitical, she kept emphasising throughout the conversation. Two Yiddisher families had lived in this block before the war, she said. She assumed they had been taken away to the camps. No one knew for certain. The only casualty her family suffered during the war was her mother-in-law, knocked down and killed by a tram in the blackout.

They had an air-raid shelter in the cellar of the block. She was down there throughout the Battle for Berlin. She said no one knew who was fighting the Wehrmacht. Most people thought it was either the English or the Americans. It was June or July, she said.

'July,' said her husband, his head not lifting from the puzzle. His hair was oiled and side-parted, short back and sides. He must have had the same haircut for the last fifty years. It was quite similar to Mark's.

I asked Frau Plenk if she had ever hated the English. Oh no, she said. Only occasionally after the bombing started, sometimes then she had bad feelings about the English. She said she knew the war was over when the eastern front was opened up against the Soviet Union.

History had just sort of happened to her, the way it does to most people. She had lived through the street-fighting in the twenties, the war, the partition of Germany, the building of the Wall. She had watched on the television the student demonstrations in the sixties and the squatters' riots in the seventies. She had seen all this, but she had never made much sense of it all. She wasn't political, as she kept saying, smiling apologetically, she never got involved in anything apart from that one time she threw a bucket of water over a stormtrooper, ruining his uniform, she added. This was because she was friendly with one of the Yiddisher families, she said, and she had been helping one of the Yiddisher girls to scrub Juden Raus from the wall of this block. The stormtrooper had told her to stop helping the dirty Jew. That's when she chucked the bucket of water over him.

She said she went quite often to visit her sister in Wassensee, East Germany. She and her sister compared notes about the societies they had inherited: the relative quality of their accommodation, the price of food, the character of the neighbourhood, the amount they got in their pensions. I asked her how much she did get in her pension and her husband raised his head briefly from the puzzle to say I shouldn't ask such personal questions. It was none of my fucking business how much money they got to live on.

'Ah, it's a shame what's happened to Kreuzberg,' Frau Plenk said, changing the subject. How did she mean? 'The *Turks*,' she said, screwing up her face a little. She wasn't a committed bigot, just a passive racist, same as most white Britons. And how did she like having an Englishman as a next-door neighbour? Oh, she was very happy having Mark next door, she said. Very happy. The English were very polite and well behaved. I thanked her very much for talking to me, apologised to Herr Plenk for invading his privacy and got up to leave. Mark stayed behind an extra couple of minutes, talking about some problem they were having with the plumbing in the shared toilet.

Coming back into his flat, Mark said he knew this Yank who had a great job, forging East German papers and tailoring perfect copies of GDR uniforms. He was a graphic artist in the employ of the CIA. Mark had met him on the junk-shop circuit, he explained, removing Goering from the turntable and replacing him with Hughie Greene, a sickly piece of English nationalism spoken against the strains of 'Land of Hope and Glory'.

'That really is pornography,' Mark said. 'Remember *Double Your Money?*'

'I preferred Michael Miles in *Take Your Pick*. Loved his double-breasted DJ with the flyaway lapels and baggy strides. And the short bald bloke waiting to beat the gong if anyone said yes or no.'

I said this primarily to please Mark, who adored reminiscences about British trash culture from the fifties and sixties, but *Take Your Pick* did have a camp charm that was entirely absent from more recent get-rich-quick shows like *The Price Is Right*. All three western armies of occupation had their own radio and TV stations. The Americans had uniformed news readers. Mark thought it was great. Like something out of *Sergeant Bilko*, he said.

Berlin's first TV broadcast took place in 1929, the same year that the *Graf Zeppelin* completed its round-the-world voyage and Thomas Mann won the Nobel Prize for Literature. Having invented dynamite in 1866, Alfred Nobel made his fortune and later managed to identify his name with Literature and Peace. One of the great PR coups of modern times, I thought, watching Mark pop up and down like a jack-in-the-box in front of his tape and record collection, choosing this or that track, changing his mind, selecting something else, playing one snatch of Morricone to prove his point about New Order being thieves of published sound, cackling in delight at the East European cover versions of western hits, mixing effortlessly from the hi-energy gay disco version of 'I'm Not Your Stepping Stone' to something by Grandmaster Flash.

Mark's flat was his museum, his stage, his radio station. Guests had to be complicit in the fantasies, to enter into the spirit like children imagining a boat or aeroplane from the quick stretching of a sheet across dining-room chairs on wet afternoons.

I told Mark I was meeting Al and Pint that night at Leydicke, a bar beneath an iron bridge off Yorckstrasse which all of us liked because it had not been redecorated since the twenties and also because it sold cheap wine made from local berries. One wine was made from the wild strawberries growing alongside the disused railway tracks that (like the spokes of a rusting bicycle wheel) met at the hub which had once been Yorckstrasse, the Clapham Junction of pre-war Berlin. The trains had gone to Paris and Prague, Vienna and Venice, Mark said. The strawberry seeds had been brought hundreds of miles by the steam trains and fallen off on the bridges and embankments that converged on Yorckstrasse and this was the history of one of the cheap wines sold to derelicts and tourists at Leydicke.

'What is To The Finland Station?' he demanded suddenly. 'It was a line in a song I didn't understand.'

'It's the title of a book by Edmund Wilson, an American historian. A history of the socialist philosophers, everyone from Proudhon to Robert Owen, people who wrote about history and made it too. The Finland Station was the place in Petrograd where the trains got in from Finland and that was where the sealed train carrying Lenin arrived in 1917. From a railway carriage on that station Lenin made his famous speech about bread, peace, land.'

'One of those allusions lost on me,' Mark said defensively, playing the track in question. I missed the name of the band, but the song was part of that growly synthesiser genre which Al called depro-disco. Mark said he'd try and make it tonight at Leydicke and meanwhile I should watch my step with the Allied soldiers.

Walking past his customised bicycle towards the blob of light indicating the arched entrance to Nostitstrasse I heard again the song Mark had regretted not recording himself with Al.

Shark Vegas were just as talented as Frankie Goes To Hollywood, but so what? Anyone who still believed in the meritocracy needed their head examined. From Mark's flat it was a twenty-minute stroll up the hill, past the Dallas Grill on Tempelhofer Damm, to Luftbrücke Platz where American, British and French flags flapped in the stiff wind. Next to the flagpoles, in the centre of the square, was a three-pronged concrete sculpture commemorating the airlift. It looked like a fat grey hand with three identical fingers sticking up.

'On this day thirty-five years ago the blockade of Berlin was lifted,' intoned the BBC voice across the PA. The RAF, the Brylcreem boys in freshly laundered grey uniforms, stood with hands entwined behind straight backs *at ease*. Pink blossom was drifting across the square like confetti. The BBC voice paid tribute to the courage of those who lost their lives defending the freedom of Berlin.

A few hundred spectators had gathered in the cold on the asphalt paths and green lawns. A few carried small West German flags and concentrated on the speeches. Others, Saturday morning passers-by, were more interested in the cut of the different Allied uniforms. The French military band wore little black pumps that looked like patent-leather ballet shoes. One of the trumpet-players had small oblong sunglasses, as worn by the Byrds in the 'Hey Mr Tambourine Man' era. Such sunglasses would never be countenanced in British military bands, even if the sun were shining.

The Berlin polizei, wearing green nylon jackets with woollen collars, patrolled the crowd with their eyes, hands limp by their black leather holsters. A group of demonstrators had already been shifted from the ceremony by the police and now stood near a bus stop 100 yards away, holding yellow placards which displayed statistics about the relative monies spent by the NATO countries on nuclear weapons as opposed to famine relief, a customary index of social sin. A bugleman blew 'The Last Post', then the French soldiers played the national anthems of Britain, the USA and France. When the band struck up the West German anthem an old Berliner turned away in disgust, mouthing obscenities, his wife following at an anxious distance.

Presaged by a long drum-roll, propeller planes buzzed the square at 11.06 a.m. Cameras clicked and veterans transported wreaths to the foot of the grey monument. A television reporter rearranged the wreaths into a more telegenic juxtaposition for his cameraman's close-up. The end of the ceremony was proclaimed in the two languages of the three occupying armies, the soldiers marching out the square carrying all manner of weapons from cutlasses to sub-machine guns. Captains and colonels skipped along behind their overdressed wives towards the convivialities at the officers' mess in Tempelhof base. Cocktail parties were another familiar feature of military life in West Berlin. Maybe I could have blagued an invitation if I had jacked up the accent a few notches and telephoned the British army PR a few days previously, I thought. Even now I might have stood a chance of hustling my way into the champagne and canapés with the press card, if only I had shaved this morning and worn a suit and tie. Not for the first time I realised my wardrobe was inappropriate for the entryist nature of my project. When I got back to London maybe I should open an account at Austin Reed or at least buy one of those seersucker suits much favoured by the ambitious journalists at The Observer. Meanwhile, I was stuck with this black Fred Perry, shiny brown raincoat, too-short Staprest trousers showing three inches of white sock and brown Dr Martens. Officers in the British army believed that only bounders wore brown shoes with blue trousers not to mention black shirts. I stood no fucking chance.

I lit up a Marlboro and considered my options. Most of the crowd were spilling out on to Columbiadamm for the 300-yard walk down to the gates of Tempelhof. A reunion group from the

1946 AACS Squadron was assembling for a group-shot in Luftbrücke Platz. 'THE GUYS WHO DESIGNED THE AIR TRAFFIC CONTROL SYSTEM USED IN THE AIRLIFT', said the explanatory blurb on their banner. One of these veterans wore crocodile-skin boots and a cream stetson. Most of the others had squadron ties and navy blazers or expensive casuals. There was a smattering of wives, their hair set like candy floss.

'All you young guys get down on your knees,' shouted the veteran assigned to take the memorial photographs. 'Right. Come on. Say cheese.'

Everyone obliged: a giggly cacophony of American cheese in accents drawn from California to New York City. One of them complained through cheese-clenched teeth that foreigners were spoiling the group shot at both edges.

'That's okay. We want some Berliners in here,' said another, extending his hand to a woman wheeling a pushchair decorated with miniature West German flags.

I joined the throng pouring down Columbiadamm alongside Tempelhof airport, the sand-coloured fortress designed by Albert Speer and finally completed in 1939. It was built in one long, slow curve punctuated by square flat-roofed towers slit like a rapist's hood. The tall rectangular windows were latticed with steel. Stone eagles stared truculently from the façade. Swastikas had made way for Stars and Stripes.

The iron eagle that had once perched on the airport's entrance arch was fifteen feet high with a wingspan of fifteen feet and had been modelled by a Berlin sculptor called W. Lenke. When the US armed forces first assumed control of Tempelhof they were in a quandary: the iron eagle was indubitably a grim symbol of Nazi power, but the eagle was also the official symbol of US power, both empires having pinched the idea from the Romans. A compromise was reached in 1967. The iron eagle's body and wings were broken up with sledgehammers, but the head was preserved and flown over to West Point.

Inside Tempelhof smoke was drifting across the base from the profusion of barbecues set up by the GIs. Helicopter blades and aeroplane propellers beat out another version of the song of the machines. Falling from the sky were purple flares and tiny flags

and men in parachutes the colours of the western allies, the
people's heads uplifted to the descending reds, whites and blues.
Mark Reeder would have said it was just like a fucking war film:
West Berlin had fallen, the Red Army was marching up the
Kurfürstendamm and helpless families were milling around the
military airport hoping they might be the lucky ones on the last
flight home.

Tanks were churning up the earth in a 200-metre circuit to give
the children a ride, though a sign said they travelled at their own
peril. Fathers and sons were joining the queue to get behind the
barrels of the 120 mm Wombat and the 40 mm M203 grenade
launcher. Once ensconced behind the sights, the boys made their
own sound-effects, pi*choo* pi*choo*. In my own street-battling days
the Tommies had fought the Krauts, but recently I had witnessed
small boys fighting imaginary Russians in English streets. With
whom did little West Berliners stage their fantasy shoot-outs?
With four foreign armies in the city, there was plenty of scope.

Other small boys were crawling all over the biggest tank on
display, the British Chieftain with the urban camouflage paint
that was unique to Berlin, an officer told a small crowd of
admirers. Black, grey and cream with symmetrical slabs of
mustard and sludge-green like a constructivist painting, the
Chieftain's camouflage was designed to hinder its detection in the
war-torn streets boulevards grey tenements rusting bridges
burning buses trams trees . . . steel caterpillars on the constructivist tank rumbling and clanking through burning Berlin. Chieftains would be more effectively camouflaged for the next war if
they were re-painted dayglo orange. Yes. Bright orange tanks and
flame yellow uniforms . . . I washed away the taste of war with a
cup of coffee, barbecued Polish sausage, Californian Ice-Cream
(made in Holland in small letters on the carton) and a pancake
sprinkled with Grand Marnier and caster sugar. Feeling sick, I
gazed at a British bubble-helicopter filled to bursting with plastic
footballs. The squaddies' racket was taking Polaroid pictures of
children inside the helicopter and charging them DM 5 apiece.
Within earshot of these enterprising soldiers a group of Irish-
American GIs were pouring pints of Guinness and playing gurgly
rebel music on a Japanese ghetto-blaster.

The Berlin Berets Square Dancing Club were appearing live in the main hangar. Outside, behind a wooden trestle-table loaded up with guns, grenades and rocket-launchers, three uniformed GIs stood demonstrating the hardware to the visitors. Each GI had his name in capitals stitched above his left breast. MILLER was explaining the workings of the M60 machine-gun.

'Yeah, it fires 200 bullets in one minute,' he said. His colleague, HERNANDEZ, was telling another Spanish speaker that he came from California. MILLER set down the M60 and picked up the Flarewell grenade-launcher, maximum effective range 200 metres.

'Can this take out a Soviet tank?' asked an American civilian.

'Sure can. It can more easily disable it. But it can also kill it.'

A jive-talking black, name of ATKINS, wanted to know why I was taking notes. I said I was a spy.

'You a *spy*, man? I'll tell you anything you want to know man. Long as you pay me.'

Walking away from the gun-display, past a US helicopter which had FREEDOM CITY written in black on yellow, I stuffed the notebook in my raincoat pocket and ran rueful fingers across my stubble. Should have shaved. Like a real spy. ATKINS was only joking, but there was a tradition of US personnel committing treason for dollars. At least the Brits sometimes betrayed their country for an idea, I thought, feeling the stirrings of patriotic pride for the first time that day.

Yellow snow-clearers and red fire engines were being ignored by the crowds, gunless vehicles having no place in the war fantasy which brought the fathers and sons to Tempelhof, where Goering made a keynote speech on 29 April 1933. An Otis Redding song was drifting out from the main hangar.

Two Hercules aeroplanes were going through their paces, flying 200 feet apart at 200 m.p.h. A female voice on the overpowered PA said, 'The Hercules is the most capable short-range airlift vehicle in the world. The Hercules can do up to 300 m.p.h. and can slow to 100 m.p.h. in its landing configuration.'

This contrast was now being established in the sky, one Hercules flashing past the other. Heads craned back to watch the performing grey planes. I continued on past the hamburger stand

being run by three genial white Americans from Morale, Welfare
and Recreation. Welfare and Recreation were fairly self-
explanatory, but I wondered what those army social workers did
to boost Morale, maintain Morale or whatever the fuck it was
you did with Morale. Maybe they held special surgeries for
depressed soldiers. Odd word, morale. I remembered mispro-
nouncing it when I was little. My mother had said that at times
morale was very low in the war.

'Moral was low?' I said.

'Morals were pretty low too,' she said, chuckling, thinking I
was too young to understand such an adult quip. But she was
wrong. I knew her joke had something to do with sex. Sexual
intercourse. Shagging. I knew some of the words, but didn't yet
know quite how it was done, although I had heard various far-
fetched theories. Lighting up possibly the eighteenth cigarette of
the day, I was returned to what passed for reality by a posh and
jovial British voice booming from the cream metal horns attached
to posts all round the running track.

It was another BBC World Service voice. Maybe this one
worked for BFBS Berlin? It was compèring an obstacle race being
staged by the RAF Motorcycle Display Team, the red riders
against the blue riders. Huddled in small groups, a crowd of two
hundred or so sat on granite steps watching the leaping motorbikes. The spectators looked cold and confused, but the World
Service voice was not discouraged. Not on your nelly! It was
going to jolly up these Krauts and recreate the House spirit right
here at Tempelhof airport. Come on you reds. Get going you
blues. It urged people to take sides.

'*Come on, red!*'

A couple of English-speaking children shouted out words of
encouragement to red or blue. I wondered what motorbikes the
RAF used, now the British motorcycle industry was more or less
dead.

'Blue's just in the lead. *Come on, red!*'

Blue just pipped red and the World Service voice asked the
crowd to give the riders a big hand please. Only a small hand was
forthcoming, but the voice was a blithe spirit and burbled on
regardless, making some hearty crack about the weather.

The RAF Motorcycle Display Team then removed the engine from a Metro and put it back all inside one minute, spectacularly boring I thought, but British Leyland was presumably the team's sponsor.

'If anyone wants their engine changing we can give you a quote,' said the World Service voice, chortling to itself. If Germany had won the war perhaps Luftwaffe stunt-riders would have put on motorcycle sideshows for the British collaborators at Biggin Hill. A Dakota buzzed the base and over the main PA the American female voice announced that a country and western band was about to start up in the main hangar. It was, we were told, an international band comprising members from America, Scotland, France and England in that order.

When the first sweet twang of the slide-steel guitar blew out across the base into the cold wind, soaring like a melodious jet above the rumbling tanks and crackling barbecues, the German cowboys detached themselves from the milling crowd and ambled towards the main hangar, their shoulders rolling. Where had they all come from? I had seen two or three of them at the Berlin Blockade photographic exhibition in one of the smaller hangars, but now there were simply dozens of these Marlboro men rocking on stack-heeled embroidered boots towards some song about lovin' and losin', workin' and driftin'. All of them had Levi 501s and some had stetsons too. They walked like cowboys always do in films, like they had shit their pants.

The day was assuming the fragility of a dream. It had become a blur of non-sequiturs running in all directions through the smoke while the aeroplanes and helicopters circled overhead like steel birds of prey. In the small fairground near the airport's entrance men and boys with flyblown hair sat in bright rockets completing whooshing circuits and girls screamed with fear or delight as the Whip snapped back their necks. Suddenly I was face to face with two men from General Electric, one in a blue suit and one in a grey suit. They stood smiling before displays of graphics and blurb extolling the virtues of their AN/FPS117 (V)2 Minimally Attended Solid State Radar. The gigantic golf ball towering above Tempelhof was part of this Minimally Attended system said the two men in suits and I believed them yes thanks very much. I fled the men from General Electric and staggered into a hall of facts where I learned that 536,703.3 tons of food were delivered to Berlin during the airlift, 1,586,029.3 tons of coal and 202,775 tons of *other*. The record for a single day was 16 April 1949 when 12,491 tons of food and medicine were flown into the city by American Skymasters and British Yorks. The total number of flights made during the airlift was 277,569. Total aeroplane mileage: 92,061,862 (156,505,400 km). Keep going. Look at the photographs of women building the third runway at Tempelhof and think in the west women only do such things in time of war. Ponder a picture of two children perched atop a derelict building watching a plane flying low overhead. 'Hope,' read the caption. 'Children watch a C-54 taking off from Berlin Tempelhof during the Berlin Airlift. This is one of the more famous photographs from the airlift effort.'

I leaned against a steel girder and thought of Mark Reeder when I saw the lovingly painted plastic replicas being displayed by the Modellbauclub IPMS Deutschland, a whole range of Second World War aerial combatants immobile on a table in a Tempelhof hangar. Alongside was the stand of the West Berlin Balloon Club which included a framed message maintaining that this sport, along with scuba diving, was suppressed in the GDR because of its escapist possibilities. Adults nodded sagely and drew the attention of their children to this bleak detail of totalitarian life. *Ordinary East Germans were prohibited from hot-air balloon racing and scuba diving.*

A US pilot named Lieutenant-Colonel Gail S. Hadrusen acquired the nickname The Candy Bomber because he dropped sweets to the children on parachutes during the Airlift. There was a photograph of this altruistic airman posing at Tempelhof in 1964 with one of his candy parachutes. Every child's dream, I thought, a bomb exploding chocolate and chewing gum.

The east banned things and the west dropped sweeties and this is all ye know on earth and all ye need to know. God help us. I lit the last cigarette in the pack and breathed as deeply as I could given the state of my lungs. I wanted to go home to the predictable eccentricities of Mittenwalderstrasse, to read a book and fall asleep and later drink raspberry wine at Leydicke with Pint and

Al and Mark if he showed up, to hear some jokes that would establish my distance from this fucking Disneyland, this high-tech historical roller-coaster celebrating the gorgeous power of Anglo-Americana and its glamorous resolution of the sins of the past. Victory is sweet and all the world loves a winner and the German cowboys danced up a storm in the main hangar, stomping those boots and twirling those stetsons and whooping for more till their throats were dry as the plains in summer.

8 *Exile on 109 Street*

I had an appointment for afternoon tea with Florence Karger. Although she had been living in East Berlin for thirty-five years, she still observed certain rituals, as is the way with exiles. Edward Said wrote that the word exile should be used only to describe those people forced to flee their country, expatriate being the correct term for those who chose to live abroad, but I wasn't sure the distinction was quite this clear-cut. Pint could have stayed in East Berlin, same as George could have stayed in Sri Lanka, the German Sisters could have stayed in Heidelberg, Mark Reeder could have stayed in Manchester, but all of them felt some compulsion to leave. The borderline between voluntary expatriation and forced exile was inexact, like most borders staked out by theory. In Johnny's case he had no sense of nationality from which to escape. He was a foreigner everywhere. His mother, Florence, belonged to another driven generation, the thirties communists flung by circumstance and desire to all corners of the earth.

Grünau was described in angular thirties capitals, painted in black on the white metal oblongs nailed to the station walls, a style of typography that had become fashionable again in the west. The S-Bahn guards wore navy-blue peaked caps circled with blood-red bands. The station was spotless, the sun shone, the greenery soothed the brightness of the light on the quiet streets outside. I felt again as if I was strolling through the opening sequence of some film. This was Germany before the storm. I took my place in the queue for the tram.

Ten stops from the Alexanderplatz on the S-Bahn, Grünau was one of the more select commuters' suburbs. It was around four in the afternoon and the first office workers were spilling out into the sunshine holding briefcases. Some could walk home from the station. Most had a further short journey by bus or tram, neither of which had conductors, only drivers. In East Germany it was a trust-system of payment. On mounting the bus or tram people slid one of their pre-bought tickets into a grey metal puncher and beat a hole with their fist or the flat of their hand. I never saw anyone trying to bunk their 20 pfennig fare. All the metal punchers had been worn down by millions of honest hands. To certain eyes the worn punchers were further evidence of a cowed population. To others the worn punchers represented an admirable sense of civic responsibility. Maybe God divided Berlin to demonstrate His proposition that facts have no intrinsic meaning.

The tram was the colour of ice cream in my first recollection of its slippery beauty, vanilla ice cream that I used to think people licked all day in heaven probably. The tram ran parallel to the road for forty yards then veered left and disappeared into a deciduous forest. It was like one of those scenic rides they have at English seaside resorts. I got off at the first stop and walked through the trees till I came after ten minutes to the beginnings of the settlement known as Intelligenzsiedlung. Young athletes were jogging down the centre of the street that skirted the banks of the Spree. Eight-man racing shells were stacked up outside the boat-houses, part of the complex built specially for the 1936 Olympics. I turned right down 109 Street, found house number 8 on my left and recognised the white Lada parked on the drive overhung with trees. The Kargers had lived in this detached two-storey house since 1951, the rent fixed at 2 per cent of Georg's annual income.

Georg was still asleep. Florence had just got up. Both of them had weak hearts. Every day they lunched at noon then took a siesta. Before putting on the kettle, Florence showed me a book of drawings and watercolours done by a good friend of hers, Elizabeth Shaw, another member of the British emigré community in East Berlin. The book was mostly devoted to English and Irish landscapes, soft Devon hills and bays, smudgy dawns in

Glengariff and Youghal. Although there was nothing in the book specifically reminiscent of the green flatlands around Wisbech where Florence grew up, the muted colours were suggestive of the quality of light on certain remembered September afternoons, her hands stained purplish after blackberrying, the weak suns leaking pinks and golds across empty East Anglian skies, all the usual fragments of colour that constitute a childhood memory.

In May students from nearby Cambridge used to come strawberry-picking, she recalled, working mainly in the fields owned by Smedley's. 'Is that still a name?' she said absently. 'Smedley's?'

I nodded. It was indeed a name in the world of jam.

Framed on the wall were some of Johnny's own watercolours and crayon drawings of the English and French countryside, engravings of old Vienna and two drawings by John Heartfield, who achieved fame as a photomontage artist in the thirties, having adopted an English-sounding name as deliberate provocation to the Nazi patriots. Heartfield, Florence said en route to the kitchen, was one of many distinguished intellectuals who decided to settle in East Germany after the war. The novelist Stefan Heym was another, she shouted out above the clinking of cups and saucers.

She came back into the living room five minutes later with a home-made sponge cake and a china tea service on a tray. Her grey hair was chopped short around a face that had once broken hearts. She wore a washed-out denim tunic. She said the house needed re-painting but she didn't like having lots of workmen in the house what with all the mess they made and everything. Johnny was out, but she expected him back soon. She asked discreet questions about the life lived by her son in London and I answered as diplomatically as I was able. She said she loved having younger company in the house. In the old days Johnny had always brought his friends round for tea on Sundays.

Over her third cup of tea Florence told me about the man Johnny was named after, the love of her life. When she met him she was working as secretary to the general manager of a firm in Welwyn Garden City. She was 22. The year was 1932. A friend of hers in the accounts department, a socialist who liked discussing politics over a few pints, said Florence should go to London and meet this friend of his, a left-wing journalist.

'I was interested in the idea of him,' she said, smiling with the casual sexual confidence of one who never had much problem finding potential suitors. 'John was a Marxist. He had a flat on the King's Cross Road. Anyway, he was the first really important person in my life. He started pouring all this stuff into me. Sometimes I said, John, for Christ's sake, I don't want to think about all these things. It's too painful. Don't be daft, he said. You've started. You can't stop now. And it's true. Once you've started reading about history and politics, it's hard to stop. Everything's connected.'

Everything's connected. I had read somewhere that being a Marxist in Eastern Europe was like being a Christian in the Middle Ages. I was also thinking that men will use whatever they have at their disposal to win the heart of a woman they love. Love me love my politics, baby. Love me love my writing, darling. Florence's relationship with socialism, which was to have such dramatic consequences for her life, began as an affair of the heart. Her devotion to socialism was mediated through John then Robin then Georg. This last romance was the longest-lived and the least passionate. George was still sleeping upstairs. Birds sang in the garden outside. Florence was re-living her days in London with John.

'I left my job in Welwyn and came to live with John. The *News Chronicle* approached him and asked him if he'd like to do a series on oil and the role it plays in the world. He was commissioned to do three articles. The first article was an absolute sensation. And what shall I tell you? The other two articles never appeared.'

She shrugged. She had been raised on conspiracy stories. She urged me to have another slice of sponge cake and wondered aloud what had happened to Johnny.

'At the time of this *News Chronicle* business John was a freelance. Very independent thinking. He didn't write things just to please his bosses. Does *Film Weekly* still exist?' she asked, eyebrows poised above her tea-cup.

I shook my head. These days the house-magazine of the film industry was *Screen International*, edited as it happened by a friend of mine and Johnny's, I said, an art-school Maoist who worked as a postman for four years before drifting into journalism via *The Leveller*.

'Well, at the time,' Florence continued, 'there was a very progressive editor on *Film Weekly*. John wrote about the way that Hollywood portrayed black people in films, always as slaves, bowing and scraping. He was a chap with a very bright and expansive mind. He's always remained an absolute example to me. A Welshman. The Welsh, you know, have strains of Spanish. He taught me how to enjoy life too. I had been used up to then to a very *pinched* kind of existence, you know, you work but you live on the fringe of poverty. John never had a lot of money, but he could never live in that pinched kind of way. There was something big about him.'

John liked a drink, told a good story. Georg was by nature a more ascetic man, primarily interested in matters of the mind, wary of the pull of emotions. Florence's journey across the systems began in the ambience of socialist London in the thirties, collecting pennies on the street for Spain, reading banned books in the Paddington Free Library. Orwell had just published *The Road to Wigan Pier*, Gollancz began his Left Book Club and Florence bought volumes at half-a-crown apiece.

'When he died it just blew a great big hole in my life. He was in his early thirties. It was the first great blow,' Florence said, sitting back in her armchair, her eyes still mourning after all these years. She joined the Communist Party in 1938 and began working for the Joint Committee for Soviet Aid in her spare time. During working hours she was a secretary at *The Lady*, the monthly magazine for upper-crust women.

At the inaugural meeting of the Left Film Club Florence took down the minutes in shorthand, following the screening of a documentary on the Jarrow March. The meeting was addressed by Cedric Bellfrage, Muriel Dickinson, Ivor Montagu and other luminaries, but Florence's attention was distracted by a handsome young painter called Robin who had just graduated from Oxford, where he had read Modern Languages.

'This young chap Robin,' she said. 'It was nine months after John's death. And you know how it is. Life goes on. That was the beginning of my affair with Robin, only six months before the war. The Left Film Club never got going because of the war.'

Florence married Robin a few weeks before he was called up. She stayed in London throughout the Blitz. So much had happened so quickly, the discovery of an ideology that brought new friends and social scenes, the emotional upheaval of the Spanish Civil War, the death of John, the marriage to Robin who had gone away to fight, so much had happened she was unafraid of the bombs. She never slept in the Underground. She was often out in the streets when bombs were falling and the skies were lit by ack-ack tracers.

By this time Florence had left *The Lady* and was working full-time at the Joint Committee for Soviet Aid. After the opening of the eastern front, British portraits of the Bolshevik leviathan swiftly metamorphosed into an heroic canvas of brave Russians battling the Nazis in the ice and snow. Girls in Britain knitted jumpers for the Red Army. Florence's job was transformed.

'Things changed almost overnight,' she said. 'Quite extraordinary. All of a sudden people were sympathetic. Tanks rolled out of Coventry with FOR JOE written on the side by the workers. It became the easiest thing in the world, this organising job. I felt I shouldn't get paid to do it. Of course, Robin was away. I never believed he'd get killed. I always thought he'd come back.'

A 25-year-old lieutenant-colonel in the Royal Fuseliers, Robin was killed in action on 8 August 1944 near the city of Florence. He was a painter. He had planned to take his wife to Florence after the war.

'His chaps, sergeants and so on, came to see me after the war. None of them knew Robin was an artist. That side of himself he had kept hidden away. He had been in the Royal Fuseliers with Monty, who he used to call that old idiot,' she said, getting up to put the kettle on. Footsteps on the floor above indicated that Georg was up and about. Soon it became silent again which meant Georg was at his desk writing: a philosophical and anthropological inquiry into the origin of music and the universal character of musics through space and time. Florence took him a cup of tea.

I'm collecting lives like stamps or coins and sticking them in my scrapbook and hoping for the best, hoping they all add up to something, hoping I can do justice to all these brave lives, I thought, while Florence was upstairs. *I never really loved him. In the early days.* Florence said this during one of our first chats. I had been shocked and also embarrassed that she should tell me such a thing. Why me? Had she told the same thing to her son? In the event it was old news to Johnny, Georg too. Georg had never been under any illusions. He knew that in later life Florence had grown to love him. He knew there were different kinds of love.

Florence had been introduced to Georg by the woman who helped him escape from Vienna through the sewers. This woman, a glamorous Jewish socialist, married Georg in London. They were divorced after two years but remained good friends. Introduced to Florence by his ex-wife, Georg invited Florence to a concert. It was Wagner, Florence remembered. She said she hated Wagner. Georg said oh what the hell? Come anyway.

'We went out a few times,' Florence said, 'but I was still lovelorn about Robin and not at all in the mood to settle down with someone else. Then, shortly before Georg was due to return to Vienna at the end of the war, he wrote me a letter explaining quite frankly that he had looked elsewhere for a wife, but his search had been unsatisfactory, it had not borne fruit. He said he could offer me a good life. He had decent prospects. Would I go to Vienna with him as his wife?'

Florence stopped to consider, raising the tea-cup to her lips.

'I didn't love him, but I respected him,' she said, choosing her words carefully. 'At the time I was thirty-five. I had the feeling, well, that I was past my first youth. I wasn't going to get a job with anyone who was looking for a dolly bird. And I had thought it might perhaps be an idea to go to Germany and try and do some good. I knew it had been bombed to pieces. Anyway, I decided Georg was a good man who would give me a good life.'

She went to Vienna with Georg, but she didn't marry him until she was eight months pregnant with Johnny. The registrar conducting the civil ceremony was sensitive to her condition. Do sit down, he told her.

Florence knew I found her emotional pragmatism hard to understand. She had met Laura the summer before when I came over to write the piece about punks in East Berlin. In my romance with Laura she saw a blurred reflection of her own love-affair with John, I knew, she had said as much. Laura was nine years younger than me. I was a journalist with bad debts. Laura was very pretty, as Florence had been. I was very sociable, as John had been.

It was such a nice day, Florence suddenly said, so English, what on *earth* were we doing sitting indoors? I followed her outside and she showed me with pride her little vegetable and herb garden, her potatoes and parsley and green beans, her rock garden.

'I love rock gardens,' she said, sitting in the blue canvas swing-chair beneath the fluted canopy. One fifty-foot-square section of the garden was overgrown with flowering weeds and grasses. Florence had read somewhere it was good to have a wild patch, somewhere for the creepie-crawlies, a planned wilderness in the otherwise immaculately tended garden. A woman gardener came a few times a week to help Florence out.

'Isn't the lilac beautiful?' she said, pointing at the purple blooms along the hedgerow which shielded the garden from the eyes of passing strangers. 'Germans are very keen on lilac for some reason.'

A plump woman wearing a purple headband and woollen two-piece walked up the drive and greeted Florence with a kiss on the cheek.

Her name was Hattie, one of Florence's best friends in East Berlin. She worked at Radio Berlin International, the GDR equivalent of the World Service, in the section dealing with international inquiries. It was an interesting job, she said, but very hard work. There were only three of them and they got simply thousands of letters from all over the world asking about the educational system, the standard of living, the system of government, oh my God. She wiped her brow in mock fatigue. Of course, she said, the most popular question from British listeners concerned employment in East Germany.

A jolly woman with an infectious laugh, Hattie had more or less devoted her personal life to caring for her sick mother and, as a result, had never married. What she found hard to understand about the west was people's self-obsession, she said. She had once written to a cousin in West Germany asking after an ill aunt. She never got a reply.

'How can anyone not reply to a letter about a poorly relative?' she asked me, genuinely puzzled. I shrugged and shook my head apologetically. Florence said nothing. Her thirty-five years in East Berlin had not eradicated a certain nationalism. Secretly she thought Hattie's criticisms applied more to Germans than the English.

'These westerners,' continued Hattie, dabbing the remains of sponge cake from the corner of her red-lipsticked mouth, 'they have so much to make life easy for them. So many appliances in the kitchen. All the fruits and vegetables in the shops to be able to cook nice meals. I envy all that very much, but *they* are never satisfied. They don't know how lucky they are. They think only of themselves.'

Hattie had recently passed her sixtieth birthday and, as a result, was permitted travel to the west. She was going to spend her summer holiday with an old schoolfriend living in Cologne whom Hattie had not seen since the Wall was built. She was much excited at the prospect. She intended persuading her schoolfriend to undertake a tour of castles and cathedrals in the southern part of the Federal Republic.

'You know, these castles that were built by kings in the tenth century,' Hattie said enthusiastically. 'Of course kings mean nothing to me. But the castles are of interest.'

A similar caveat was inserted into her account of the cathedrals: 'Of course religion means nothing to me, but the cathedrals are very beautiful.'

Hattie's ruminations on these contradictions were interrupted by the high-pitched splutter of a Trabant, Johnny's voice thanking some friend for the lift home, the door slamming, Johnny striding into the garden where he played as a child. Kisses pecked, hands shaken, Hattie reached into her handbag and plucked out a present for Johnny: a small knife in a leather sheath.

Johnny couldn't even remember who Hattie was. He felt too embarrassed for his thank you to carry much conviction. Florence made matters worse by laughing and saying, 'Oh dear. She's forgotten he's grown up.'

While Hattie made a tactical retreat to the bathroom Florence explained that Hattie had always been a loyal friend. 'I always had my friends, the ones who loved me. The others? Fuck 'em I always thought,' she said.

Swearing was an article of faith for Florence, but I always liked the self-consciously anti-bourgeois fucks and shits she dropped into her speech. Georg avoided vulgar expletives. John the journalist probably had a fruity turn of phrase, I decided, as the afternoon light softened towards evening and conversation gradually turned towards the cold war. Big subject. Big book? Yes, I'd love a glass of Bulgarian white. Johnny poured. Florence proposed a toast to peace. Despite all her travails she had somehow remained an innocent. Long live innocence, I thought, feeling the juice trickling coldly past my teeth and sliding down to the warm spot inside.

'Oh, we had to build the Wall,' Florence was saying. 'They were just bleeding us dry. Anything at all that could be sold for profit in the west went there. Even the lilac.'

A gleam in her eye, she added that the Wall had brought other advantages too. All the westerners who used to come over to the eastern lakes and parks, for example, you couldn't move for them. They were getting four ostmarks for each deutschmark. Everything in East Berlin was dirt cheap. Florence, for one, was glad those people didn't come any more.

'The green heart of Berlin,' said Hattie, 'that is ours. They have Wannsee and the Grunewald, that's all. The green heart of Berlin is here. We were very lucky the way the border was drawn.'

The Wall prevents crime too, Florence said. Once Georg's Lada was stolen from the centre of town. It was recovered within a few hours, but if the Wall hadn't been there that car would have been over the border like a shot, the number plates changed before you could say Jack Robinson, no hope of ever seeing it again, she said. The vandalism, the mugging, the disrespect for the old, the drugs, all those things were kept away from the east by the Wall. Hattie was nodding agreement.

Johnny was grinning, but for many people the Wall was not a sinister thing of dogs, wire and watchtowers. For them the border was a blanket, cosy defence against the excess and violence they

associated with the western way. In western societies the middle
class favoured strengthening the police for similar reasons. Save
me and my children from the things I see on television. Let me live
my life in peace. Please Mr President, Mr Policeman, keep the
nastiness away from my neighbourhood. Build a wall around us.
Do whatever's necessary, I don't care. I'm scared. Jesus. Make
things safe. Let everything be nice.

People want the world to just go away and leave them alone. In
summery gardens east and west it's the same story. Florence was
in her element chattering in the garden on such a beautiful
evening, her son home from London, her son's friend too, nice to
have some younger company, plus lovable loyal Hattie. God, it
had been different when she first arrived, she said. Absolutely
miserable for the first two years, you couldn't imagine. Threat-
ened to come home many a time. But she stuck it out, learnt
German, got a job. Little by little things improved.

'In a way I'm quite at home here now,' she said, cradling her
glass of wine.

'You have been here quite some time,' Johnny said.

Ignoring her son, Florence went on to explain how she felt
during the exile imposed by the Stalinist period, when western
communists were unable to return to their capitalist homelands.

'It sounds stupid, but when I finally got back to England I felt
like kissing the earth, I really did,' she said. 'Johnny was about
nine. We were treated like royalty, weren't we? We stayed with
relations in Thetford, they had a little village shop, and Johnny
worked for a while behind the sweet counter. I remember asking
him if he was enjoying the work and he said: yes, I like it very
much, but I think I've eaten all the profits.'

Johnny smiled, bashful as any son when the mother tells stories
in front of his friends, particularly those stories which are
supposed somehow to crystallise the offspring's burgeoning
personality. *I think I've eaten all the profits.* The child of
communism. Johnny sat next to his mother on the swing-chair,
smoking a cigarette. The three tall pines shading the garden had
been planted when he was a baby, Florence reminded him.

A bespectacled man in his mid-thirties cycled past on the un-
metalled road beyond the Karger's hedgerow and Johnny exhaled

the smoke thoughtfully through pursed lips. That cyclist had been a good friend of Johnny's twenty-five years ago, but now he didn't talk to Johnny any more. Johnny was a traitor. He had gone to the west. Three years ago they had a conversation on the street and the former friend asked Johnny why he had left East Berlin. Johnny told him what he tells everyone when they ask that question: he had a dead-end job in East Berlin and needed to travel in order to find more challenging work. I knew that was only part of the story. I knew about Juliana and I also knew that Johnny himself had a yen for the bright lights. I knew further that he was a bit ashamed. Sometimes I felt the same way myself. You can hate pornography, but it can still cause tumescence.

Georg finally emerged blinking from his labours. He was almost completely bald, and old age had given him a stoop which had subtracted five inches from his former height. Georg's old suits fitted Johnny perfectly. Florence said she hoped everyone was hungry because there were delicious potato pancakes for tea, home-made by a woman who helped out in the house sometimes. Hattie said it was most kind of Florence to invite her, but really, it was getting late and she had to be hurrying along. Florence walked with Hattie to the garden gate and then she went into the kitchen to prepare the tea. Sockless in his sandals, Georg wore the round glasses popular among avant-garde intellectuals in the thirties and a high-buttoned denim tunic in the Mao mode. His fingers were long and white, pianist's hands unroughened by manual work, hands that had danced across the keys in Berlin beer-halls before the Nazis came to power. The small-talk in the garden came abruptly to an end once he had taken Florence's place on the swing-chair. Evidently engrossed in his latest book, he wanted to canvass my opinion on the subject of musics across space and time.

'One of the beauties of music . . .' I began hesitantly because Georg was an intimidating man. He fixed me with that stare through those thirties spectacles, placed his elegant hands in an attitude of prayer, his whole face seemingly twitching with new ideas as I attempted to speak.

'Yeah. One of the nice things about music is that it's inherently irrational and not subject to materialist explanation, beyond the kind of instruments used and so on. Music has no technical function, no real usefulness, and that's the source of its power.'

'That is one possibility,' Georg said doubtfully.

'The whole point of music, in fact,' I said, quite carried away by this banal notion, 'is that it is universally useless. Unnecessary.'

'But it may be emotionally necessary,' Georg said.

'Like love?'

'Of course.'

Florence called everyone into the dining room. The potato pancakes were supplemented by sausage, cheese and green salad. Georg's mind was still inside his manuscript. By comparison to ancient African drum music, he said, jazz was very simple in its structure. In fact, *all* the musics of the metropolitan societies had more in common with each other than *any* of it did to the musics of the pre-industrial societies. Elvis Costello said writing about music was like dancing about architecture. I thought this, but did not say it, although Georg would have welcomed the challenge. Johnny had once brought Georg along to a *Leveller* collective meeting in London. Georg had said nothing, but I remembered watching my words more carefully than usual. Georg had a certain presence, even in those days when I had no idea of the torments he had survived. Georg himself never spoke about such matters. Everything I knew about his pre-war life I had gleaned from Florence or Johnny. It was Florence who told me that Georg's mother had flushed his Communist Party badge down the toilet. Best place for it, Georg's mother had said. Georg's family was very bourgeois. His father was a composer of light operas that were still performed in Austria. The Kargers would continue receiving a percentage of the royalties until the year 2000.

Georg made one glass of red wine last all meal. Florence apologised for the strawberries from the deep freeze still being hard as ice.

The travel restrictions, I said over coffee, that was the most common complaint I heard against the East German government. Yes, Georg replied, I was right. It was a grave source of discontent and it was indeed a terrible infringement of people's liberty, which did not help at all in winning *the argument*. Personally he was in favour of the travel restrictions being lifted.

'And yet,' he added, his long index finger erect, a mannerism he must have used at the conservatoire, 'and yet there are some very intelligent people here who say it is not possible, and they have good reason. The problem, you see, is that the west will do anything to sabotage the way of life in the GDR. If our most talented and well-qualified people were permitted to travel, they would, I think, be offered fantastic inducements to stay in the west. They would have to be saints to refuse. For our country this would be disastrous. We have, for example, just a few hundred specialists in computer software. If we were to lose these people it would be an unmitigated disaster. I don't know. But, still, there must be *some* solution to this problem.'

Georg felt the problem would outlive him. He rose from the table and returned to his study. When you embark upon a book at the age of seventy-seven you must race to the conclusion and hope you still have some life left for revision.

'Do you know Eduardo?' Florence asked out of the blue. I said I met him once at a gay disco called Heaven, in London, but I didn't really know him.

'He studied at Weimar with Johnny. He's Spanish really. His parents emigrated after Franco won in Spain. Where does he live now?'

'Paris,' said Johnny.

All these displaced people. All the millions of miles travelled from one idea to another. From one love to the next. I drained my glass and considered the life lived by Frau Plenk in the flat next door to Mark Reeder. She was about the same age as Florence. She had never travelled, never known more than one man sexually, never learned any words of foreign tongues, never felt committed one way or another to the various wars of ideology that had dogged and determined her life. Florence and Frau Plenk. Was there any connection? Both women's lives had been dominated by men, I suppose. Neither of them had the chance to be themselves, the way their men were. Their menfolk had the same first language and were on opposite sides in the Second World War. Now they lived in different neighbourhoods of the same city: a poor immigrants' ghetto and a rich communist suburb. *The compass is broken. The black arrow spins round and round. The wanderer gets lost in the map. Ideologies melt like freak snowfalls in May. In Berlin.* I said goodbye to Florence and Georg and sometime before midnight Johnny drove me to Friedrichstrasse in the 1600 cc Lada.

In the years to come I often had cause to think of the life Florence manufactured from a broken heart. Lovers may die or disappear but love survives the loss. In Florence's case the love had survived John and the Spanish Revolution and grown old with her through other men and wars. Her sorrow was decent and truthful and, in those years of which I am speaking, I often drew comfort from the sad romances of Florence from Wisbech who became Florence Karger, wife of the respected musicologist, mother of one of my best friends, inhabitant of Intelligenzsiedlung in Grünau, a bit of a girl in her younger days, cheerful traitor to Queen and country, convinced communist and lover of rock gardens.

9 The angels and the fishermen of Kreuzberg 36

Out in the garden Ulrike and Uschi were discussing their latest project: the opening of a new nightclub. Charlotte was busy digging valleys in the sandpit with her yellow plastic trowel, piling up mountains, tracing parallel waves with her tiny fingers outstretched. The sun was still high enough in the blue for most of the garden to evade the sharp shadow thrown by the fire-wall.

'Berlin needs a new nightclub,' pronounced Ulrike. 'Everyone is bored stupid with the Djungel, but everyone still goes there just because there's nowhere else.'

With only the slightest suspicion of doubt in her dark eyes, Uschi murmured assent. She didn't really believe Ulrike's plans would come to fruition, but if by some miracle enough money was raised to open a nightclub then Uschi would work there alongside her sister. And if the nightclub never happened, who cared? Uschi was too abstract to be bothered by such things, especially when a child was growing inside her.

Ulrike was more worldly. She felt she couldn't stay forever bored, broke and beautiful. She was always making plans and probably one day the plans would materialise into money. I could imagine her rich in a chic apartment someplace, a fast car and a slim boyfriend some years younger. Champagne for breakfast, that was one of Ulrike's dreams. Enough money to tell the world go fuck yourself. Meanwhile, the fire-wall shadow was lengthening.

'Don't ask,' Uschi said, when I asked if I could borrow her

bicycle. In her view the English wasted all their breath asking permission and saying sorry. I pedalled west along Gneisenau-strasse, one of hundreds of bicycle lanes installed by the city council in recognition of the lifestyle militants who had planted their flag in Kreuzberg, this township of cracked tenements bursting with immigrants and dreamers. City without cars! Country without frontiers! World without weapons! Sir Thomas More published *Utopia* in 1516. Between the Afro-German Shop and Mehringdamm U-Bahn I counted six glass-recycling domes, five feet high, like bright green diving bells waiting for the flood.

Swerving to avoid Alsatians and children and pigeons, plus anarchistic cyclists travelling in the wrong direction, I had the usual nightmare of some slow-witted pigeon getting mangled in the spokes of my front wheel: a broken wing, a petrol-coloured breast spilling blood, a heap of grey in death-agony throes on the tarmac. Would I have the courage to pick up this flapping corpse and snap its neck? Shuddering, I consoled myself with the thought that pigeons were incredibly fleet-footed for their size and, also, I had never seen a pigeon meet its end in the wheels of a bicycle. I concentrated instead on the forthcoming interview with Peter, the newly arrived refugee from East Germany who was going to Nicaragua in the same brigade as George. He lived somewhere in Schlesisches Tor, near the only border crossing exclusively for pedestrians: an arched bridge across the Spree. The only way I knew of getting there was to cycle to Checkpoint Charlie and then travel east following the Wall. I had plenty of time on my hands. Along many of its sections the border was built down the middle of a street, impassable now for cars but perfect for bicycles.

I turned right at Kochstrasse U-Bahn station, past a fleet of tourist coaches waiting for their passengers to finish looking round the Wall Museum. Farther along, at the end of Jakob-strasse, five small boys were playing football, using a section of the Wall as their goal.

A burned-out orange 2CV was abandoned on a piece of waste ground, by a gigantic billboard of full-colour cowboys against a dusty backdrop of cattle and mountains. It carried the copyline, Go West! West, a brand of cigarettes packaged red-and-white to

look like Marlboro, was also advertised on the walls of Friedrichstrasse underground station and sold in the duty-free shop on the
platform there, I remembered, wondering if the copywriter who
wrote the slogan realised his words would be published on
posters a stone's throw from the Wall? Maybe the campaign was
specifically designed for West Berlin. Opposite the billboard was
a squatted tenement which had converted a former shop into an
art gallery. The dirty window showcased a greenish corpse on a
bed. Above the corpse hung green light-bulbs. The Hotel
Stuttgarter Hof, next door, had painted artificial windows with
grey window-frames on its bricked-up façade. Beneath the
artificial windows were window-boxes containing real red carnations.

The road alongside the Wall came to an end, but it was still
possible to cycle down the track of dried mud that led through the
overgrown grass and flowering weeds. The track ran parallel to
the cream-coloured Wall, curving left, till the Rauhaus came
into view. A dark red building surrounded by mature trees,
the Rauhaus had once been a Catholic hospital, but it was
abandoned after the Wall was built and later the hospital was
squatted by the young homeless. The Rauhaus was the oldest
squat in the city. Fading yellow paint on its roof said YANKEES
GO HOME in English. As I was cycling past, a dishevelled girl
leaned out of a third-floor window and asked what time it was. I
shouted back that I didn't know. Maybe about four. She shut the
latticed window.

These days there were some forty-five more or less permanent
residents at the Rauhaus and another thirty always passing
through. It was a rooming house for runaways from all over
Europe, the Americas and Africa. I had been there a few times,
met Rastafarians from Africa, revolutionaries from Latin
America, anarchists from Ireland. I had once considered writing a
magazine piece on THE SQUAT OVERLOOKING THE WALL,
but I never got around to it. The last time I went to the Rauhaus
two black GIs had been lounging against their Chevrolet in the
car park. The Danish punk showing me around (a friend of the
Danes staying at Mittenwalderstrasse) had said he wasn't sure if
they had come to buy or sell drugs, but drugs was the only reason

GIs came to the Rauhaus. Down in the basement electric guitars had been rehearsing another version of the Mauersound. From the window of the room where my Danish acquaintance was staying there was a crystal-clear view of the watchtower the other side of the Wall, just twenty yards away. I met some women who complained that the border guards often ogled them with binoculars while the women were in the communal toilets. One of these women, a German, told me she had got so irritated by the constant harassment that she went out and bought a black balaclava and a toy gun. One morning, having completed her ablutions, she donned this disguise and leapt out of the toilet, holding her gun two-handed like they do in American cop shows. She said the guard in the watchtower dived for cover.

The story may have been true or it may have been a fantasy that slowly through time the German woman had decided to report as a fact. People often end up believing their own lies, I thought, bumping along the mud path past some trashy psychedelic murals painted on the Wall by a Rauhaus resident considered by some to have talent.

Walking towards me along the path was a tall young woman in black and her seven-year-old son, also dressed in black from head to toe. I stopped to say hello. I remembered them from one of my visits to the Rauhaus. She was Italian. She loved having her photograph taken. In her room at the Rauhaus she had a collection of smashed mirrors whose jagged edges represented some danger to her son, I had thought at the time, although maybe jagged mirrors were the least of his problems. Until much later in life children never realised their lives had been anything out of the ordinary. *I lived in a multi-national squat in West Berlin right next to the Wall. I never went to school. My mother was a punk. She had a steel pin through her nose and used to wear tight black skirts. Whenever photographers came to the squat they always wanted to take pictures of me and my mother together in our room, which had a view over the Wall. Sometimes I used to wave at the people who sat out on the corrugated-maroon balconies in the pebbledash block of flats the other side of the border. Usually they waved back. Those flats were only forty yards from our bedroom window. I spoke Italian with my*

*mother and German with most of the other people in the squat. I
also spoke German with these Turkish friends I had. We used to
play soldiers on an abandoned building site just down the street.
Among themselves they spoke Turkish. My mother told me the
Turks came to West Berlin more or less as slaves and were only
allowed to do the most boring and low-paid jobs. She said
probably I would meet people who said Turks were dirty and
violent, but I wasn't to pay any attention to that kind of talk.
People always said those things about foreigners. There were lots
of musicians in the Rauhaus and sometimes it was hard to sleep at
nights.*

Mother and son continued strolling back to the Rauhaus,
holding hands. I pressed on. A Turkish family was sprawled out
on a lawn behind the Rauhaus, two men supervising the grilling
of the kebabs on a coal barbecue.

You Are Now Entering The American Sector, said an ancient
enamel sign at the corner of Waldemarstrasse and Luckauer-
strasse. When there was free traffic between the Berlins the signs
had some purpose. Now they just looked stupid, addressing their
welcome to the Wall. Why had no one bothered taking down the
signs? Might as well ask why no one had bothered doing anything
to repair the general dereliction, I thought. Krieg dem Imperial-
ischen Krieg was written in red on a tattered banner strung across
the façade of a squatted tenement block. Most of the windows
were broken, patched by plastic and cardboard. In a way it was
surprising the west had just left these zones to rot. Surely there
was some propaganda initiative to be gained by tarting up
Kreuzberg 36, improving the view from the other side of the
border? The only new building in the neighbourhood was a low
concrete church named Saint Michael's. I leaned the bicycle up
against a viewing platform built from planks and scaffolding,
garishly painted blue and purple. Two Turkish women, their
heads wrapped in silk, sat at the base of the structure, embroider-
ing cloth. I climbed the wooden steps and received the conventional greeting from the guard in the lookout: the two glass
eyes of his optical instrument focused on me for some six seconds.

A sash window was lifted open on the fifth floor of one of the
tenements adjoining the Wall and the guard promptly switched

his binocular gaze to the face at the window, a woman in her twenties who probably needed some fresh air or a quick break from looking after the kids.

Border guards must get to know all the faces at the windows. Perhaps the guards sometimes had romantic feelings for certain familiar faces. Perhaps they dreamt about the women at the windows, erotic dreams based on the view through the intimate lens, nights of forbidden pleasure in the watchtower, the lovers brought together on these occasions by secret tunnels leading to the tenements' basements. Anything was possible. For the people living in rooms which had windows giving out on the Wall it was simply a drag, of course, being stared at through binoculars every time they opened their window.

The particular guard in my vision took off his peaked cap, stuck his head out of the watchtower window and ran some fingers through his short blond hair. Though the light was mellowing, the sun was still hot. I noticed his watchtower was full of potted plants, a homely touch. One of the guards must have been a keen gardener. When this gardener was first assigned to border duty he must have looked at the watchtower and thought: *an elevated greenhouse.* Maybe he grew tomatoes up there too. Tomatoes were not always easy to find in East Berlin.

I dismounted the viewing platform and checked again Peter's address in Schlesisches Tor. Peter had no telephone, but George had told him to expect me sometime late afternoon, early evening. George had been helpfully vague about the time. Going by the sun, it was around five. Ideal. I was about to resume the journey when two small girls dressed in white-lace full-length dresses came running out of Saint Michael's church. Carrying white wands topped with silver stars, they raced up the steps of the viewing platform pursued by six more children in the ragged clothes more commonly worn in the neighbourhood. Their shining hair tied by ribbons, the two girls in white stood on the platform waving their wands at the guard, their silver stars leaping like fish above the Wall.

The two girls were dressed up for their first communion, I guessed, but why were they carrying wands? I never found out if the guard returned the wave, but I somehow hoped he did. I hoped he had sufficient grace to raise a hand to the beautiful girls in white, to acknowledge that brief appearance of the angels on the viewing platform. *First communion.* Perhaps the priest had delivered some homily about the need for the young to stretch their hands across the walls built to divide nations and peoples. Perhaps he had even urged them to go run up that platform and express their faith to the guard in the watchtower. It was a Berlin version of Christmas Day football on the battlefields of the Somme. The girls remained on the platform for two more minutes and then led their six scruffy followers on a dance through the ruins.

I smoked a cigarette and watched the white angels till they disappeared into an adventure playground. The visitation was over. I pedalled off down the street, avoiding the broken glass and taking note of some H-Block graffiti on a block of flats which was built in the sixties but was no less run-down than the turn-of-the-century tenements. The Wall opposite the flats was spraypainted with the names of English football teams and further political slogans. Realism regained its control of the scenery. God's maverick artists were banished from the streets.

Along metalled roads, tarmac paths, dirt tracks overhung with trees and lined with hedgerows, I followed the irregular meanderings of the Wall. Smooth and cream, the Wall is made of concrete slab and stands between 3.5 and 4 metres high. It is 10 centimetres thick and reinforced with iron. Its dome is the consequence of concrete piping (average diameter: 35–40 centimetres) running along the top. During experiments conducted over many years at Jüterborg, members of the National People's Army were unable to scale the Wall because of the scientific impossibility of obtaining a good grip on this concrete piping. The total length of the concrete-slab section of Wall is 107 km. Circling West Berlin, there is a further 55.4 km of metal-lattice fencing, 4.8 km of barbed wire and 9 km of Wall improvised from the remains of house façades and vacant lots. There is no statistical information on the number of people who live in apartments right next to the Wall, but probably it runs into tens of thousands. Snatches of music fell out of open windows and doors. The base of the Wall was fouled with dogshit. People sunbathed on balconies and roofs. Boys with nothing better to do hit plastic footballs ceaselessly against the walls.

An old woman stood by her open window in a tenement somewhere near Mariannenplatz. Her dress was black and her face looked sad, but maybe this sadness was too swiftly imposed on the design of her face. The trace of anguish may have been a slight attack of wind or heartburn, but I doubted it somehow. She belonged to that class of Berliner which was invisible unless you looked up, the old female faces at the windows. The city had nothing much for them. They lost their husbands in the war. The streets were too crowded. The cars drove too fast. The things in the shops were too dear, the price of coffee and cake, not to mention brandy, made socialising too expensive. So they remained at their windows.

The streets round Schlesisches Tor threaded a mosaic of car dumps, warehouses, waste ground and, here and there, tenements that had survived the British bombs. I freewheeled down the hill, past one apartment block painted luscious colours, lemon and pink and green and violet, like a jar of boiled sweets in the tangled wreck.

Down on Gröbenufer, a concrete promenade overlooking the Spree, men were fishing on a small jetty reached by steps leading down from the prom. Pigeons sat on the iron railings and sauntered among the debris. Alsatians fought and flirted while their owners waited for the fish to bite. A couple of the dogs went for a swim, causing a certain amount of merriment on the part of the fishermen. No one was enjoying much luck with the rod.

In this part of Kreuzberg the Spree defined the border. Floats attached to rope divided capitalist waters from communist waters. Every once in a while the East German river police cruised past, the launch flying the flag. One scene from the televised version of *Smiley's People* was shot here on Grobenufer, the leather soles of Alec Guinness's black Oxfords echoing significance on a cold night by the river frontier, the *clip-clop* convention of the spy films.

Three old ladies shuffled across the iron bridge, the Oberbaum Checkpoint, two walking to the west and one going east. Down on the jetty a few derelicts swigged beer from bottles and cans and chewed the cud with the fishermen. Were there any fish in that grey river? I got off my bicycle. This scene down by the jetty made most sense as theatre: the frayed theatricals of the down-and-out, the grim humour of the well-sussed, these fishermen of Kreuzberg 36 casting their lines into the divided dead river. It was a rum do, methought, fishy as fuck.

On the opposite bank of the river stood a new high-rise building with bronze reflecting windows, the Dallas-influenced architecture which primarily reflected the Party's ambiguity towards western glitter. Looking on the bright side, it remained possible that the whole vogue had begun life as an architect's prank, a multi-storey pun on the theme of structural contradiction. If this was the case the prankster had also managed to imprint his or her vision on the skylines of Dresden and Leipzig, making the prank truly *awesome*, as young Americans tended to intone when they mounted the viewing platforms. Across the river, the red flags from May Day were still waiting to be taken down.

Peter lived one minute's ride from the Spree, in the Hinterhof of Falckenstrasse 17, a first-floor apartment he shared with three other exiles from East Germany. Turkish children were playing in the litter-strewn courtyard.

The flat was plain and neat: white walls, books, records, black-and-white photographs of his friends. Beethoven was playing on the GDR stereo. Peter had been allowed to bring his things with him. He had legally applied for an exit visa and, with 30,000 others, had arrived in the west in the new year. He brought through coffee in a white pot, matching the white cups and saucers, the white linen tablecloth. An oak table stood beneath the sash window.

'You never got far from the border,' I said.

'That's Kreuzberg,' he said, looking out the window. The Wall was less than 100 metres away.

Peter was twenty-one. A tool-maker from Jena, he decided to come to West Berlin because he didn't want to go into the National People's Army. He would not have left the GDR had it not been for the conscription. He would not do national service in the west either, he added.

So many exchanges with refugees from the east began with this kind of cold-war joust. Peter was taking pains to distance himself from unwanted ideological constructions. George had recommended me. George was a reasonable credential, but this was a funny town and I was, accordingly, to be treated with suspicion. The mess of cold-war preconception cannot just be wished away. It takes time for the cartoons to blur into something more abstract.

Peter's thin blond hair was loosely tied with an elastic band. Strands fell across his pale cheeks and, every now and again, he wiped them away. I knew that his home town, Jena, had been a kind of base for the unofficial peace movement in East Germany. I mentioned this.

'The peace movement in Jena,' he said, grunting. 'Yeah. You hear a lot about it here. In the west.'

One of his flatmates came into the room carrying some books. Dark-haired and shy, or hostile, she said hello and went into her bedroom. Peter said she had been a teacher in Jena, but she hated the military training children received in school. He got up to change the record, came back to the table and said the coffee we were drinking was Nicaraguan.

'One thing the east does teach you is some idea of global relationships,' he said, gazing out the window. 'These people in the west who have spent years studying at the expense of others who work, and who then go on to get highly paid jobs, expensive flats and cars, without ever thinking about the relationship of their lifestyle to the poverty of the southern countries. I don't understand how they can be so blasé about their life. But there's lots of bourgeois types in East Germany too. They work hard at their careers so they can buy nice things for their house and maybe buy their own dacha for the weekends. They need to have the latest models of everything, televisions and washing machines. It's similar in that way to the west.'

His own parents weren't that way inclined, he said. His father had worked at an optics factory in Jena for the last twenty-seven years. His mother was disabled. He had one sister still at school.

'I miss my parents and sister, but that doesn't mean I can't live without them,' he said. 'Still, it is an abrupt break. You can't go back and you do leave a bit of yourself there somehow. I miss some of the places I used to go for a drink or a walk. It's sad also for the people in the east. There's one less person around for whatever it was you were all doing.'

I had a memory of a night at the Quartier Latin, the winter of '79, a band from the east called Wind Minister making its debut in the west. Most of the audience was originally from the GDR too. The first song had the chorus, 'You're never never never never never *never* going home'. The last song was the first song repeated. Wind Minister never came to anything in the west. Another flashback. Conversation in London. Laboratory technician nicknamed Bootsman. Newly arrived in the west. Confused. The man who gave Pint's name to the Staasis. You can never go home, Bootsman said. That's an interesting thing, he said. That's a reason to go, he said.

I asked Peter what his parents thought about his leaving for the west. He said they were worried he was going to get mugged, he wasn't going to find a job, he was going to get ill and wasn't going to be able to afford the hospital fees. He smiled.

I went to the bathroom. *Krieg dem Krieg*, it said above the toilet seat. War against war. I picked up a newspaper someone had left on the toilet floor. Danny the Red had become a Green. Tottenham Hotspur fans had gone a-rioting in Brussels. One of them had been shot dead by a barman in the red-light zone. I pulled the chain, washed my hands and hoped Peter would become less defensive. Clearly, he had been an activist in the Jena peace movement. He just didn't want to talk about it. Back at the table I tried again, in a roundabout fashion, asking some vague question about the political space that existed in East Germany for the expression of opposition on the part of people like himself, libertarian socialists, pacifists, whatever. His reply was, in its way, a classic cold-war text.

'There are a lot of young people in the GDR who don't fit in,' he began. 'It can be for very trivial reasons, like the way you look. Even long hair is still regarded as a threat in the GDR. But it can be because you have been involved in the peace movement. For whatever reason, you are soon singled out and it makes it hard to continue studying. Things like that. Most of the university students have, you know, served their time in the Free German Youth. But still, it's easy to tell horror stories about the east. The fact is that I'd still be there if I hadn't had to do military service. The real reactionaries are here in the west.'

Peter was not going to play Judas, the west could keep its pieces of silver. He was instead a prisoner of the merry-go-round. The painted horse bobbed up and down on its ceaseless revolutions. Stories critical of the east led swiftly to the horrors of the west and back again, round and round. Living at the very centre of the vicious circle, Peter was haunted by the compulsion to compare. At every turn he was snatching his words from the gaping mouths of the greedy propagandists. EVERYTHING IS RELATIVE! That was the slogan writ large on the spinning carousel.

'There are two Germanies,' Peter said, scraping the hair from his eyes. 'People my age have grown up with this fact. We have no sentimental longing for reunification. That's something for the old folks. For us it's no big deal that we grew up in the Soviet-occupied zone rather than the American-occupied zone. We have the same language, but we don't have any feeling of belonging to a particular racial group. It's like English and Americans speak the same language.'

We drank more coffee. The cries of the immigrant children wafted through the open window. East Germans, no more than Turks or Yugoslavs, never became West Germans. Even if they spent some time in jail before their emigration, they refused the embrace of the west. They retained a kind of pride in their *eastness* which was similar to class pride. They knew they had something which westerners would never really know or understand, however hard they tried.

The west was pretty much what Peter expected. When he was in Jena he had friends from the west who used to come and visit. His view of the west in those days was based on what his friends told him, not what he read in the newspapers or saw on the television. The only thing he did find a bit bewildering when he first arrived in West Berlin was the plethora of political groups, the long shopping lists of good causes.

'At first it seemed exciting,' he said. 'But then I realised it was just based on a kind of trendy consensus that didn't threaten anything. There's so many people in West Berlin, particularly in Kreuzberg, who just assume the correctness of all the socialist and ecological causes going. They support everything from saving the whales to disarmament and the Greens, but they do nothing, these people, apart from token gestures, like buying Nicaraguan coffee or going to a solidarity demonstration. Sops for their conscience. It gets on my nerves, all this talk and liberalism. Lots of these people, they've studied for years, they have a nice flat and car. They themselves live off the third world.'

Peter said all this quite calmly, without raising his voice. His anger was sober and controlled. A symphony by Mozart accompanied his speech against the shabby self-deceptions and hypocrisies that were traditional to the western way, the rich leftists casually dismissing their privilege by quick recourse to the concept of contradiction, *the* favourite word of the guilt-dogged bourgeois. The social and political sciences were the west's confession booths. Sociology was an elaborate excuse, the obvious clothed in the esoteric, the injustice sweetened by science. Personal responsibility was burned on the cross of determining forces. Blame it on history. Pass the wine. Peter's cool rage had led him to enlist in the Berlin Brigade. He would be spending the summer in a war zone, a small village 60 km from Nicaragua's border with Costa Rica. He would be building houses for refugees.

Maybe it was the only way he could gain some respite from the merry-go-round. The view of the Wall from his first-floor window constantly reminded him that he had abandoned the struggle in his own country. He felt guilty about that, I knew, and he was tired day in day out explaining to everyone. Yes, I did come to the west from the east, but it's not what you think . . . I didn't come here to be another phony hero peddling his past at the cold-war circus. I neither love capitalism nor hate communism. I want neither fast cars nor fancy apartments. I have no interest in careers. I want only to live an honourable life. I came here because I had to. It was personal.

Going to Nicaragua was a way of proving to himself and to others that he meant what he said: as a libertarian socialist he was opposed to both manifestations of Germany.

Peter had lived in both bits of the north and now he was heading south, to help David in his fight against Goliath. He was leaving a city of three million for a country of three million.

I said that little countries only became world-famous after they had revolutions. Before 1979 the only thing the west knew about Nicaragua was that Bianca Jagger was born there. I told him I also wanted to go to Nicaragua. His eyes lit up. Peter felt relaxed for the first time since I had entered his house.

He said it was kind of ironic, but he was unable to travel to Nicaragua with the other 33 members of the brigade on the Aeroflot jet from Schönefeld airport. Peter couldn't get a transit visa. His route was more complicated, an Air Iberia flight from Madrid to Havana. He would arrive in Managua the day after the rest of the volunteers. I wished him luck. It was dark now and the sodium lights burned all along the Wall. The fishermen had packed up their rods, the homeless had gone to their cardboard beds in the derelict buildings. Border patrol cruised up and down the river. I cycled home with another life in my pocket.

10 Road to Golgotha

Al was wearing a pair of sunglasses he had bought in Czechoslovakia. He sidled up alongside and spat *passport* in my ear, holding out his hand like a secret policeman, alluding to a prank he pulled in Prague. It was 9 a.m., Mehringdamm U-Bahn station, the northbound platform of Line 6, three stops to Friedrichstrasse.

On the platform by the Intershop at Friedrichstrasse there was the usual huddle of small-time smugglers. Middle-aged men broke open cartons of 200 and secreted the individual packages down their trousers and in their pockets. Others stashed bottles of vodka and brandy in briefcases. An old woman on crutches bought six vacuum-sealed packs of coffee. Al bought a packet of Camel.

He was planning to do some shopping in East Berlin. Some fucker had nicked the blue short-sleeved Free German Youth shirt he liked wearing to parties in West Berlin, he said, adding that Berlin parties were a big improvement on those sordid English affairs where half the people hid their booze down the back of radiators, in the cooker, in the coats room, and the other half spent the entire party looking for it. He also wanted to visit the haberdashery department of Centrum, he said, to buy this black PVC kind of Marlon Brando hard-core high-energy gay-disco number.

In the queue at Friedrichstrasse Al met a friend of his, Norbert, who played in a band called Laloora. Norbert was going by train to visit a sick uncle in Dresden. Originally from the east, Norbert had been allowed to come to the west on account of a rare kidney condition, Al said, when Norbert had disappeared through the grey metal door.

Friedrichstrasse was a doddle. Only a short queue. Nothing in our appearance to much bother the guards. I was wearing my shiny brown mackintosh with the concealed buttons. Al was wearing what he always wore: Levi red-tags with turn-ups showing two inches of white sock, black trainers, a zipped navy cotton jacket over a T-shirt. His thin sandy hair was shaved at the back and sides. He looked like an off-duty squaddie who was into Tamla Motown.

It was Wednesday. At noon there would be the weekly changing of the guard at the Schinkel-designed Memorial to the Victims of Fascism and Militarism, the goose-stepping ceremony which Al considered to be further reflection of East Germany's hopeless sense of PR.

'That's a job I'd like,' he said, walking up the Unter den Linden. 'The Saatchi and Saatchi of the Ostblock, department specialising in anti-western propaganda. I know some fucking great locations. Kirby New Town. The Byker Wall man.'

His thin lips stretched into an approximation of a smile.

Near the Alexanderplatz, in a church bombed by the British, there was an exhibition entitled Berlin 1939–1949. A penis-shaped missile stuck in the grass outside the ruins carried this message: Den Kapitalisten bracht ich Millionen Profit: Den Völkern Europas Tränen Leid und Tod.

'Quite good that,' Al whispered from the corner of his mouth.

Small family groups trooped through the ruins inspecting the blown-up photographs on the walls. In Hitler's time the trees were uprooted from the Unter den Linden and giant swastikas planted in their stead. The fathers had their own stories to tell their sons on the ten-minute tours of the ten troubled years. By the age of eight or nine children in East Berlin knew a good deal about Nazism and the war. The same was true in Russia. I wondered out loud what percentage of nine-year-olds in the US realised the commies had been on America's side in the Second World War.

Al grunted. He had hitch-hiked across the USA, worked in

various bars and diners. America had its good points, like films and soul music, but history never really caught on over there, he said, suggesting a quick tipple in the garden of this seventeenth-century Weinstube he knew. In the event the place was closed for renovation, scaffolding up on the crumbly yellow façade. Opposite the Weinstube was a clump of grey rocks on a grassy mound. 'That's the original Berlin Wall,' Al said.

The town was first immured in 1250 by German princes of the Holy Roman Empire. One of these early rulers, Albert the Bear of the House of Askanier, made a name for himself as an oppressor of the Slavs. The bear was adopted as the official symbol of Berlin and, to this day, the Berlin Bear featured on the postcards and tourist maps sold in the shops round Zoo Station.

Al himself had a flat in Neukölln that was only sixty metres from the modern Wall. He had a rich store of anecdotes about the various ways visitors of his from Middlesbrough reacted to his flat in particular and the city in general, but the one I liked best was about a cousin. First thing she did after she got to Al's cramped flat was rush outside to the nearest viewing platform. She stood up there looking all along the Wall, waiting for some action. After a couple of minutes she got a bit dispirited. Come on, she said, where are they all?

'She thought it was going to be like *It's a Knockout*,' Al said. 'You know, people swinging on ropes, pole-vaulters, hot-air balloons, the business.'

It was ten minutes by foot and tram to another of Al's favourite cafés, on Leninplatz. A sullen Lenin cast in red stone, thirty feet high, stood in the centre of the square. Bouquets of red carnations lay at the base of the statue. Pursing his thin lips, Al nodded slowly at Lenin's stern gaze, the proud mouth and the purposeful eyes.

Al never let on very much. I'd known him two months before I found out that, in addition to being the lead singer of Shark Vegas, he was a painter and a photographer. Hanging in his kitchen at Neukölln was one of his oil paintings, a black prisoner in a US jail being comforted in the cell by his wife. In his bedroom he had done a mural after the style of Malevich, red circles and wedges, black lines and triangles, a genre born of the love-affair with the powerful new machinery, the steel mills and the power stations that would march all over Russia waging war against the ancient superstitions of the poor. Lenin said socialism is soviets plus electricity. The dream had collected some rust. Behind the monument in Leninplatz rose three high-rise apartment blocks, three giant steps: 16 stories and 19 stories and 23 stories high.

I had been here the summer before with Laura. *The Observer* had asked me to do a travel piece for the colour magazine, part of some tedious series that was probably called OFF-BEAT HOLIDAYS, I couldn't remember exactly, but I had managed to swing it so that Laura was the official *Observer* photographer. We spent a week touring East Germany, staying in Berlin, Dresden and Leipzig. Laura and I had separate rooms in all the hotels. Officially, we had only a professional relationship. We had to keep remembering not to hold hands on the back seat of the grey Volga in which we were driven around like royalty by an anarchist called Heinz. He had been conscripted into the eastern front at the age of fifteen. His hero was Willy Brandt. Our guide was a young woman called Petra with whom we became quite friendly except we got her into trouble by mistake once. Laura was taking some photos of cops at a market in Potsdam and we were picked up by a Staasi in a green anorak who took us to a caravan and interrogated us for a while, made telephone calls, it all took time. Afterwards Petra seemed very crestfallen. She said maybe she'd never again be entrusted with western tourists. I hoped everything worked out all right for her. She cried when we all came to say goodbye. For a woman like Petra the travel restriction cut deep. She told us she had no desire to live in the west, East Berlin was her home, but she hated the thought of never setting foot in the west.

Anyway, the photo Laura took of the Lenin statue was the only one of hers *The Observer* used, much to her disappointment. For me the whole thing had been a scam, a free holiday, but Laura had been hoping the trip would help launch her on some photographic career which of course never happened. In the article I wrote I said, 'Go on. Be a devil. Take a holiday in the heartland of the enemy.' I got a couple of letters from people who sounded like old CP members, saying how dare I describe the GDR as our enemy. I meant to write back explaining it was a joke.

I followed Al across the wide clean square to the Café Espresso. Its sign was modelled on the Coca-Cola logo.

Al had a round-shouldered slouch, rolling aggressive shoulders, swinging arms, the head rocking from side to side. His slightly duck-splayed swagger fitted the neat turn-ups on his Levis. I never found out what his parents did for a living, but his walk clearly established his allegiance. You can tell a lot from the way people walk and, over the first coffee and Weinbrand, we discussed the various modes of perambulation, from patrician through yuppie to lumpen.

As I said to Al, the Café Espresso was like a camp version of an English mod hang-out in the sixties. Bronze triangular lamp-shades were pendent over each white Formica table. The windows were covered by frilly net curtains. Flowers sprouted from white boxes enclosed by black wrought-iron. On our table a pink carnation stood lop-sided in a black plastic vase. The coffee was served in clear Duralex cups and saucers. Probably we both had sentimental reasons for spending so much time in East Berlin. Al came over here as often as he could, whenever he had enough cash to pay the entrance fee at the border, about once a fortnight.

Feeling the faint glow of the first of the day, we paid the bill and walked north up Friedenstrasse. There were four Peace Streets in East Berlin, two in West Berlin and one in London. Whenever I was with Al there was always another point of comparison, *as if you couldn't tell*. When the Greater London Council tried to change the name of Jubilee Gardens to Peace Gardens the royalist press waxed livid and the scheme was dropped. Later the council itself was abolished.

'He is perfect to whom the entire world is as a foreign land,' wrote a twelfth-century monk, Victor of St Hugo.

'That's a job I'd like, film censor in the GDR,' Al said, having perused a poster announcing a season of Wim Wenders films. The bill was one of many pasted to a circular pillar, seven feet high and four feet in diameter. Scraps of long-gone cultural events were still visible beneath the brighter colours of the newer advertisements. East and west, these pillars were survivors from the twenties, punctuating the streets like fat exclamation marks.

'Think of all the films you'd get to see,' Al said.

There were, I agreed, worse jobs. We turned off Friedenstrasse and walked into the People's Park of Friedrichshain where Al's attention was attracted by a bronze statue of a sword-slashing warrior on horseback. A heavy metal monument, Al thought, probably done by an early mescaline enthusiast. The swordsman had been wounded by bullets and shrapnel.

Nearby was another sculpture commemorating the German volunteers who went to Spain in 1936 and died fighting Franco. A bas-relief in black, it showed hundreds of tiny frightened faces, mouths open in pain and horror, whole crowds of refugees fleeing the bombs, burning buildings, squadrons of fighter-planes wheeling in the sky and one figure dwarfing everything else, shaking an angry fist at the cruel destruction. Al said it reminded him of Victorian paintings of Dante's Inferno.

Opposite the bas-relief was a kindergarten, on the ground floor of a pebble-dash block overlooking the square. Was kindergarten the only German word which had established a meaning in English? Off-hand I couldn't think of any others. East Berlin had 297 nurseries for infants to the age of three and another 514 kindergartens for children aged between three and six. The total kindergarten population of East Berlin was 62,200 – 83 per cent of all kids in the age group. CHILDREN NEED PEACE LIKE FLOWERS NEED LIGHT, said the cotton banner strung across the kindergarten in the People's Park. Did the people who wrote this stuff really believe in it or were they no less cynical than advertising copywriters in the west? Hard to say, but there was a kind of innocence expressed in banners, statues, street-names and the ideas of peace and justice manifest in clumsy exhortations across the façades of factories. It meant something. People did believe in different things here.

I mentioned I needed to buy some stationery and Al said he knew a good place on Karl Marx Allee. We walked down to Frankfurter Tor U-Bahn station, to a huge open-air café in the main square there. A few drunks were bent over the concrete tables, but the place was pretty much deserted.

'That's a job I'd like,' Al said. 'The Alan Whicker of International Low-Life.'

Friday afternoons, he said, the concrete tables were full of drunks, chock-a-block. Factories in East Berlin shut down for the weekend at noon on Friday and the workers went straight out on the town while the children were still in the nurseries and schools. Friday afternoons the open-air café in Frankfurter Tor had live entertainment: an all-male five-piece in matching red shirts that did Credence Clearwater Revival numbers. Like many such bands in East Berlin, the lead singer didn't know all the words to the English songs in their repertoire. Words the singers didn't know they faked, making English-sounding noises. Al said 'Bad Moon Rising' in ersatz English was a gas.

Plumes of smoke reached up to the pale sky from a red-and-white striped chimney somewhere behind the square, maybe a kilometre away. I lit up a cigarette. I could hardly remember what it felt like to be physically knackered after a day's work, heavy-limbed, falling asleep in the armchair, alarm clocks ringing in the dead-of-night morning, running to the fucking bus stop to get there on time. Facing each other at opposite corners of the square were two expensive restaurants, Haus Budapest and Warsaw Café. According to people who claimed to know about such matters, Al said, both restaurants had served decent grub in times gone past, but the chefs had changed or some fucking thing.

At the stationers' on Karl Marx Allee I got a new address book. My old one was falling apart at the seams. I had bought it just after I started writing for *The Leveller*, about eight years ago. These days I couldn't put a face to half the names in the stained and tattered pages. Al bought a diary. It was small, A6 size, with a laminated plastic red cover saying 1984 in white on the front. He also got some 2B pencils.

We walked down the prestige boulevard, the cambered dual carriageway lined with the wedding-cake façades of apartment blocks in the Stalinist style, the shops on the ground floor. Ornate functionalism had somehow drifted back into fashion. Further down Karl Marx Allee, Al bought a new Free German Youth shirt.

Crocodiles of square-jawed tourists were being led round the Alexanderplatz. Lovers sat by the coloured fountains. Hustlers wearing newly-washed Levis or Wranglers prowled the open spaces seeking westerners, a cinch to spot, offering them a rate of four to one for their deutschmarks.

Al dived straight into Centrum, took the escalator to the second floor and spent five minutes in haberdashery looking for the black PVC kind of Marlon Brando hard-core hi-energy gay-disco number. No joy.

He tried on a tweed Bavarian huntsman's cap, the obligatory shaving brush stuck to its side, then we decided it was time for lunch. Some years ago both of us would have said dinner, we reflected, strolling towards the Tele-Tower, but in London we had been forced to mend our ways. Dinner-I-mean-lunch was too awkward a construction, particularly over the telephone.

'In London,' I said, 'lunch means business and dinner means sex.'

Al said he never moved in those circles.

We dined in the self-service at the foot of the Tele-Tower. Meals were served in plastic dishes with three compartments: one for potatoes, one for sauerkraut, one for beefsteaks and gravy. It reminded me of school dinners, costing five bob for the whole week, two shiny half-crowns every Monday morning, steaming metal dishes of mashed potatoes, custard that left terrible stains on navy-blue blazers, flirting with the dinner-ladies so they'd give you a bit extra, of course love, growing lads. School dinners have remained my favourite kind of food. Ditto for Al. We ate ravenously.

I told Al the story about Alan Winnington, the East End Jew who reported from China for *The Daily Worker*, accompanying the Red Army on its triumphant entry into Peking. When the Korean War broke out he was one of the few western correspondents reporting from behind communist lines. For his pains the British government deprived him of his passport. For the last thirty years of his life, therefore, Alan Winnington made his home in East Berlin, earning a good living as a writer of popular detective stories. He wrote in German. He was a good friend of the Kargers. Johnny knew him well. Alan Winnington's German stepdaughter had been permitted to attend his funeral in London, where Winnington had said he wanted to be buried. A wake was held afterwards at the Marx Memorial Library in Clerkenwell Green, a five-minute walk from my flat in Wilmington Square. *I was in a web spun by Johnny*. Laura was now in the flat, maybe wondering if I was going to call tonight. I felt a rush of panic love from the stomach to the mouth, a surge of electricity that heated the skull and stung the eyes. You Hurt Me. That was the title of the latest single by Shark Vegas, Al sounding a little like Lou Reed. He wrote the song. Someone must have broken his heart. The matter had never been discussed, but I knew someone had, broken his heart that is. Once he gave me a tiny clue. He said he managed to stop smoking for two years. I asked what made him start again. Life, he said. Exiles always had personal reasons. Heartbreakers were good for the airline industry.

I recovered concentration in time to hear Al saying he had read in *Stern* that 180 soldiers had gone AWOL from the British Army of the Rhine over the last year. 'Another example of the kind of story you don't get back home,' he said, gathering the final remnants of baked potato to his tin fork.

He knew personally one squaddie who had gone AWOL with a Sterling sub-machine gun. Trying to rob a bank, he was shot in the arse by the MPs. There was another story about a squaddie he met in Kreuzberg who claimed to have killed a bus driver in Aden. The streets everywhere were awash with stories no one saw fit to print. Ulrike knew this. She had African princes and Turkish smugglers living on the same street. She shared drinks with people who had once been in the Red Army Fraction. She knew the score. To her it was obvious: official sources fed a few scraps to the people and stored the rest as secrets. East and west it was the same story. Certain plain truths were unavoidable in Berlin. It was like catching yourself unexpected in a café mirror, seeing yourself the way others see you, turning quickly back to the folded page of the newspaper, listening to the song on the radio.

Al was talking about the wartime lies. How many English people knew some thousand soldiers were killed at the dress rehearsal for D-Day in the Bristol Channel? Relatives of the deceased were informed they died heroically in action at the Normandy landing. Al once met a Newcastle publican who had been an RAF fighter pilot during the war. The publican was boasting one night about his wartime exploits, describing an action his squadron undertook against a nazi convoy in the North Sea the very day before the cessation of hostilities. There happened to be an amateur historian at the bar who informed the publican he had attacked a convoy carrying concentration camp inmates from northern Germany to Norway.

'The bloke was really sick, you know. Up till then he'd been a jolly publican who thought he'd done a good job in the war and everything,' Al said, nodding his head in the noiseless chuckle.

At the window-seat behind us, alone, was a fortyish woman with a peroxide Helen Shapiro, panda eyes, a red shift-dress and pointed white high heels. Al rolled his eyes in her direction. I smiled back. Nothing more was said. We liked the way she looked. We finished off our drinks. The last of the beer clung to the plastic glasses like soapy water. Outside, two skateboarders were turning tricks at the foot of the Tele-Tower.

'Flash bastards,' Al said.

Picking our way through knots of people eating currywurst from grey cardboard plates, we neared Alexanderplatz station, a glass palace girded with steel. The curved arcs of glass were always spotless, but they refracted light like water. Figures standing on the platforms were rendered bent and indistinct, like quick watercolour impressions. We decided to go to Köpenick, the suburb where Pint spent his childhood. Al said he fancied visiting the chateau at Köpenick. Maybe we could take a ride in a boat, too, he said. It was nice, having no particular plans.

The S-Bahn train snaked through the city, slowing down to negotiate all the railway points at the gigantic terminal of Ostbahnhof: arriving passenger trains from maybe Prague or Moscow, expectant faces standing at open windows, goods trains loaded with coal and new cars, passenger cars awaiting renovation on sidings, men in peaked caps in signal-boxes, junkyards, iron bridges. Al said he liked railway landscapes.

Leaving the edge of the city, beyond Ostkreuz, the train ran through acres of allotments, patchworks of vegetables and flowers and freshly-dug earth dotted with wooden sheds. Middle-aged men in rolled-up shirtsleeves were digging, weeding and pruning.

The train stopped at Rummelsburg new town, the S-Bahn connected to the high-rise blocks by a walkway through the lawns. The other side of the station a factory was belching smoke.

Heavy industry looks almost quaint these days, Al said. In the English context, he said. The train reached Köpenick. Al bought a newspaper at the kiosk outside the station.

A cream tram skidded to a halt. Its driver had blonde hair and high cheekbones. She wore red lipstick. She was chewing gum. The automatic doors snapped shut and the streetcar went off down the hill, clanging along rails bedded in the cobblestones. Al put on his Czechoslovakian sunglasses and we strolled down the main street. Walker by name walker by nature, my father used to say, in his mock-hearty way.

Most of the shop-fronts were painted brown. The street was like a sepia photograph. Window-displays made the most of scarce resources. Three shops sold only German sausage. Tall stacks of canned vegetables and meats in one window resembled 1920s Manhattan skyscrapers. Eventually we came to a red bench by the river. Al sat down, lit up a Camel and started reading *Neues Deutschland*. Its back page showed a photograph of a British cop frogmarching away a young miner. A woman in orange crimplene pants came by, her coiffured poodle on a leash. Pleasure cruisers from Treptow ruffled the water at regular intervals.

At Köpenick the Spree widens and disperses into lakes, blue blobs at the easternmost edge of the map of Berlin. Al was reading about the Iran–Iraq war. The Americans and the Russians were both supporting Iraq.

'Let's go to the chateau,' Al said, folding up the newspaper and leading the way along the paved promenade to a busy street where a white-gloved traffic cop had evidently decided that if you had to stand in the middle of a road junction all day you might as well pare down the signals to a fine art. The cop twirled his baton with the chutzpah of an acclaimed conductor. The streets were his concert-hall. His orchestra was the traffic. Most of his ensemble was composed of two-stroke Trabants, their soprano splutter supplemented by the bassier rhythms of the bull-nosed Wartburgs, the roars of the MZ motorcycles, the thunder of the buses and trucks and the cries of their air-brakes, the occasional hum of idling Golfs and Volvos. Who was it who told me East German intellectuals felt unembarrassed about owning Golfs but

could not quite countenance Volvos and Mercedes? Pint probably.
Or maybe Johnny. The magician flashed his white gloves again and
the traffic obeyed. Walking across the street, I felt the hot rush of
carbon monoxide on my legs, a pleasant enough sensation.

The chateau walls were the colour of weak mustard. Here and
there the paint was peeling, the masonry crumbling. Assorted
goddesses of love, carved in stone and weathered by the years,
kept watch over the chateau's gardens. At the farthest corner was
a huddle of shabby men who I assumed were sharing a bottle and
some stories. On closer inspection these men were standing
around a lifesize game of chess, discussing each move, exchanging analysis and predictions the way men do. The pawns
were the size of toddlers, the knights and bishops the height of
half-grown adolescents.

'It's like an advert for the workers' republic,' Al said out the
corner of his mouth.

Only six moves old, the game was still a struggle for the centre.
After long consideration, index finger vertical on his lips, the
unshaven player of the white pieces decided upon a queen
exchange to prevent black castling. The wooden queen was as big
as himself. He wrapped his arms around her and lugged her seven
squares, the length of the board. He stepped back five paces to try
and get the gigantic game into perspective. Hauled from the
board, the black and white queen stood alongside two captured
pawns and the other spectators.

A Russian tourist detached himself from a group being led
around the gardens and strode beaming towards the game. In his
twenties, black-haired, he wore a navy suit and carried a Praktika
in its leather case. Maybe he was hoping the chess might spark
some contact with the locals, a chance to practise his German, a
few pleasantries on the subject of Kasparov's attacking play,
Karpov's profound concentration, the beauty of the game in
general. But no one paid any attention to his smiles. I felt a bit
sorry for him. After taking one photograph of the scene he
returned to his tourist group.

White castled. Black fianchettoed his bishop. Opening hostilities were over. The game probably had another hour to run. My
money was on black.

Al decided to return to Köpenick to make a few telephone calls. He wanted to see a friend of his who was engaged to marry a Swedish pop star that Al and Mark had brought across on a day-trip to East Berlin.

'Another passport marriage?' I said.

'No, this is the real thing. Big love job,' he said.

As we were crossing one of the bridges over the Spree a white pleasure-cruiser chugged past. The security personnel atop the boat looked like shirtsleeved British policemen, a blue-and-white check circling the brim of their peaked caps. Upon the open deck aft middle-aged men in blue and brown and grey suits were dining. The party was wholly male. White wine was cradled in silvery ice buckets. Waiters, white napkins folded neatly over their left arms, replenished the glasses at intervals. Everyone walking across the bridge stopped to stare.

'They live well enough off our money, don't they, the bastards?' said one squat man to his wife. He wore a brown PVC jacket, belted at the waist. He was carrying an empty shopping bag. As the vision of the good life slowly disappeared downstream he continued watching, muttering curses. Probably his wife had to endure further speeches on the matter when they got back home.

'What do you reckon?' I said to Al. 'A beano for party high-ups or a visiting trade delegation from Sofia or someplace?'

He shrugged.

'Definitely professional communists,' he said.

Not one of the telephone kiosks was vandalised, Al observed, waiting for one to fall vacant. Surreal, I said. Al made two calls. The first established that the woman engaged to the Swede was out of town. The second arranged to meet Ralf, leader of a band called Jessica, at Rummelsburg S-Bahn station, eight o'clock.

Jessica were befriended by Mark while he was doing research for *The Tube*. Mark had a lot of trouble with various commissars for cultural affairs who wanted Pudy to represent communist pop on the programme. Pudy had been around in the days when Johnny was a pop star in the east. Mark tried to tell the cultural officials that Pudy on *The Tube* would be a public relations disaster. British pop fans didn't want to see forty-year-olds doing sententious songs about peace. Mark had hoped to feature one of the underground punk groups on the show, but this was clearly impossible. Pondering his problems one afternoon in the A-Platz, he spotted a sharp-looking young man with a guitar case. Mark rushed after him. It turned out to be the lead guitarist of Jessica. The four members of Jessica were all registered musicians. They didn't play in churchyards. Jessica were the compromise agreed between Mark and the pop commissars. After their appearance on *The Tube*, of course, the band achieved a new status in the eyes of East German promoters and programmers. Mark had inadvertently made Jessica famous.

I sometimes wondered what the commissars had made of Mark during their various meetings. What had Mark been wearing?

Al and I repaired to Mecklenburger Dorf, a mock-village composed of concrete cottages with thatched roofs, a scaled-down concrete windmill, tables and chairs set in reinforced concrete on the gravel. It was a place for teenage hard-cases, lovers and serious drinkers who sat at those concrete tables nearest to the bar. At 60 pfennigs a glass of beer you could get quite drunk on the fruits of two hours' labour. Feeling peckish again, we bought potato pancakes and *apfelmus*.

'A good hard-times meal,' Al said with relish, taking alternate mouthfuls of pancake and apple sauce from his white plastic fork. Sparrows and pigeons scavenged leftovers from cardboard plates on the tables and gravel. The radio was being broadcast from white loudspeakers suspended in the trees. It was the six o'clock news.

'Other countries which are refusing to participate in the capitalist Games in Los Angeles include . . .' A list of African and Asian nations followed.

'It's just like *The Prisoner*,' I said.

'I was about to say the same,' Al said.

The news was over. Birds sang in the thatched roofs. The pinball machines gurgled, bleeped, trilled, clunked and rang up the score. Teenage maestros wrestled with the gaudy glass tables, fingers working the flippers, eyes tracking the silver ball and the clicking numbers, cursing TILT and celebrating REPLAY.

I was pursuing the subject of *The Prisoner*, the pretentious TV series inspired by the LSD anarchism of the sixties. It had also been on the cold-war merry-go-round, I said. I had always seen it as some acid-head critique of consumer conformism and state terror, but others could see only Eastern Europe in the well-regulated paradise conceived by Patrick McGoohan. I suppose they were the same people who saw nothing of Britain in 1984, I said.

Al said we had time for a swift half before going to Rummels-burg. I concurred. Al said it was true what I said about 1984. Orwell went spare when he saw how his book was being packaged in the USA. He tried to withdraw it from publication, but it was too late and anyway authors only have so much power. Big Brother was recruited by the imperialists. Strapped to the horse El Cid-style, he was sent into battle against the communist hordes. People who had never even read your man pointed east and shouted *Orwellian! Nightmare!* The disfigurement of Orwell was a fucking disgrace, we agreed, leaving the phony village.

The light was dying, the streets quiet. On a red placard running the width of some factory gates it said, THE PRESENT FULFIL-MENT OF THE PLANS IS MAKING OUR CONTRIBUTION TO THE PEACE.

'I don't see how they work that one out,' grunted Al. The would-be Saatchi and Saatchi of the Ostblock thought a shade more originality in the conception of slogans would be no bad thing.

We sat on a bench outside Rummelsburg station, waiting for Ralf. In the high-rise blocks purple neon lights were glowing in a hundred different windows. I thought maybe it was some code, the colour of tacit opposition, but Al said the purple lights helped house plants to grow. Every five minutes or so the S-Bahn trains unloaded another few dozen workers who traipsed across the path to their homes, clutching small bags and briefcases. It was a hot night. There were the first rumblings of thunder.

Ralf didn't look much like a pop star. A serious-looking man in powder-green denims, training shoes and gold-rimmed spect-acles, he was a student of classical music during the day. The bassoon was his specialist instrument. He played keyboards for Jessica. He was also a reservist in the army.

On the S-Bahn into the centre of town Al and Ralf exchanged stories about the travails of the rock and roll life. Al hadn't played live for two months. Shark Vegas had insufficient equipment and Al was broke. Ralf was doing about three gigs a week. He said Jessica could afford more equipment. Their problem was that the stuff they wanted was only available in the west. As a student Ralf got 215 marks a month. Each time Jessica played, he made an extra hundred ostmarks, more for television appearances, of which there had been a number since *The Tube*'s Berlin special. By GDR standards, and also by Al's standards, Ralf was rich.

I asked Ralf if Jessica had ever played an illegal gig in a churchyard.

'Why should we?' he said. 'None of us are Christians.'

'Fair enough,' Al said.

Walking down the steps from the Alexanderplatz station, Ralf suddenly stopped in his tracks and asked us what we thought of East Berlin. You always got this question, it was the standard way of checking out westerners, but it was always hard to answer in a couple of sentences. Yeah, we mumbled, we liked it here. Life was less manic, fewer cars and hustlers and more sense of space.

'In West Berlin,' Ralf said, 'the buildings are higher and closer, a breeding ground for claustrophobia and angst. Are the buildings like that in London? I've always wanted to go to London.'

I said that in London the rich tended to live in low buildings, the poor in high buildings. It was the opposite of Manhattan.

'Are you left or right?' Ralf asked me out of the blue.

'Well . . .'

'*Commie*,' grinned Al, through clenched teeth. Ralf looked confused. He took us to a smart café at the corner of Judenstrasse and the Alexanderplatz. We sat on the terrace and Ralf went inside to phone round the other members of the band.

Al thought this was the kind of joint which probably served fancy drinks so we ordered gin and tonic. The waiter took the order then came back two minutes later saying they didn't have any gin. Ralf was needlessly apologetic. 'Vodka?' Ralf said hopefully. The waiter shook his head.

Whatever their formal political views, East Berliners always assumed westerners were accustomed to Babylonian luxury. Taking westerners out for a drink or a meal was, therefore, bound to be a harrowing experience given the inevitable shortcomings of the menus and the service in East Berlin. All the time the easterners were thinking, *What are the westerners thinking? Isn't this very drab compared to what they're used to?* The westerners in turn went out of their way to compliment their hosts on the positive aspects of their way of life. Casual socialising became such a mess of unspoken anxieties. The cold war sabotaged the best of intentions. Al explained that gin and tonic was not in fact his normal tipple. He hinted he inhabited somewhat seedy circumstances in Neukölln. Ralf looked dubious.

I remembered Mark telling me about a visit he made to a priest when he was fixing up the Toten Hosen gig. Showing Mark around his house, which was spacious and light, the priest said it must seem very primitive compared to what Mark was used to in the west. Mark said he lived in a one-room flat that had no bathroom; he shared a toilet with an old couple across the landing. The priest didn't believe him. People in the east knew about the western poor but could never believe that anyone they might meet personally could be touched by the poverty they had read about in *Neues Deutschland*. It was a blind spot, I thought, sipping my East German brandy. Somehow it reflected a deeper problem: almost 70 years after the October Revolution the communist vision of the good life was still determined by the imagined luxuries of Paris and London. The communist project was to attain the goodies while circumventing the misery, but it just wasn't possible. Eastern Europe was a second-rate industrial power, it couldn't organise its production globally. Races for more luxury were always going to be won by the west, the east bringing up the rear with its ersatz reproductions. See! We can do it too! Western versions of utopia had colonised the world's subconscious. The west peddled dreams that captured everyone, everywhere, from the suburbs of Moscow to the shanty towns of Mexico City. Paradise needed re-building. ASAP. Meanwhile, I was drinking up the moments, feeling lucky.

Ralf picked up my packet of Marlboro and noticed it said VENI VIDI VICI in small capitals on the gold crest. He went on to inquire after my class background. I told him. He seemed reasonably satisfied. He proceeded to outline the class composition of the television crew that had filmed Jessica for *The Tube*.

'The producer, John, he went to public school and Oxford and he was like the God of the group,' Ralf said. 'Everybody obeyed him, even though he was much younger than most of the others.'

Al was chuckling noiselessly again, tight lips suppressing the smile. In Ralf's eyes the British were a strange tribe arranged in ancient hierarchies. His innocent anthropology was music to our ears. *It was all so laughably true.* The rest of the band turned up in dribs and drabs, the bassist then the lead guitarist then the drummer. The manager came too. About the same age as Al and I, he wore a tailored denim jacket and spoke fluent English and Russian. He was a professional cultural worker, employed by the state. He had a number of bands on his books, but Jessica were his most important act.

Ralf glanced at his digital watch. It was 21.38. Time to get something to eat, he considered. He had no particular class advantages, but he was without doubt the bossman. He led the way to a chicken broiler house, one of those places where you could have a quarter of a chicken, half a chicken or a whole chicken, with or without French fries, accompanied by a small or a large beer. There was no table big enough for seven, but the waitress told us to wait a moment. She wore those shoes all East German waitresses wear, black, a hole where the heel should be, tied with laces above the ankle. She went to a table occupied by a black GI and his girlfriend, halfway through their chicken and chips. She asked them if they wouldn't mind moving to another table. Reluctantly, the couple got up. Two tables were joined together. Our party sat down. The waitress must have seen Jessica on television.

The drummer, Ollie, was looking more tired than the rest of the band. His chubby cheeks were pale and sagged, there were black patches beneath his eyes. He closed those eyes momentarily every time he ran a hand through his shock of black hair. I asked him why he was feeling so weary. I had to ask in the slightly suggestive way which is expected among gatherings of men. What have *you* been up to, me old son?

'I'm the only genuine proletarian in Jessica,' he said, smiling. 'I work in a light-bulb factory.'

'He's also the only member of the band who's married. No coincidence he's the fattest,' Ralf added unkindly. His sense of humour was subtle as his sociology. Ollie ignored the quip. The drummer's dream was one day to tour the west with Jessica. On his lapel he still wore the tin *Tube* badge the posh producer had given him.

Sometime after eleven Jessica's road manager arrived at the broiler house. The main reason he had come was to give myself and Al a lift to Friedrichstrasse. Someone must have telephoned him. He was thin as a rake, hollow-cheeked, his hair a symmetrical bush of tight curls. His girlfriend or wife (my money was on girlfriend) had cropped dark hair and wore a leather mini-skirt. East and west these artisans of the pop music industry, the roadies and sparks and soundmen, exuded similar atmospheres, a kind of proletarian cool, the sardonic boredom of the insider. Seen it all before, pal. The roadies knew about the folly of ambition, they had watched the driven egomaniacs come and go. Humping the gear from the stage, sitting in the dressing room after the gig, steering the truck through the rain at night, they had seen the catchpenny dreams dissolving into nothing. They just carried on doing their job. It was better than working in a car factory.

Al was a romantic too, but he had the arrogance of those who do not need success to confirm their nervous talent. Secure in his wit, he was one stage beyond careerism. He was also leaving it a bit late to become a pop star. He took the days as they came and went dancing Saturday nights. He read and painted and wrote the odd song. He was sufficiently idle to have time for reflection, to hone his thoughts and stories, *to think*, to listen to the pitter-patter of daily news from the leaking mouths of the city. He had time to notice the mackerel skies and the statues in the parks and the colours of the worry-beads rotating on the dark-skinned fingers, to listen to the songs sung by optimistic children in the mornings and by crack-voiced drunks at night lamenting the world that did them wrong, to know all this and not be made bitter by the knowledge. Al had time enough to spend a day with me in the east doing nothing much in particular, seeing what was happening, compiling more bits of personal evidence against the stupid lethal conventions endorsed by millions too busy to think, too overwhelmed by repetitive days and nights of work television sleep work television, too tired. The business, the tiredness, it would be the death of us all. No more work television sleep work television, only the peaceful snoring of the frazzled cities, a few scared survivors crying their eyes out in the dark, the dirty rain falling, the weeping of the powerless gods. The survivors will think it's too late to write poems, but maybe a few lines will get set down anyway, iron age verse carved on the ruins, something for the next world.

Al was listening to Ralf saying that two of the band had yet to do their military service and that it was going to be very disruptive, Ralf was worried about it. Al asked him if he had enjoyed his time in the National People's Army.

'Armies are the same the world over,' Ralf said.

Not true, I thought.

We had one last large beer for the road. People proposed toasts to each other's health and happiness and the spirit of rock and roll, which I secretly felt was poorly represented by Jessica's watered-down reggae, sort of early Police, I had heard a tape at Mark's. We left the broiler house at five to twelve.

'Look at that,' Al whispered, directing his chin at the floodlit Tele-Tower. Its illuminated concrete pillar flowed up to the silver globe like a special effect from the Hollywood version of *Moses*. I nodded at Al and he shook his head in further wonderment, the alphabet of head movements often being preferable to the routine recital of words-fail-me superlatives: fucking incredible beautiful Jesus amazing great wow shit ace knockout epic lovely A1 fucking hell. Superlatives went in and out of fashion like haircuts.

Outside Friedrichstrasse the roadie told us we better hurry. We said we were old hands at this game but, yeah, probably he was right. It was a few minutes after the witching hour. The roadie didn't want the border guards asking us who we had been with and why. He jumped back into his old green Wartburg and bumped around the semicircle of cobblestones that led to the rich tarmac. He accelerated up the hill to rejoin Jessica. The post mortem on the Englishmen was doubtless in full swing. Funny pair. Friends of Mark though. Probably okay. Thought Al would be younger. Didn't look much like a pop singer. Wasn't too sure about the journalist. You know the kind of crap they all write about East Berlin. But Mark must have checked him out. Mark wouldn't send anyone untrustworthy. Maybe they're good contacts. We need someone to take that broken amplifier back to the west to get repaired. Next time maybe. Anyone get their phone numbers?

It took only five minutes to traverse the thirty feet from the end of the queue to the Formica booth. Friedrichstrasse was much busier at the weekend. The uniformed functionary looked quickly at my passport, then placed it on the edge of his work surface. He flicked it up like a beer mat, caught it after one revolution and held it out with a flourish, quick and stylish. His smile said: *fuck the ideologies.* I smiled back. The border guard repeated the performance for Al. Al liked it too, I knew. Must have been pissed, he said, in his downbeat way, but I knew he enjoyed the coded message of the spinning passport and the peaceable smile. In time the incident would become incorporated in one of his straight-faced stories.

The harsh-lit train to the west bore its usual midnight load of lost drunks, peacock revellers, tired workers travelling home, others headed for the nightshift, foil-wrapped sandwiches in their canvas bags. Those sober enough to focus concentrated upon the advertisements for furniture and vitamin pills, reading every pushy word over and again, doing this to avoid getting trapped in the crossfire of drunken leers, counting the stations and hoping for the best, the deafening rhythm of hundreds of accelerated heartbeats in the creaking crowded carriages.

'It's like being back in the zoo,' Al said. 'And, yes, the first thing we see is one, two, three, four, no, *five* policemen.'

This was at Kochstrasse, the station adjoining Checkpoint Charlie. The five cops were a snatch squad looking for illegal immigrants and drug smugglers. Most of West Berlin's heroin entered the city by this route, Turkey to Bulgaria to Friedrichstrasse to the west. The police made a swift tour through the cars searching suspicious faces. The necks of the travellers were lathered in sweat. Prophetic lines in their palms were washed by nervous streams. The doors wheezed shut and the scared train lurched forward.

'Let's go to Golgotha,' Al said.

'Golgotha?'

'It's a bar. On the highest hill in West Berlin. It's where you go to get absolutely fucking crucified.'

11 *Big love job*

I went to Tegel to meet her. A BMW K100 RS, incubated in glass on a stand, had attracted a crowd of admirers. Her flight was twenty minutes late. I still had no intention of writing about her. I was supposed to be writing about the cold war and I didn't honestly see how I could introduce her into what was already a pretty shambolic narrative, messy as my life, people drifting in and out, things left undone, debts and story-lines piling up and increasingly small chance of getting things in order, the whole thing only kept on the road by faith and luck and the tolerance of others. I was waiting for the silky voice to announce the arrival of her British Airways flight.

I knew Laura coming to Berlin was a risk, a professional and emotional gamble. I was supposed to be researching a book not swanning around the city with my lover, days by the lake and cande-lit suppers and long afternoons in bed saying whatever came into our heads, kissing each other, saying *I love you* at regular intervals, taking it in turns to fix the drinks, maybe playing cards, reading out loud to each other, stroking each other's skin and hair, licking each other like cats, dozing when we felt like it, dreaming nice things, waking each other up with kisses and murmurs, remembering our dreams out loud, making impractical plans, fantasising about our children, what we would call them, for example. I liked old-fashioned names like Reg and Sam and Sid, Eileen and Rose and Rita. Laura went more for whimsical names. Her tastes were in general more whimsical, it should be said. She had grown up in a different class at a different time. She had no hatred, only sorrow. She often cried when she saw sad things on television, sad plays, sad documentaries, even a sad face in what was otherwise supposed to be an entertaining kind of programme. Sad things made me angry and her sad. We used to argue about that. She used to say I was tough as old boots. I said she cried because she felt guilty. She cried because she despaired. She didn't really believe in much, apart from love and later she stopped believing in that too. She went on peace marches and once drove down to Greenham Common in her mother's white Cortina estate car, but for the most part she just wanted the cruel world to go away, she didn't want to get depressed thinking about poverty and war. The Falklands War started up soon after we became lovers. I was still living in Holsworthy Square, the third-floor flat that cost only £6 a week, just off the Gray's Inn Road. Every night I sat seething before the television news. Laura thought the war was stupid and cruel too, but it had never really occurred to her there was any way of preventing the stupidities and cruelties. At that stage my rage was a sort of novelty for her. I think she even respected it. Later, it became a problem, my raging and drinking, the bitter speeches and drunken tears.

Her own family was rich. Her parents, as was normal among the metropolitan bourgeoisie, were divorced. Her father had re-married a younger woman. Her mother was going out with a man who was only two years older than me. In fact, her grandmother was going out with a man who was only seven years older than me. When we were all together, the times Laura's mother did a big Sunday dinner, I found it a little weird, though it had its charming aspect, three generations of women whose lovers were separated by only seven years. No one in my family, none of my aunties or uncles, was even divorced. None of my parents' friends were divorced. None of my friends' parents were divorced either. I just didn't come from divorced society. My parents still slept in the same bed. I knew things had been a struggle for them, especially when they were younger, but I also knew that this struggle was what had helped keep them together. People who had never struggled could more easily take off and go when the mood took them or when the first offer materialised. Some people were just spoilt, it was simple as that. Laura wasn't spoilt. She was the first-born in her family and she had had to help her mother with the younger children after her father ran away to France when Laura was eleven or twelve. I sometimes thought her despair was the consequence of her father running off and of seeing her mother so upset. Her grandmother, too, had been unlucky in love. Laura learned young some of the emotional stuff I only learned later. But, still, her parents were rich. Her guilty father took her on two holidays a year, a skiing holiday in winter, a beach holiday in summer. She had been to an expensive school which taught her nothing till she was sixteen, then she went to a comprehensive in west London, but she was always bunking off, she never took any exams, she drifted away into the demi-monde occupied by all the other poor rich children of the metropolis, living in squats and dressing up for parties and going skiing once a year.

She met me when she was nineteen and I was twenty-eight, a sunny Sunday afternoon in Swiss Cottage, a market of junk stalls that has since been closed down by the council. I was trying to buy a football, it was a long story, she was picking through the rusting useless treasure dumped any-old-how on the wooden trestle tables. When I saw her, this is such a cliché I know, my mouth sagged open in hopeless physical desire, I felt queasy in my stomach and nothing, I mean *nothing* else that had happened that day had the slightest significance, the tiniest importance. She was wearing ballet shoes and trousers that finished in the middle of the calf and a pink pullover, her hair falling in careless wisps. I wandered the junk market in a daze. She looked at me twice, slow brown-eyed inquiries that made me gulp, the dry gulp that often precedes vomiting. I suddenly felt that if I didn't open my mouth and say something now, *now*, I would never have the chance again and I would regret it all my fucking life, she would still be wandering through the junk shops of my dreams when I was a pensioned off lush with bitter-sweet memories of the last twenty years of the twentieth bleeding century. So I did, speak, jabber, a flood of apologies for doing this, waves of sorries overwhelming each stammered vital phrase, a deathly two-second pause when I had finished my piece, the glimmer of a shy smile and the agreement to write down her telephone number on the back of a small red out-of-date membership card for the Seven Dials Club. The first time we met for a drink she explained she had a boyfriend and I said I didn't care, I was happy just to see her, whenever she had time, a cup of tea, a glass of beer, a quick bite, I was easy. For two years it went on like this, then one night we kissed on the traffic island at the junction of the Gray's Inn Road and Rosebery Avenue and two months later we became lovers, two days after that, she moved into my flat. It was a very long honeymoon, nine months, from the Falklands War to Christmas, I couldn't remember when I had been so happy. People noticed and wondered maybe if I'd got hold of some new drug from the United States that made you feel permanently content, but I told them, well, you know, I'd met this girl. Usually I didn't say anything about love.

I had my own stupid pride to consider, my own reputation among editors as a fast-living grammar-school boy who could safely be dispatched to the ghost towns of the north and come back in one piece. In retrospect this was a purely commercial idea of myself. I was my own swaggering advertisement. I never brown-nosed, I treated people with the contempt they deserved and I was respected for it. Suspended between the classes, I played one off against the other. I aped the cocky self-assurance of the poor in my dealings with the rich, to whom I sold stories about the poor, but actually I belonged nowhere. I was the journalistic equivalent of a life insurance salesman, knocking on doors and giving them the spiel, telling lies and getting commissions. Anyway, love fitted uneasily into this bizarre self-advertisement, in the same way that Laura fitted uneasily into a story about the cold war, *another reason to write about her*, I thought. It was high time to own up to the complications, to admit love, to place the stories in the love-struck mind in which they took shape. Why not? I had nothing much to lose now.

I was beyond caring about editors and commissions, I thought, grimly, waiting at Tegel Airport, chain-smoking, pacing up and down by the continuously changing crowd of BMW oglers. Some of those men would ogle Laura, too, when she finally emerged from passport control. They would desire her with that same cold passion with which they lusted after the BMW K100 RS. It was horrible to think, but maybe there were a couple of men among the gaggle of car admirers who would feel what I had felt when I had first seen her. It was possible. I wanted to be special, but I knew I wasn't. There was a chemical chain of desire linking us all together, the communist and the fascist alike, links of love lust that bound us like animals in factory farms, east and west, it was only a change of scenery, the farm managers wore different clothes. In communism and capitalism love was what made people happiest and saddest. Maybe there was a cold-war angle in this after all, the equalities of joy and misery wrought by love in the competing systems, now and through all time, the glorious terrible lowest common denominator of all places and ages, billions of broken hearts and oceans of private tears. I had to try and get myself in some kind of shape. Her flight was due in ten minutes, according to the latest Tannoy message, broadcast in German and then English, like the sub-titles on the menus.

She was already part of the story, she had flown with me to this airport the year before, the day of her birthday as it happened. We had drunk champagne on the aeroplane and, as we came in to land, I had pointed out the Wall, a thin brown beach through seas of grey, a year earlier when the love still smelled fresh as hotel-laundered shirts, the aeroplane whining to a halt on the runway at Tegel and a bourgeois Brit complaining in a loud voice to his younger business associate. *It's a question of national pride. For the Krauts. Getting first off the aeroplane.* We had collapsed in champagne giggles and staggered euphorically through Tegel being met by a driver from the East German Reisebüro whose name sounded like Gay Bar which also seemed funny at the time, driving to the gold-shimmering Palasthotel next to Museum Island where we had separate rooms with huge soft beds and talked to each other on the internal telephones like children who get toy plastic phones for Christmas, myself and my sister, for example, when we were seven and six respectively, waiting now with this headful of memory, surrendering to the hopelessness of love like an oblivious drunk being driven over the cliff, the car fluttering to the sea like a falling leaf, slow motion, like in a made-for-TV movie. We had spent a week in the GDR as undercover lovers and then gone together to West Berlin where we stayed in a hotel on Fasanenstrasse, *The Observer* picking up the tab. I ran around during the day making contacts for the story I proposed to write on punk rockers in East Berlin (this was the colour magazine route into the cold war, I had decided) and in the nights I took Laura round town.

I introduced her to Pint. Johnny was in Berlin at the time too. We had one incredible night at some bar in Kreuzberg, I could never find my way there again. The barman wore dark glasses and played Tamla Motown singles on a Dansette that just stood on the bar. We drank till five in the morning then drove to the Reichstag at dawn. Laura drove, I remembered. It was a grey Alfa Romeo owned by a guy called Hans, a physicist from East Berlin. He lived in a flat with Pius, who was Astrid's boyfriend. The Doors were playing on the radio, I recalled, a song with the line *the west is the best*. Hans and Pint laughed like men possessed. It was a messy grey dawn and we strolled along the banks of the Spree, in the grounds of the Reichstag. Johnny took lots of pictures with his new Olympus automatic. In those days Laura was still very shy and always turned her head whenever Johnny pointed the lens at her. I saw some of the photographs afterwards, everyone looking in different directions, mostly with their backs to the camera, the doors of the Alfa Romeo open, the green river bank and the grey dawn, another long night that seemed somehow *important* at the time, as if the combination of alcohol and love and Berlin had managed to raise me briefly above my circumstances. I felt connected to my time, privileged. It was a bit like the night Pint and I scaled the wooden watchtower in the snow. I felt that each step on the frozen ladder took me further away from the categories that had tried to claim me, a feeling of being alive in a particular space at a particular time, a feeling that others ascribed to God.

Needless to say, Laura had fallen in love with the city too. She had met enough wastrels in London, but she had never before met people who had freed themselves so thoroughly from expectation, people who belonged neither to the west nor to the east, who neither sought wealth nor glamourised poverty, romantic sceptics who thought for themselves and, when they chose, let go of reason, abandoning themselves to uncertain adventures through long nights concluded by café breakfasts. It wasn't like getting drunk in London. We went back to the east together too, holding hands, thinking it would be embarrassing if we bumped into either Heinz or Petra, the driver and the guide on our one-week package holiday in East Germany. I took her to meet Tommy and Vera in their beautiful apartment on Kollwitz-Strasse.

Tommy cooked a curry. Laura fussed over the baby.

Laura had never been in the habit of reading newspapers or watching television news. She had bunked off history classes at school. She knew next to nothing about the historical background to the division of Europe, we didn't talk much about that kind of thing. She only knew what she saw, for example that people's complexions in East Berlin were much clearer than complexions in the west. She noticed the absence of female flesh on advertising billboards and she always said she felt so *safe* in East Berlin. No one ever bothered her on the street (as I had done when I first met her). She liked the sixties decor in the cafés, the minimalist designs upon the wrapped sugar cubes and the napkins and matchboxes, all of which she collected assiduously. She liked the cream trams and red fire engines and the way the children looked walking to school, neat hair and clean clothes and little satchels on their backs. She liked the fathers in their swimming trunks playing with their children in the Neptune fountain, the soldiers strolling hand-in-hand with their girl-friends, the old men sitting on park benches reading the com-munist version of the daily news. She loved the fast lift to the top of the Tele-Tower where we had once had an hilarious dinner with the head of the East Berlin Reiseburo, both of us trying to sound like serious professional travel journalists, not that anyone actually believed us, but we had to go through the motions.

If Laura had been a bit older and a bit less beautiful we might have had more credibility, I thought. Her beauty was actually quite a problem. Whatever she wore, even when she was doing odd jobs round the house with the Black and Decker drill her father had bought her for Christmas, she looked like a film star. She was always being followed along streets. Occasionally photographers would stop her and offer her hundreds of pounds to pose nude in their studios. She sometimes thought it might be a good idea if she shaved off all her hair or something, but that would probably have been useless too. It wasn't that she flounced around like those girls who know the sexual effect they are having upon men. She was timid, she walked with her head down, the attentions lavished upon her she found baffling, irritating and sometimes frightening. Her beauty had begun to make me self-conscious as well. In the early days I was too drugged with love to notice the glances but recently I had started to feel the heat of all the eyes. Whenever we walked into a bar I knew conversation at some of the tables would abruptly halt, heads would turn and men would say things about Laura: nice piece, cracking bird, lovely arse, state of the tits, wouldn't mind giving her one. I wanted to spray the bars with bullets like air-freshener. I wanted the bottles to explode like bombs in their dumb drunken deluded faces. I had moody times too when I made excuses because I just couldn't face going out, the thought filled me with dread. In public I had lost my anonymity. Every time I walked through a human crush I felt like beauty's personal bodyguard. My nose for trouble had pre-empted many a scrape, but I had begun to regret this susceptibility to the atmospheres in people's faces and movements. I had begun to wish I had the loud-mouthed insensitivity of the average public schoolboy, his blissful ignor-ance of the resentment written in tight mouths. I had also spent a good deal of time pondering the matter of beauty. Clearly it was not something absolute, its definitions and manifestations changed through space and time, but at any one place at any one time there were people and things widely considered beautiful. Beauty was not democratic. There was a hierarchy of beauty in all human society, however kind people tried to be about those rendered ugly by misfortune and ideology. (The notion that beauty existed in the eye of the beholder was an ideology invented by ugly people, I had said one time, for the sake of a cheap laugh.) Beauty was an ancient form of social division, as old as the generation conflict and the struggle between the sexes, but these ruminations had not much helped my condition, my aching abstract *jealousy*, my fear of the coming hurt.

I saw her. She bobbed up and down in the queue. We both did noiseless I-love-yous in such a way they were easy to lip-read at thirty paces. She came running from passport control, ran into my arms and stayed there two minutes. Clinging to one another, we recited over and over the childlike incantations. I love you darling love me? course baby my angel I missed you my sweet I love you and I always will kiss me oh tell me again I love you and I always will. *Promise?* Promise. There was the further language of hands and eyes, the eyes-closed love-sounds, the nuzzling recognition of each other's smell, the allaying of the animal fears, the temporary isolation from everyone and everything else. Unclaimed suitcases travelled round and round on the spinning metal bars. Airports were depressing. I carried Laura's suitcase to the taxi rank. In my other hand I held her hand, stroking it and squeezing it, too many messages and too few means. We should not expect too much from love, I thought. We should live in the now and be thankful for the trickle of moments. Love died when lovers tried to organise it, plan it, think it too far ahead. We should just enjoy being here on the green leather seat of this taxi, cuddling like teenagers at the pictures, driving through dark irrelevant streets, together in Berlin again. We had two years of shared stories and here was one more episode, another bright handful of possible days and night. The taxi-meter recorded the journey in clicking numbers. You can't choose who you fall in love with. You have no power over love.

12 Doughboy City

Laura was still sleeping. She lay curled up on the polystyrene mattress, the white sheet dappled with sun from the latticed window, her face still as stone, a limp hand hanging above the copy of *Franny and Zooey* she had been reading the night before. I kissed her on the forehead and whispered see you later. Her eyes closed, she made a kissing sound with bunched lips, raised the limp hand briefly to my hair then returned to her dreams. I stole out of the house at eleven o'clock. No one else was up.

I had a date with Captain Genser at the General Lucius D. Clay Headquarters. I was feeling a little nervous about it. Surely the US military had noted with displeasure an *Observer* feature I did on USAF Lakenheath, the F1-11 base in East Anglia? I had made the base sound like a kind of militarised Butlin's on dope, with undertones of race war. I remembered being taken by the Lakenheath PRO to meet what was supposed to be a model Anglo-American family, a US serviceman who had married an Englishwoman, the couple living off-base with their son. The PRO thought the family would give the piece a hands-across-the-Atlantic feel, two Nato powers united also by romance, etc. It turned out that the Anglo-American son was in fact the product of the Englishwoman's first marriage and had no American blood whatsoever. A six-foot-two skinhead, towering above his American stepfather, he despised all Americans, including his stepfather. Throughout the evening he referred to Americans as *yanks*, pronouncing the word like he had a slice of lemon on his gum. The PRO gloomily contemplated his medium-term career prospects. The photographer and I had stomach-ache from the muscular work of repressing the laughter. Happy days, I thought, pedalling under the long series of iron bridges on Yorckstrasse. It was a long ride across town to the Clay Headquarters on Clay Allee. Would Captain Genser have been handed a file on me which included the mischievous report on Lakenheath? If so, would he deny me the opportunity of spending a day with the GIs, as I had requested? And if I did get turned down did I really care? The sun was out, Uschi's bicycle was running well, I was a thousand miles from my London creditors, zippedidoodah-zippedeeay-my-oh-my-what-a-wonderful-day.

Was it *wonderful* day or *beautiful* day? It was definitely three syllables worth of superlative day. Plenty of sunshine coming my way.

I cycled past Winterfeld Platz, the cabaret bar where I had seen Sugarmoon embarrassing all the tourists. I left a trail of old songs all the way from Kreuzberg to Clay Allee.

Another reason I was happy, apart from the obvious, was that Laura had settled in well. Within three days she had become fast friends with Ulrike, despite Ulrike telling me beforehand that she very rarely liked English women. I had been apprehensive introducing Laura to Ulrike. I had watched Ulrike sizing her up from head to toe, from the white ribbon in her brown hair to her flat pointy black shoes. When Ulrike had presented her daughter to Laura, Charlotte had grinned with all the fearlessness of children accustomed to strangers. Laura had taken an immediate shine to Charlotte and this was an important factor, I felt, in the friendship between Ulrike and Laura. Ulrike soon felt confident about leaving her child to play with the effervescent English-woman. On Laura's side, she was most impressed by Ulrike's sang froid, her cool languor, her shameless idleness, her fashion-able boredom with the night life, the whole range of Berlin poses that were so charmingly manifest in Ulrike. Laura saw in Ulrike an attractive way of dealing with the world. Laura had begun painting a watercolour based on a photograph of Ulrike eight months pregnant with Charlotte, the elegant naked mother-to-be looking bored and arrogant, neither euphoric nor apologetic about her pregnant state. *I am with child, for good or for ill,* her face said. *Look at my hard bloated stomach, my enlarged breasts. Look as long as you like. I have no fear, no regrets. I bear a beautiful fact.*

In one week Laura had established her independence, going to the lakeside beaches with Ulrike and Uschi, meeting the colourful cast that dropped by the house, painting and playing. It left me free to pursue my researches on the cold war, gunning Uschi's bicycle down Clay Allee, past the 1930s cinema which had been appropriated by the US military. It was showing *Blame On Rio*.

Isn't anybody going to listen to my story all about the girl who came to stay?

In Dahlem, this bourgeois neighbourhood on the edge of the Grunewald, the Kreuzberg principle of unlocked doors had few adherents. Steel gates, walls, barbed wire, Alsatians, burglar alarms, the shuttered mansions had the usual paraphernalia of private security. The back gardens were shaded by pines, the children's faces polished as the Mercedes and the BMWs. German capitalism, I reflected, had always been embodied by the names of car and weapons manufacturers, while US capitalism was more commonly symbolised by makers of soft drinks and fast food, which was not the kind of conversational gambit which was going to cut much ice with Captain Genser.

She's the kind of girl you love so much it makes you sorry, still you don't regret a single day.

Atop the white stone steps the white helmeted MP stood erect as the pillars. He looked askance at my lady's bicycle, windblown hair, Staprest trousers neatly tucked into white cotton socks highlighting the dirtiness of my shoes. I told the MP I had an appointment with Captain Genser. The MP told me to leave my bicycle in the lot down the street. I thanked him profusely.

The Clay Headquarters was built for the Luftwaffe in 1936 under the command of Marshal Goering. It was confiscated in 1945 under Allied Law no. 52 pertaining to properties of the Third Reich. Since 1949 it had served as the office of the US Commander, the headquarters of the US Mission, Berlin (State Department) and of the Berlin Brigade. My passport having been inspected, I was shown into the waiting room outside Captain

Genser's office. Through the open door I could hear Captain Genser briefing an American reporter.

'Of course you must understand that we are only two miles from the biggest Soviet spy operation in the world,' he said. 'I can't be as free with my information here as I would be in Chicago or someplace. And some of the journalists here, you know, are not exactly friendly. It's just not like back home and you'll have to understand that.'

'Sure,' said the American reporter.

Oh girl. Lennon's cracked voice snuffed out by a psychopath on the edge of Central Park. *Oh girl.*

The Captain came from Chicago, Illinois. His short-sleeved khaki shirt displayed muscular tattooed forearms. He was around forty, proud of his trim figure. On the wall behind his desk framed certificates attested to the miles he had jogged in good causes. He had seen service in Vietnam, he had been in West Berlin only four months. He gave me a bone-crushing handshake then said he must introduce me to his boss, an older, balder man in a bigger office.

'The less sympathetic press,' said the boss, dumping a copy of *Taz* on his desk. I smiled sympathetically. The boss said it was very nice to meet me, but he was sorry, he had a luncheon appointment, he had to go, he would leave me in the capable hands of Captain Genser. So far so good. No detectable hostility.

I took out the Chinese-made red-and-black hardback notebook, set it on my crossed knees, flipped the pen from my top pocket and narrowed my eyes in a stagey approximation of the serious journalist. I could still play the part, I discovered, after a few warm-up questions establishing there were approximately 6,000 American soldiers in West Berlin and another 8–9,000 family members, that the average tour of duty was three years, though many extended for a further year, and that no restrictions were placed on GIs' social activities.

'Would they be an occupying force rather than a protective power guaranteeing the freedom of Berlin,' he said, 'then perhaps there would be certain restrictions.'

Sure, I said.

I asked what, in practical terms, the US Army did on a day-today basis to guarantee the freedom of Berlin? Given there was no war going on at the moment, I added jokingly. The Captain sniggered politely.

'Show the flag,' he said. 'That's our mission here. It really boils down to showing the flag.'

I wondered how many flags, approximately, the US Army had in its possession in West Berlin, that would be a colourful fact, but I couldn't think of a way of asking it without arousing the Captain's suspicion. I tried to picture a flag factory . . . women in white overalls, churning looms, vats of dye, huge rolls of material being mechanically sliced into individual flags.

'All American soldiers are taken on a tour of East Berlin as part of their preliminary orientation programme,' the Captain was saying. 'Helps the young soldier to better appreciate why he's here. So, yes, all new soldiers are taken on a trip to the other side. *Almost without exception they come back angry and totally drained.*'

I was unprepared for the abrupt change of tone. His under-lining of the last sentence demanded I return his gaze and nod understandingly. This I did.

'You see, for an American it is a traumatic experience,' he continued. 'A lack of freedom is a concept they have never experienced. They've all heard about communism in theory. To see it in practice is quite sobering. Even though many of them have experienced Vietnam and Korea. It is still very different.'

The Captain spoke of freedom as if it were easily identifiable as good or bad weather. He was a regular guy, he recommended I try the Irish coffee at the Irish Pub in the Europa Centre, or else I should go to the Kudorf, this mock-village place off Kantstrasse. A lot of fun, he said, a manly twinkle in his eyes. I had been there. A pedestrianised warren of bars and nightclubs, a nightlife theme park of neon-lit rusticity, the place was full of loaded tourists and whores and soldiers, but I returned the Captain's suggestive smile and said I was definitely going to check it out. The Captain loosened up and said, well, you know, he was here with his wife, but really this city was quite something for the single guy. When he first got news of the posting lot of guys he knew were ringing him up and congratulating him, saying, Steve, you got yourself some city there. Right now the Americans were getting 2.74 to the dollar which was really a good deal and made Berlin even more attractive, financially speaking. All GIs were entitled to get an American car shipped over from the States, but he had got himself a European car and personally he was very satisfied with it, it was very economical on gas for one thing. Yeah, he reckoned Berlin was a pretty good deal for the career soldier. All in all. The apartments were as nice as a US Army soldier was going to get anywhere. The size of the apartments was determined by family size and also by rank. Personally, he had three bedrooms and a bathroom and a half.

The Captain was now completely relaxed and he had to tell me, boy, had he been forced to learn a lot in the four months he had been here? Like his wife. She went and got out the map soon as she knew she was coming to Berlin. *She couldn't find the city because she was looking for it in West Germany.* I laughed. I was prepared to bet any amount of money it was Captain Genser himself who couldn't find Berlin on the map, but it was a good story, too good just to quietly forget on the grounds that it showed yourself in a pretty poor light. Better therefore to keep the story and just find someone else to be the fall-guy. Who better than your wife? No one expected wives to know any goddamn thing anyway, it didn't even reflect particularly badly on your wife. For Christ's sake how many Americans *do* know that West Berlin isn't in fucking West Germany? But obviously, yeah, I'm working in Public Relations. Guess people would think it was bad, guy working in PR didn't know where Berlin was, especially those snotty European bastards. But I reckon it's pretty safe and okay for the wife not to have known. You have to admit, it is a funny story.

When I first spoke to the Captain over the telephone I said I was maybe doing a couple of stories for *The Observer* and, also, researching a book. The Captain now wanted to know exactly what type of book I had in mind. Buying time, I said I wasn't sure, I'd only been researching the thing a few weeks, but sort of vaguely what I had in mind was the reporter's notebook approach, you know, lots of interviews with people living and working here, describing the atmosphere of the place, plus some

of the historical background and, you know, puncturing some of
the myths about Berlin. Like what? he said. Well, like the idea
that it's a grim grey city whereas in fact you got all this greenery,
all these rivers and lakes and beaches. Stuff like that.

'You done much work in East Berlin?'

'I've been over there a couple of times,' I said. 'But, well, you
know what it's like. It's not that easy to get talking to people.'

'No one on the street right?' the Captain said brightly.

'Exactly.'

*You see, for an American it is a traumatic experience. A lack of
freedom is a concept they have never experienced.*

I was thinking about Laura. Probably she had got up by now
and was having breakfast down in the basement or maybe
playing with Charlotte in the garden. I asked the Captain if it was
all right if I smoked and he said go right ahead. There would be no
problem, he thought, arranging a little tour of the US installations
in Berlin. Maybe I would be interested in seeing Doughboy City?

'Doughboy City?'

'It's kind of an artificial town we built for exercises. Built in '75.
It simulates the kind of urban environment we have here. We even
built our own S-Bahn station there. Yeah. Doughboys was what
they used to call GIs. It was World War One slang.'

'Because they made a lot of dough?' I said, thinking *over-paid
overweight and over here.* Or was it over-paid over-*sexed* and
over here?

'No. Because they ate a lot of dough. At that time you got to eat
a lot of dough in the American army. How's Monday looking for
you,' he said, looking through his diary.

'Monday's fine.'

'Okay, let's say two o'clock Monday. I'll arrange transport.'

The weekend went too soon. Friday night a crowd of us went to
Berlin Mitte, a bar in Kreuzberg named after the old section of
East Berlin. The drinks were all named after famous people from
the Warsaw Pact countries. We drank Yuri Gagarin cocktails.
There was a woman there who had two white rats on each
shoulder of her black leather jacket. On the back of her jacket was
a huge decal of the East German flag. Ulrike said she was famous

in Berlin, the two-rats woman. She had been raped a year or so ago and the rapist had killed her two rats, so the rats she had now were the second generation. Saturday night I took Laura to the hi-energy gay disco at the Metropol. Al and Mark both came too. We left at six and got the U-Bahn home. Al said West Berlin was the only city in the world which had machines dispensing glucose tablets on the underground platforms. Slept most of Sunday. Pint came round in the afternoon and got stoned in the garden with Ulrike. I tried to carry on working, but things were happening too quickly now. *When we get back to London I'm going to leave you*, Laura said, Sunday night.

I suppose the rot had set in sometime before. I think she felt trapped by my love, by my relative success too. I was doing more or less what I wanted to do, writing stories I more or less believed in, getting a few foreign assignments. She didn't want to be a kept woman, but she found it dispiriting doing shitty low-paid jobs and she was too proud to ask her father for money. Although in the early days she had pleaded with me to marry her, I think she had begun to think she was too young to settle down with someone nine years older who had a steady job. The trouble was I respected and loved her all the more for wanting to leave me. From her point of view it was self- evidently the right thing to do. You couldn't live only on love. You should have adventures while you were still young enough, even if it meant you were going to be lonely sometimes. (Later, after she had left, I said to people she was right to go, I would have done the same myself in her circumstances.) For Laura the flat in Kreuzberg was an EXIT sign, showing her how it was possible to live without the securities of a regular lover and job. Laura lionised Ulrike. Ulrike encouraged her in her revolt. 'She's going to leave you, English Boy,' Ulrike had started saying to me, often when Laura was present. Usually I smiled and shook my head in a *maybe* motion. Laura's smile was tougher to decipher.

But that Sunday night was the first time Laura herself spoke those dread words. I sulked, cried a little, all the usual theatre. I hoped it was one of those cruel things people said in the heat of the moment. Everything would be all right, it was only a lovers' tiff. Laura had become intoxicated with Berlin. Nobody ever asked her what she did for a living, where she came from or where she was going. It was like suddenly being released from jail, from the earthly obsessions of London life, the worthless gods of career and money, the unfreedom of love, even this, oh baby, I knew what you meant. Everyone we knew here seemed part of the same conspiracy, people without a past or a future, only a permanent freewheeling present, a life as I have said without clocks and routines, without reference points, without news and television, a life that was as near to a successful escape as it was possible to find in dying Europe. I found it seductive, too, but finally it was another illusion, more fool's gold.

All you respect is suffering, Laura said that same Sunday night. *You don't like people just having a good time.*

I left the house on my own and toured the local bars getting bitterly drunk. Back at the house Ulrike gave me an ironic knowing look. Laura had gone to bed and was sound asleep. I sat at my blue Silver-Reed portable.

In the remorseful morning Laura and I kissed and made up, but in retrospect it was a phony peace. Things cannot be unsaid. The seeds were sown. Love stories were so predictable. I showered, shaved and thought myself into the next part: bourgeois journalist. I presented myself at the General Lucius D. Clay Headquarters at two. On the fucking dot.

'How you doing?' Captain Genser said gaily.

'Fine,' I said, shaking him by the hand, gritting my teeth.

'Best get going right now. I arranged transport.'

Leaning up against a navy-blue Cortina was the driver, Peter. His suit was the same colour as the car. Dandruff from his flyblown blond hair speckled the collar and shoulders. He had deep rings beneath his reddened eyes. He was German. He made no attempt to hide his contempt for the Captain. He was not the average kind of chauffeur, he never said sir. I wondered if he was maybe a spy. He gave me a funny look when we were introduced. Probably we shared the same suspicions.

'Where do you want to go?' he said when we had all got into the car.

'BB Housing to start with,' said the Captain. Peter stuck a Marlboro in the corner of his mouth, lit it and kept it there, the ash falling down his front as he toured the leafy streets.

'The area round here is called BB Housing,' said the Captain, pointing through the window at some plush apartment blocks. 'Further down the street is housing for majors and colonels. Really very pleasant.'

Next stop was Andrews Barracks. Commissioned by Kaiser Wilhelm in 1873, this redbrick establishment was the first cadet school for the new army of the United Germanies. During the Third Reich it was the headquarters of the SS regiment, Leibstandarte Adolf Hitler. A short queue of GIs was waiting to be served at Tony's Diner outside the barracks.

'Gold-mine, that place,' said the Captain. I felt like death warmed-up. It would be embarrassing if I had to be sick out of the car window.

I said, yeah, Tony's Diner was certainly ideally situated, commercially speaking. Inside the barracks the Captain asked Peter if he couldn't drive more slowly, he was trying to point things out for the journalist from England here. Peter said nothing, but slowed down.

Inside Andrew's Barracks a few black soldiers were playing basketball and a white soldier was carrying two pressed suits wrapped in cellophane from the dry cleaner. We drove past something called the Morale and Support Facility.

'There is a good deal of contact, formal and informal, between the Americans and the Brits,' the Captain said. 'Less so with the French. Because of the language problem.'

'Where now?' Peter said outside the barracks.

'How about going to Potsdamerstrasse?' suggested the Captain.

Scathingly, Peter replied there were four Potsdamers and which one exactly did the Captain have in mind? The Captain said he had been thinking of the Potsdamer where the air traffic control centre was located, where the Americans, the Brits, the French and the Russians worked shoulder-to-shoulder, he said, although on second thoughts we wouldn't be able to see a great deal from the outside of the building.

'Let's go to McNair,' the Captain said.

'McNair,' repeated Peter mechanically.

'Some people think McNair Barracks used to be a Luftwaffe base,' said the Captain. 'It's a kind of romantic idea, but it's not true.'

Romantic? I sucked hard on my cigarette and pretended to be wrapped up in the view from the window, the blue Ford bowling down Dahlemer Weg. I wasn't talking enough. All the good work of the previous meeting was being undone. I was too hungover. I was also intimidated by the driver, who I felt sure had got my number. I should be asking more questions.

'How is the social life for soldiers stationed here?' I said lamely.

'Video is big,' said the Captain.

McNair Barracks was home of the 2nd, 3rd and 4th Battalions of the Sixth Infantry and of Battery C, 94th Artillery. Formed to fight the British in the War of 1812, the Sixth Infantry fought against Mexican troops following the annexation of Texas in 1836. For the next twelve years the Sixth was scattered across the western frontier, fighting the indigenous populations of what are now the states of the Dakotas, Kansas, Missouri, Nebraska and Wyoming. The unit saw action in Cuba during the Spanish-American War and also helped crush the Philippine Insurrection of 1899–1900. Captain Genser had been stationed in the Philippines, when he was still a single man. He made some joke about *extra-curricular activities* in the Philippines. I idly wondered how many whores he had lain with.

The Sixth won battle honours in the final year of the First World War and, following the US entry into the Second World War, fought in Algeria, French Morocco and Tunisia before participating in the Italian campaign. During the Second World War, the Sixth was, like all US regiments, segregated into black and white units. Segregation was not abolished until the end of the Korean War. Vietnam was the first war fought by unsegregated American troops. The sixth fought in the Tet '69 Counter-Offensive. The regiment's motto: UNITY IS STRENGTH.

Arms akimbo, GIs in white vests stood on a lawn listening to their PT instructor. We drove past a sign which said Holiday Inn Transit Billets. The Captain pointed out the two schools for servicemen's children, an elementary school and a high school.

'There is also the John F. Kennedy School in town, a bilingual establishment where some of the officers choose to send their children,' he said. He was bored too. I was twisting my face into various expressions of surprise and interest, but he sensed my boredom. Peter had the radio tuned to AFN. He made a U-turn, an insolent cigarette still dangling from the corner of his mouth.

'Where *now*?' Peter's tone strongly implied he thought the whole excursion was a complete waste of time. Probably he was right.

'Drive round the rest of McNair,' ordered the Captain. '*Slowly!*'

Before it was requisitioned by US Forces, McNair Barracks had been an electronics factory owned by Telefunken Corporation, the Captain said, telling Peter to pull in at the museum. He told me to hang on a minute. He had to find the guy with the key to open the place up, the museum was only open certain times. It took a few minutes to find the guy. Peter and I said nothing. He turned up the radio. I remembered I had eaten nothing all day. Maybe there was some kind of café in Doughboy City.

The museum was dominated by dummies dressed as cowboys and Indians and by Nazi artefacts: Luger pistols, Waffen SS helmets and black uniforms. Looking at the swastikas in the glass cases I said it was illegal to buy or sell Nazi insignia in West Berlin. Possessing a swastika was still officially a punishable crime, though it was easy enough to find Third Reich souvenirs in the Kreuzberg junk-shops.

'Right,' said the Captain. 'But in the US the memorabilia is very much sought after.'

'So Americans are allowed to buy the memorabilia?'

'Yeah. Well, people do.'

I quickly scanned the section of the museum titled The American West, From Indian Wars to Foreign Wars, 1865 to 1898. The only item of interest was a nineteenth-century recruitment poster: WAKE UP AMERICA! There was a map on the wall showing the partitioning of Germany. Near the museum's exit the Captain paused before a display of Berlin Brigade products: ties, tie-pins, scarves, badges and flags.

'I've been meaning to get one of these tie-pins for some time,' he said, rummaging in his pocket for six dollars. He had to go and find the guy with the key again to open up the glass case. I bought a tie-pin too, the same design as the shoulder patch worn by all US soldiers in Berlin, a flaming Crusader's sword upon a field of blue and, above the sword, a rainbow emblematic of the colours of the Allied flags.

A shabby little museum, I thought, getting back in the car. Peter turned down the radio a notch in deference to the Captain. Doughboy City here we come! Peter was driving fast to the border.

'Our combat soldier here only has to walk a short distance to the Wall. The reality of why they're training is right there. It's a real job, a real mission,' enthused the Captain.

Was there a trace of melancholy behind the Captain's sudden outburst, a faint recognition that in recent years the US Army had not always been on the side of right? The Captain had been in Vietnam, after all. He must have seen things there which complicated the official anti-communist rhetoric of his government at that time. Most Vietnam veterans were justly bitter at the way they had been used, lied to, treated like lepers when they got back home. The Captain had also seen service in the Philippines during the hey-day of Marcos, corrupt dictator and great friend of the USA. Probably the Captain had suffered doubts in the Philippines too, which was why he was genuinely happy to have been posted to Berlin. Aside from the fact the exchange rate was good and it was generally a cushy number, the Captain believed that at last he had found himself in a place where the US Army was popularly seen as being on the right side. *He was on the free side of the Wall.* He was defending freedom. As far as American soldiers were concerned everything was so beautifully simple in Berlin. Soldiers, same as everyone else, wanted to feel noble once in a while. They didn't want to be scared of the history books. They wanted to be able to boast of good deeds to their grandchildren. The Berlin Wall, Americans believed, was the most powerful image in the western arsenal. The Berlin Wall made them feel good. *It's a real job, a real mission.*

'Berliners know why we're here and they want us here. In certain parts of West Germany that's not always the case,' the Captain said.

I quizzed him further. I squeezed him gentle as a new toothpaste tube.

'Yeah, well no problem at all with those fifty and over because they all have memories of the war. And those from the late thirties to the fifties we don't have much problem with either, they're old enough to know what's going on and they're fairly positive,' he said, pausing and wondering quite how to say the last bit. 'We do sometimes have a problem with the younger age groups.'

That last sentence was my half-pinch of toothpaste. The gentle pressure takes some time to force out the minty truth. Then the squeezing must stop and the top must be carefully and tightly screwed back lest unwanted truth spills out overnight, which is just a waste of damn good money.

The Captain flashed his laminated ID and a portly GI saluted, then opened the gates to Doughboy City.

'What you see here are replicas of the different types of city construction,' said the Captain. 'We got the older type of housing, the tenement type, and the newer kind of apartments too. Look. Over there we've even got our own S-Bahn station and S-Bahn train.'

The white station had a small platform on a mound of earth. Mechanical diggers painted army-green worked away at its base, steel jaws gobbling the dusty soil. Uniformed labourers wielded spades and pickaxes like in a prison film. Constructed from bare concrete blocks, the buildings had no windows, no doors, no roofs. Doughboy City had no cafés either, it wasn't that kind of town.

'The Wall is right there,' said the Captain.

For a moment, foolish thought, it occurred to me this Wall was phony too, another authentic detail in the city built for war games, but the two observation towers rising up from the other side, the guards up there with their binoculars, these details established its realness. The Americans had built their own watchtower too, so the guards of the respective empires could spend their days examining each other's physiognomy through the binoculars while the phony war raged in Doughboy City. The Captain was explaining that the dirt hill at the edge of town was built a couple of years ago to obstruct the view from the East German watchtowers.

'They were just watching all our manoeuvres, it was ridiculous,' he said.

So why did the Americans build their phony town right next to the Wall? I wanted to ask this, but I choked too long on the Captain's use of *ridiculous*, the inference that a man-made hill subtracted in some way from the sum of ridiculousness piled up in this small neighbourhood of windowless flats connected by dirt roads like a third-world city. It was a stage-set designed to suggest the wails of the sirens and the wounded, a place to rehearse the next war with the weapons of the last, to prepare for the apocalypse by playing soldiers in boy city. Beyond the city walls were green fields and hills.

I lit a cigarette and decided I ought to say some thing. Silence between strangers was quickly translated into hostility. I still needed a press pass for Allied Forces Day on 16 June, which Captain Genser had told me was kind of our answer to May Day.

'Why is there so much building work going on?' I said, for it was true that the mechanical diggers and uniformed workmen were everywhere. The Captain smiled knowingly.

'There's always a lot of construction going on here,' he said.

'Right,' I said.

'Back to Dahlem. To Trumanplatz,' he said.

The reluctant servant drove the Ford in second gear to the gates. I still felt sick. Going through Mexikoplatz the Captain was saying he actually preferred the Italian restaurants in West Berlin because the Italian restaurants were the only ones which didn't make a fuss about accommodating children.

Along Argentinische Allee the Captain told me he once got through the Helmstedt–Berlin checkpoint (en route to West Germany) very quickly because the Red Army soldiers were watching American cartoons on the television. The Captain felt proud that Russians were watching American cartoons. I mean, how many GIs sit around reading Yevtushenko of an evening?

Trumanplatz was a shopping mall for the troops and their families. We got a bowling alley, four cinemas, each changing their programme every three or four days, plus the Commissary, a post office, a dry cleaners, souvenir shops, a bookstore, everything you need. The Captain was describing the facilities in this platz named after the president who approved the atom bomb attack upon Japan and also went to war against North Korea. Peter parked the car and the Captain took me into the Commissary.

'All good fair prices,' he said, walking past shelves loaded with Hershey's syrup and Jacko pudding pops. 'Not particularly cheaper than the USA, but there you have a selection of stores to go to. So here it's a fair price for quality goods. All the merchandise is guaranteed.'

I had a look through some of the records. They were arranged in categories: Country, Pop, Soul and Classical. I picked up GOSPEL COUNTRY USA – 50 SONGS AMERICA LOVES TO SING. No other country doubled as a personal pronoun in quite this way, I thought. The USA had taken the name of a whole continent for itself. Its critics were simply *ant-eye American*. Some people were ant-eye every goddamn thing, anarkisseds, communists, those kind of people, got a lot of them in Europe, ant-eye establishment. I followed the Captain into the hi-fi department, one room stashed with the Japanese post-war miracle: Hitachi, JVC, Pioneer, Sanyo, Sony, Toshiba, matt black and sparkling chrome and digital displays, flashing lights all the colours of the rainbow, steel eyes shooting perfect sound at the *just-looking* GIs lifting up their price-tags. This was how the Japanese had gained their revenge. It had been a long march, and once westerners had made jokes about Japanese radios, but now the empire of the rising sun had broken through. It had treated its slaughterers with due respect, it had not been ant-eye American, but it had won the economic war and begun to re-arm. Japan was the joker in the capitalist pack.

'Everyone wants this stuff,' said the Captain, pointing at the Japanese VCRs. 'Video is very big here. We can get AFN and the BBC too.'

He remembered he had to pick up a couple of suits from the dry cleaner's. The sign facing the queues at the Commissary checkout stated BAGGERS ARE PAID BY YOUR TIPS ONLY. Baggers were mostly soldiers' children.

All the women working at the dry cleaner's were black. Behind the Formica counter was a girl of about nineteen, her hair in

black-pride plaits, her mouth working some bubble-gum. While
the Captain rummaged for his slip, she blew pink bubbles and
cracked them expertly, loud. After much foraging through
pockets the Captain located his slip and handed it to the girl, who
took her time drawing herself up from the lounged pose on the
counter. She sauntered out back, returned with the two suits and
handed them to the Captain without saying a word.

Outside in the breeze, cellophane over the suits flapped like a
panicked bird. I stopped by the bookshop. A pictorial biography
of Rommel had pride of place in the window display. Down from
Rommel was another book in the same series, on McArthur, and
a big-format glossy called *Lost Berlin*. Prancing on its cover were
thirties dancers dressed skimpily in black.

'Everything from girlie to the classics,' said the Captain.

He was such a blithe spirit. He needed some stamps. A black-
and-yellow poster in the post office was headed TERRORISTEN.
Beneath black-and-white photographs of alleged members of the
Red Army Fraction the poster offered DM 50,000 for information leading to arrest. Such posters were everywhere back in
1979 when the RAF, the *Berusverbot* (the law banning communists from public employment) and the squatters' riots in
Berlin were making the running on the front pages. I said
something along those lines to the Captain, who humphed,
mumbled that the terrorists were still a big threat and led the way
across Clay Allee back to his office.

I noticed that one of his jogging certificates had been awarded
in Puerto Rico, ceded by Spain to the USA in 1899 and still under
gringo rule. The Captain had brought me back to his office to sum
things up.

'The mission is the raison d'être,' he said. 'Showing the flag.
Supporting the Berlin Brigade's reason for being here.'

I was puzzled by the tautology but I thanked him for his
trouble. We shook hands. The Captain wished me luck with the
book. I said I'd need it. I walked up Clay Allee a little way to an
Imbiss patronised mainly by Americans. I stood in the queue
behind two teenagers discussing in loud voices the merits of
peanut butter on a hamburger as opposed to peanut butter on a
pancake. A black GI sat on a nearby wall explaining to his

comrades the hassle he was having due to the loss of his passport. His accent was from one of the southern states: 'Aw, shit, you know the way folks up here run things. It's not like in the States.'

I remembered some postcards I had bought at the Greyhound bus station in Birmingham, Alabama. At one angle they showed Christ on the cross. Turn the card through thirty degrees and Christ was resurrected. A trick of the light. I drank a coffee and felt a shade better. I reclaimed my bicycle from the General Lucius D. Clay parking lot and, fifteen minutes later, ordered a late breakfast in a café at the top of the Kurfürstendamm, opposite the Bhagwan Far Out Disco on Lehninerplatz. I sat by the window facing a cinema showing *Der Liquidator* starring Charles Bronson.

Over the next ten days George was making his final preparations for the Aeroflot flight from Schönefeld Airport to Augusto Sandino Airport. (Having fought the US Marines who occupied Nicaragua in 1926, Sandino was shot dead in 1934 on the orders of the first member of the ruling Somoza dynasty, which ran the country until the 1979 Revolution.) George was learning a few words of Spanish from a tape cassette. Ulrike kept saying maybe she would join George in Nicaragua, she was bored with Berlin. Every time she said it George's face lit up. He failed to understand this convention of people saying things they didn't mean.

Laura's painting of Ulrike pregnant was as finished as it was ever going to get. It hung now in our bedroom alongside the paintings by the Swiss artist. Life went on. Murat was spending more and more time in the house, getting more and more drunk. Every now and again his mother kicked him out the house until he dried out. Ulrike's daughter, Charlotte, had a bad fall in the garden one day and the wound above her upper lip turned into a scab which resembled Hitler's toothbrush moustache, as I remarked once to Ulrike. She found the suggestion shockingly amusing and, over the days, repeated it to her friends who came by. The English Boy says she looks like Hitler!

For George's going away party one of his fellow exiles from Sri Lanka prepared a curry dinner. Four other Tamils, who I had seen before listening to the BBC World Service with George in Andreas's room, were invited. Murat brought six bottles of

Buzbag. Everyone living in the house assembled down in the kitchen basement at nine. Johnny came too. Everyone got drunk, but it was a melancholy event, George's last supper. I proposed a toast to George and to Nicaragua. I may have said death to the imperialists, I can't exactly remember. Everyone proposed different kinds of toasts and hopes (which are really the same thing) concerning George and Nicaragua and most of us were thinking it was dangerous and heroic what he was about to do (safe and selfish what we were all going to carry on doing) and that he would be badly missed. George had somehow kept things in perspective. He had been the constant reminder of another world, a dusty place of palm trees, barefoot children, bright birds, dirt roads, tropical rainstorms, women carrying loads on their heads, soldiers with gold crosses pendent on their chests, we had only the haziest picture of this world, a collage of magazine articles and television documentaries and translated novels, but we knew it was a harder place where people fought with bullets for bread and independence. We tried to imagine George in this hot country, maybe it would be similar to the hot country that was his home? Would he come under fire? Would he fall in love? We silently considered these matters, but said little beyond the well-meaning platitudes that fall routinely from mouths at goodbye dinners. Stay in touch. Don't take any risks. Look after yourself. Write sometime. Be good (nudge, nudge). Have you had all your injections? Remember you can always come back. You'll always be welcome here. Any time. Really any time. Bon voyage.

In the morning George came into my room and shook my hand the revolutionary way, hands facing upward like men arm-wrestling on a bar. He said he'd see me in Nicaragua some day. I wished him well. Laura was still sleeping at my side. She half-awoke to murmur goodbye, but she had never really got acquainted with George. Probably she had been too scared to interrogate him about his life and beliefs. She knew him as a cheerful man who had had an unhappy life. She didn't want to know any more. She didn't want to become burdened by his sadness and rage. She knew it would only make her feel more guilty and helpless, the way most westerners felt when they watched famine documentaries, the flies clustered in the black children's eyes. I didn't blame her.

George walked out the unlocked door for the last time. His departure marked the beginning of the end of the household. We would soon be flung apart as randomly as we had come together. The contents of this house would soon be scattered like the ashes of the dead across the world's magnetic field.

An hour or so after George had left for Schönefeld Airport Ulrike and Uschi found dozens of notes hidden beneath piles of clothing, under books and magazines and stacked plates, tucked behind the paintings on the walls. Scrawled in George's large untidy hand these notes all said the same thing: I HAVE TWO HOMES, ONE IN SRI LANKA AND ONE IN MITTEN-WALDERSTRASSE. LOVE GEORGE.

He had gone to find a third.

13 God and the guestworker

Murat, whose name meant peace in Turkish, was down in the kitchen basement talking about God. It was another languid Saturday afternoon, not that Saturday afternoons were noticeably different in character from afternoons named after other days, except for the fact that on Saturday nights I went dancing at the Metropol with Al and Mark and anyone else who wanted to come along, and therefore, on Saturday afternoons I was pleasantly aware that the night was taken care of. I thought probably tonight I would wear my shiny Tamla Motown suit, bought for twenty-five dollars in a second-hand shop in Dallas. Its bronze silk reflected blues or greens, browns or golds, according to the light and also your idea of these colours.

Murat, Ulrike and I were sharing a bottle of Buzbag. None of us were yet drunk, but Murat had started earlier than myself and Ulrike and he was in the garrulous mood that preceded his brooding depressions. Murat was in love with Ulrike. Whenever he was in this lively pre-drunken state he talked endlessly about his pantheist beliefs and mystic experiences. I think he thought this was the route to Ulrike's heart. She had her own weaknesses for magic and mystery, but faced with Murat's mysticism she always became the worldly cynic, rolling her eyes and laughing and saying he was a romancer.

No one ever listened very intently to Murat's stories. He didn't seem to mind, he was content enough just to be in the house, away from the cramped quarters he shared with his mother. Ulrike had

first met him in a local café. He had entertained her with his jokes
and his tragi-comic black eyes and he had quickly got into the
habit of dropping by with his bottles of Turkish wine, expatiating
upon the God he thought was everywhere if only people would
bother to look and listen.

One of his problems was that he had been boiled down to a
type by Ulrike, who had a penchant for quick classification.
Murat had become another element in her carefully constructed
self-image. Her friendship with him was a public declaration
of her generous anti-racism, her un-German cosmopolitanism.
Murat played mystic and jester to the court of Ulrike. She had
never seen his home.

Opening another bottle of Buzbag, Murat inquired after
Charlotte, who had been taken out for a walk by Laura and
Uschi. Murat had grown very fond of Charlotte for whom he
spent hours contorting his face in weird expressions and making
the little girl laugh. And Charlotte's affection for the funny man
with the dark hair and big nose was clean and uncluttered. Murat
was uninterested in parties or nightclubs (or so he always said)
and therefore came in handy as a babysitter. At least once a week
he would spend all night with Charlotte while her mother
whooped it up at the Paris Bar or the Djungel or wherever was the
place to be on any particular night. His car was useful too. He
often drove the German Sisters to the beach or took them
downtown at night in his red Ford Cortina, which had a furry dog
hanging from the rear-view mirror.

Ulrike could never have made friends with a German or an
Englishman who wore flared trousers and had a dog hanging
from his rear-view mirror. She tolerated such things in Murat
because he was Turkish. Although he must have been aware of
her condescension he was blinded by love. Their relationship was
corrupt and necessarily so. My own friendship with George was
probably open to similar analysis. Friendship couldn't abolish
history. Even love could founder on the tiniest nuance of
historical difference. My own love for Laura was mocked by the
ghosts of the class war. We liked our tea made in different
strengths. Ensuing discussions about the optimum relation of tea
bags to water reflected tastes inherited from different classes. The

poisons ran deep. We argued and made love as members of different classes. The Berlin Wall became famous as a hand-wringing symbol of ignoble division precisely because the German peoples it divided had so much more in common than Ulrike and Murat, the German and the Turk, the hipster and the guestworker. Private walls, electric gates, burglar alarms, guard dogs, laser security systems, such things were sometimes necessary to repel the enemy within, but this public monstrosity zig-zagging around West Berlin was another matter altogether. It was indiscriminate, democratic, separating *all from all* without consideration for race, creed or criminal record. It was outrageous.

Murat was born in a town called Nigde on 27 March 1953. His mother was a French teacher, his father a clerk in a judge's office. Murat had one sister a year younger. He was thirteen when his mother took her two children on the train from Istanbul to Berlin, a journey of two days. In Murat's view his mother wanted to escape his father, who had been found guilty of embezzling 66 million Turkish lira and sentenced to two months in jail. The father was an alcoholic. Murat hadn't seen him in years. His mother found work on an assembly line at AEG-Telefunken and the family of three shared one room four metres long and two metres wide in a Kreuzberg tenement. Murat still lived there with his mother, though his sister had done better at school than Murat and had qualified as a draughtsman before marrying. Murat's first job after leaving school was as a woodcutter in Lichtenrade, a fifteen-kilometre bicycle ride from Kreuzberg. For two years he chopped wood and cycled thirty kilometres a day and was reasonably happy, it was the best job he ever found in West Berlin. After he was fired he worked in restaurants and hotels, washing-up and waiting on tables, the usual immigrant occupations, then he was conscripted into the Turkish army. He considered dodging the draft. He had been living seven years in West Berlin at the time of his call-up, but guestworkers received only work permits from the authorities in Berlin and had no rights of citizenship. To this day Murat had to go to the police station once a month to renew his work permit. Probably nothing would have happened to him had he refused to join the Turkish army, but at the time dark rumours were circulating among the Kreuzberg Turks that young men who evaded national service would be dealt with severely. So Murat returned to his homeland and spent two years in the Panzer division. It was during this time that he discovered God. Murat was now telling this story. Ulrike had heard it before. She communicated this information to me by arching her eyebrows and making a circular motion with her manicured hand.

God did not come to Murat in one flash of revelation. It was more a series of coincidences. The first incident occurred on 24-hour leave from the British Chieftain tank in which he had been sweating for some two months. Browsing through a market in Ankara, he chanced upon a tiny leather sack, one inch high, and inquired about its purpose. According to Murat the man running this particular stall was old and wise. He told Murat the leather sack held a book containing all known human wisdom, the writings of Abraham, Moses, Mohammed and Christ, all in miniscule Arabic script. Murat bought the book.

He plunged a hand inside his high-collared shirt and fished out this leather sack, threaded by a thin gold necklace. He wore the book around his neck at all times, he said solemnly. Three weeks after the purchase of the miniature book, Murat was travelling in a bus that was bombed.

'It was a miracle I survived,' he said. 'Before that I didn't believe in God.'

When he returned to West Berlin after his two-year national service he got a job in a dentist's laboratory. One day he had spent eight hours filling flasks with cobalt chloride. He went home, drank a beer and collapsed. His mother found him on the bed and revived him with artificial respiration. Murat had been poisoned by the cobalt chloride.

'I was clinically dead,' he said.

Two years later he met a German voodooist who possessed diabolical powers. For example, Murat said, he made a German woman speak fluent Turkish. She had no prior knowledge of the language.

'The only one who heard her talking was Murat,' said Ulrike, lighting a cigarette. 'And he was stoned.'

While he was sitting in this flat with the voodooist Murat noticed a spider on the floor and crushed it with his shoe, he said. He saw the spider in a pool of blood. The voodoo man extinguished a cigarette in the palm of his hand and the spider was re-born. There was still a pool of blood on the floor, but the spider was crawling.

'Then the German who spoke fluent Turkish tried to get Murat into bed,' said Ulrike, laughing.

Murat raised one eyebrow, cocked his head to one side and smiled so broadly that his clipped moustache became perfectly horizontal. His black eyes shone liquidly. I could well imagine those eyes clasping ideas and gods unknown to the likes of Ulrike and I. Ulrike had cast him as the clown, however, and everyone else in the household (with the exception of Ana, the recluse pursued by magicians) tended to follow Ulrike's direction. It was her show, she had assembled the characters and she wrote the script. It was an entertaining enough production, but it had never seriously occurred to the main players that they had anything to learn from Murat's life, let alone from his stories of omniscient books, of cheating the deaths proposed by bombed buses and fatal poisons, of voodoo miracles with spiders and tongues.

English and American pop singles on AFN had supplied the soundtrack to the guestworker's speeches. Ulrike got up from the table to turn off the radio and play instead a tape by Erik Satie, the melancholy piano of Europe. The two bottles of Turkish wine were empty.

'More old fascists coming back now in the CDU,' Murat said. 'It's getting worse for foreigners. The old Nazis are in power again. It says Turks Out on the walls. But I don't like capitalism or communism. What do either of the systems have to do with *feeling*? I would prefer a system built on instinct.'

'A romancer,' Ulrike said.

'I would like to live in a country which has no borders,' Murat said, his eyes unfocused as if he was adressing his remarks to the music, to whatever pictures the melody had painted in his mind, maybe slow-motion ballerinas leaping from stone to stone across the dark rush of the river, maybe the patterns made on fields and seas by different kinds of weather. I shut my eyes. There was a mood of dreamy resignation in the slow rise and fall of the tunes, not to succumb to the sadness but somehow to transcend it, exist beyond it and render it into something beautiful, to insert art and music in the dark voids where fear and panic did their work. 'It doesn't matter where we live,' Murat said. 'No borders and no countries. The time will come when it will be like this.'

The phrase, iron curtain, commonly attributed to Winston Churchill, was actually first used by Goebbels, I said. No one knew how much shit they had in their mind, I said, but Murat wasn't listening. He was in a world of his own, the introspective netherland between the happy drunk and the sad drunk, that point on the chemical continuum when those of us who like to drink believe ourselves to be on the verge of saying great things. Murat continued his conversation with the melancholy music.

'God is millions of people,' he said. '*Millions.*'

Ulrike smiled indulgently and got up to make a pot of filtered coffee. I was writing everything down. I needed a chapter about a guestworker. I needed to get showered and shaved and dressed in the suit of many colours. My heart aches and a drowsy numbness pains my sense, as though of Buzbag I had drunk. I drank up the rich sweet coffee and thought that jokes (unlike music?) were trapped inside borders. Certain jokes died a quick death when they escaped across the barbed wire. The cartographers of world humour would have to be beautiful abstract painters and sages to boot. I watched Murat fall into a brown study that was soon overwhelmed by drunken slumber, his face buried in his crossed arms. His thick black hair on the kitchen table looked like a fur hat. The Satie tape finished. The Hitachi clicked as the PLAY button sprang back from its depressed position.

Laura and Uschi returned with Charlotte. Laura said she didn't want to go to the Metropol tonight, she was too tired, she wanted to do some drawing then have an early night. I was secretly relieved. I was never fully relaxed in public with Laura. I was too self-conscious, that was the drab truth, too aware of what others might think, too nervous of the way she re-defined me. I just didn't notice things in quite the same way when she was around. Anyway, I preferred dancing alone.

In addition to the silk suit I wore a black Fred Perry with both buttons done up, white cotton socks and black shoes which I would have polished had the relevant materials been available. I decided against shaving.

Waiting for the number 19 I considered what Murat had been saying. In my circles it had long been fashionable to pour scorn on those poor unfortunates who believed in God (another rare word passed into English from German). God was alienated man. How many times had I said that? I had begun even to bore myself. The custard-coloured bus hove into view.

I dropped the silver coins in the black plastic dish and the driver handed me a ticket. God is millions of people. The phrase repeated itself over and over, the bus crossing the lights at the Mehringdamm crossroads and continuing on past the New Yorck Café on Yorckstrasse where the gentrifiers of Kreuzberg drank their cocktails, eyed up the talent and exchanged information about their careers and love lives.

For me the teenage rejection of God had been a signal event. At the age of sixteen I was introduced to Albert Camus and Bertrand Russell by my then best friend, Mick Kenny, a painter who later dropped out of Chelsea Art College and spent seven years working at his parents' health food shop in Leeds before living in exile in Sweden and then Turkey. Mick and I got the same sense of illegal pleasure from Camus and Russell as we did from the sex scenes in the James Bond novels.

I remembered one week at school when the sixth form was permitted to take school assembly. Monday through Thursday it was mostly sixth formers playing acoustic guitars and singing well-meaning songs about how everyone should love one another and everything, which was pretty much what the school hierarchy expected and wanted. The headmaster and headmistress stood on the platform during these performances, smiling beatifically at the sweet unthreatening longings of youth. On the Friday, therefore, Mick and I decided to stir things up. It was our turn to do the assembly. We had dramatised the last bit of *The Outsider*, where the priest comes into the cell and tries to convince the prisoner of the existence of God. Mick played the evangelist and I was the prisoner (as unshaven as was adolescently possible). The headmaster and headmistress didn't like it. They liked it even less when we followed up our playlet with readings from *Why I Don't Believe in God* by Bertrand Russell. During Mick's reading the headmistress intervened, telling Mick to stand up straight and not slouch on the table. Mick turned round to stare at her. He curled his lip insolently, ignored the command and resumed his reading. Blasphemy was as central to my enjoyable memories of youth as the mod movement or certain well-taken goals in football matches. To entertain any sympathetic ideas on the subject of God was tantamount to betrayal, yet it had occurred to me while Murat was speaking in the basement that God was after all only a word, a word whose meaning was open to a million definitions. Why be so scared of a word? At a talk given in Caracas in 1981 Rudolf Bahro recruited Moses to his cause (the reclamation of the God that will overthrow Mammon and prevent the apocalypse) and dug out this quote from Beethoven: 'We finite creatures with the infinite spirit'. Bahro was now with Bhagwan, but he would not stay there long. We had to keep moving. I got off the bus at the end of Yorckstrasse and met Al inside Leydicke, the oldest, dirtiest bar in the city. He was halfway through a bottle of raspberry wine. His lips were stained scarlet.

He went to the bar to procure another glass and came back with a six-foot-six Berliner called Horst, a friend of Al's. Horst had the deepest voice I had ever heard. 'A voice pickled in vodka for twenty years,' Al said when Horst had returned to his other mates at the bar. Al wasn't sure if Horst worked or not. He thought it unlikely. Most of the Leydicke regulars sported ARBEIT NEIN DANKE badges, a re-working of the ATOMKRAFT NEIN DANKE badges and stickers, the red letters on yellow suns that were the most popular motif of West Berlin's green world. Al supported the cause, but mocked the cliché. The raspberry wine done, Al felt we should try a bottle of the strawberry. It was half ten. There was no point getting to the Metropol before midnight.

When Mark Reeder dashed into the bar around 11 his entrance was attended by the usual commotion. He was well-known to the Leydicke regulars. They raised their arms in the Nazi salute and paid short tribute in speeches and toasts to the heroism of the

Englanders who defended the honour of their nation and the
Falkland Islanders against the Argie marauders. I remembered a
rainy Sunday marching from Hyde Park to Trafalgar Square.
Malvinas Argentina's! Mark took the jesting in good heart. He
was no more in favour of that criminal war than any other
decently unpatriotic English exile.

'Poor old Mark,' muttered Al. 'Whatever he wears he ends up
looking like Goebbels.'

Tonight Mark was wearing his cream double-breasted raincoat over his demob suit, white pressed shirt with a starched
collar and thin black tie. His hair was slicked back like Monsieur
Poirot.

I happened to mention I had spent the afternoon with Murat,
talking about God. This was Mark's cue for a story about his
Dad.

'Nutty as a fucking fruitcake. Worse than his son,' said Al, who
had met him and who also knew the story Mark was about to tell.

Mark's father was still working at Manchester Liners when his
father died in Newcastle. Mark's father being very handy, he
decided he would make a beautiful wooden cross to take to the
funeral. He spent a whole day sawing, planing, sanding and
staining this cross that measured six foot by three. He experienced some difficulties at Manchester Piccadilly station, but
finally succeeded in persuading British Rail officials to let him
take the cross on board the train without incurring any additional
cost.

'He had this big suitcase, so the only way he could carry the
cross was over his fucking shoulder,' Mark said, his turquoise
eyes gleaming. Al grinned in anticipation.

The train arrived at Newcastle and Mark's father staggered out
of the station under the weight of his cross. A stranger to
Newcastle, he had to ask directions to the bus stop. Various
Geordies asked him if he was sure it wasn't Calvary he was after?
Mark's father eventually found the right bus stop and stood there
waiting. When the bus turned up the conductor looked in horror
at the huge wooden cross and said there was absolutely no way he
was going to allow such a monstrosity on his bus. (Conductors
could be very proprietorial about their buses.) Mark's father

remonstrated, but to no avail. The bus went off. Having waited another twenty minutes for the next bus, Mark's father had the same problem with the second conductor. You must be fucking joking if you think you're bringing that thing on board, etc. He decided there was nothing else for it. He abandoned the wooden cross at the bus stop in Newcastle.

'I think it's a really sad story,' Al said, chuckling noiselessly.

Al said no new churches had been built in East Berlin since the war. This was true, I said, but many had been restored and Article 39 of the GDR Constitution granted all citizens the right to profess religious beliefs and perform religious rituals, although those teenagers who took the Jugendweihe (a ceremonial oath of allegiance to socialist principles) stood more chance of getting into university than those who took first communion or got confirmed. There were 73 Protestant parishes in East Berlin and 126 out of 198 vicarages were occupied by professional preachers. The Catholic Church had always refused to recognise the division of Berlin. Bishop Meisner, head of the Catholic diocese of Berlin, lived in the east and travelled regularly to the west. He chose to live in the east.

The bluish smoke swirled like storm clouds through Leydicke, staining ceilings and walls the colour of the autumn leaf. Tobaccanalians coughed their messages in the dark to others who drank and joked and felt sick after all that wine. One more Saturday night.

I was trying to keep my end up with the northern soul joker and the Nazi impersonator in the oldest, dirtiest bar in Berlin, but I was too in love to concentrate properly. I never dreamed about God. I dreamed about Laura all the time. Later, when she left me, they turned into rejection dreams, different kinds of imagery but the same dread theme. I couldn't read my Berlin notes without thinking about her being in Berlin with me. She ran away to Barcelona which happened to be an anagram of *a lone crab*. I was alone. She was with some body else. Eventually I ran away too and wrote about the cold war in the shadow of a hot one. I didn't come to Berlin to discover God. I didn't come here to witter on about love. It wasn't my fault what happened. I came here to escape *The Observer* and make a few extra bob. I came here to

have a good time and write a long letter home, but somehow in
the process I lost my bearings. In my memory I was drinking
strawberry wine. A crowd of Scandinavian tourists briefly
overwhelmed the bar, much to the dissatisfaction of the slack-
faced regulars. The Scandinavians were tall, rich and young.
Some of the NIGHT-TIME BERLIN tours run by bus companies
working out of the hotels included in their itinerary a quick stop
at Leydicke, on account of its being the oldest, dirtiest bar in
Berlin. I was a voyeur too, but I was losing my thread.
Contradictory ideas and elements were escaping like steam from
a singing kettle. But I always hated automatic writing, Kerouac
was so *unprofessional*, and anyway I hadn't yet done with the
Berlin religions.

There were 6,000 Jews still living in the west and 400 in the
east. The Jewish community centre in the west was on Fasanenstrasse, the site of a synagogue burned down by Nazi mobs in
1938. Turk, Arab and Pakistani Moslems had between them built
twenty mosques in West Berlin. In East Berlin there were no
guestworkers and no mosques. In West Berlin there was a
Buddhist temple in Frohnau and a Russian Orthodox cathedral at
Hohenzollerndamm. Tai Chi, Hari Krishna, Holistic Masseurs,
Hypnotherapists, Mongolian and Tibetan Overture Chanters
(with Mantra and Sonic Meditations), astrologists, Bhagwan,
Re-birthers, Tarot and Psychic Counsellors, Primal Screamers,
these people all had buildings in West Berlin too, advertising their
spiritual services in the classifieds of *Tip* and *Zitty*, supermarkets
for lost souls.

In the east Christ had been re-born as Marx and Engels. In the
west Christ had been re-packaged as a capitalist hero waging holy
war against communism (the Antichrist). Never had the Second
Coming been more badly needed, I said to Al and Mark and there
were predictable jokes. We downed our drinks and headed for the
Metropol. *Men!*

A posse of police cars advertised their importance with flashing
lights and panic-scream sirens. People on the streets pretended
not to notice. It was a ten-minute walk to Nollendorfplatz.

Taking the tickets at the door of the Metropol was another
Englishman. His name was Henry and he had been exiled in West

Berlin for six years. Very camp, he kissed the girls' hands and said charmed I'm sure. He modelled his style on Bertie Wooster. His hair was short and oiled. He wore a black dinner suit and a monocle. Mark had heard a rumour he was 37th in line to the throne. Al said that was rubbish: Henry was just a gay aristo whose family sent him a few hundred marks every month to keep him out of the way.

With each step, negotiating the drunks on the staircase, we felt the floor thumping harder, the music growing louder, a black female vocal flying like a bird above the rich mechanical beat.

Emergency. I need someone to keep me company.

Al said it was a myth that hi-energy gay-disco music was produced in the USA. Most of the singers were black Americans, but the records were made in England, France and Italy, it was Euro-disco. He said he wasn't going to start dancing just yet because once he started he could never stop. Also he preferred it later on when all the straight couples had gone home and it was just the hard-core. Al was straight, but he celebrated dancing as an end in itself. He hated those for whom dancing was a form of foreplay. He identified himself with the outsiders. He was a genuine hipster.

Al went to get a beer and Mark took me through a door guarded by security, up a staircase leading to a glass box perched above the cavernous dancefloor. When the Metropol had been a cinema, this was the site of the projection room. A man wearing dark glasses and a Hawaiian shirt sat before what looked like an electric organ. He was composing the light show. His manicured fingers flashed across the keys like a concert pianist doing a Jerry Lee Lewis number.

Red, green and yellow lasers shot out to the crystal globe that hung above the dancers. The crystal shattered the beams like comic-book explosions, brief flashes of colour lighting up moustachioed men, split-skirt vamps, skinheads, transvestites, Mohicans, angelic boys in expensive sportswear and beautiful girls who came to the Metropol because they didn't get hassled the way they did in the straight discos. Mark said those girls were one of the reasons he came here every Saturday night. Oddly enough, I'd always thought of him as asexual. He once said he had never had a steady girlfriend because no one could come to terms with the fact he was a kid who liked nothing better than building and painting model aeroplanes.

'Lasers are a weapon,' he said, smiling boyishly. 'They're banned now in England. If that bloke turned up the power on the machine, he could kill everyone in the Metropol.'

Blue jagged neon ran like streaks of lightning above the mirrors lining two walls of the dancefloor. The pianist in the Hawaiian shirt touched the keys on the beat and pumped dry-ice smoke into the gaudy swirl. And the black birdsong soared sweet.

Burn it up, burn it up, Mr DJ. Burn it up.

By three o'clock the crowd had thinned out and Al was lost in his jerky mod-boy flailing on the slippy wooden floor. He was still stuck on the dance ethic from remembered teenage years at northern soul all-nighters, the diet of amphetamines, soft drinks and rare soul served up Saturday nights at the Wigan Casino once upon a time.

Hi-energy was the high-tech update of the fast black beat from Detroit, motor-town, *Motown*. It's the same old song. Some of the moustachioed men had taken off their shirts. The synthesisers surged up and down the scale. Drum machines thudded, regular as heartbeats. Saxophones snorted, synthetic orchestras swelled, ersatz waves fizzed on the beach. It was a toytown of sound built by boystown computers, sweet as sugar and sleazy as hell.

Don't you want some body to love? Don't you need some body, wouldn't you love some body to love? You better find some body to love.

Shrill and repetitive as ringing phones, bland as television, pitiless as production lines where human hands worked at the pace set by moving metal to make cars in Motown, disco music made the factories sing. It trapped the city's chatter and turned it into dance tracks, adding lipstick lyrics as required. All known noise was sculpted to the beat, even war noise, the crunching beat of marching soldiers, the rat-tat-tat of an M16, the whine of the warplane, the siren wail, the whistle of the falling bomb and the heart-busting explosion on target. Computers stuck the noise together and wrapped it in a love song.

It was only last week that we first met when I was walking down the street . . .

Criticising disco was like criticising the weather. Disco didn't care, the dying made the same noise as the loving. Disco was amoral, disco was the way it was. Disco was a drug swallowed unseriously by dancers. Disco was a way of forgetting. Disco was no more and no less than we deserved.

. . . hi-energy, your love is lifting me.

Who cared about the words? Who cared about any fucking thing at all in this narcotic laser-lit cathedral? The only thing to do was lose yourself, half close your eyes, move yourself in time, submit to the hypnosis. The DJs said nothing, no break between tracks. One song was slowly superimposed upon another – a climactic cacophony – the battle of the beats – until the new rhythm had finally overwhelmed the old. Fade-in fade-out. Men blew tin whistles when they liked the mix.

The earthy reek of sweat mingled with the perfumes. I had wet patches showing under the arms of my Motown jacket. I kept the middle button done up.

I'm looking for number one.

I had loved dancing ever since winning the twisting competition at the first-form Christmas party in Park Grammar, Swindon. I wore a brown foam-backed Beatle jacket with gold buttons. I learned my soul spins in the sixth-form centre of Prince Henry's Grammar, Otley. Dancing was like love: when I danced I often thought about past dances. Someone wrote a play about forty years of French history unfolding in dance steps. I saw the film. At four in the morning I took a break and joined Al at the bar.

'Just the fucking hard-core,' he said approvingly, swigging Schultheiss from the bottle.

'I like him,' I said, 'the bloke in the flower-power shirt and the flares. He hasn't stopped dancing for three hours.'

'Yeah,' Al nodded. 'Hard-core. He's a barman at Backstage.'

Backstage was a club near the café-with-no-name. The psychedelic revivalist, who never worked Saturday nights, spun round and round, his eyes closed, a thin man in a flowery shirt with high pointed collars, beige flared trousers flapping at his ankles.

Emerging through the cacophony of the mix and the shrieking

whistles was the hi-energy gay-disco version of 'I'm Not Your Stepping Stone', the old Monkees hit. It was Al's current favourite. He dashed back to the dancefloor. I went for a leak. Men were eyeing each other up, standing around chatting, boasting of their conquests, telling jokes, something of the camaraderie that women always claimed to find in their public conveniences. From inside locked cubicles came groaning sounds of love.

I live among the creatures of the night. I haven't got the will to stay and fight. I know that life is not the way it seems.

The next line rhymed with dreams. It was the nighthawks' anthem, even more popular than 'I Am What I Am' by Gloria Gaynor. I had sweated the alcohol from my system. I wasn't tired, only a bit regretful it was the fag-end of the night, some time after five. Mark noticed the look in my eye, the melancholic glaze, a speciality I shared with others of my ilk, escapists who dread sleep and sobriety, the resumption of responsibilities and reasoned positions, the chemical depression that my father called boozer's gloom. Mark leaned up against the bar, the blue fluorescent tubes picking out every speckle of dust on his double-breasted serge suit.

'All the flotsam and jetsam,' he said, swivelling round to indicate the clones, the transvestites, the young girls in black, Bertie Wooster, the clown who had flashing lights inserted in both ears, the psychedelic revivalist, the leather boys and the peep-show models.

'All we're missing is the two-rats woman,' I said.

'All the dregs,' he continued. 'They all end up in Berlin. Look at him!'

Mark was pointing at his best friend, Al.

'And me,' Mark said, sipping his peach juice. 'And *you*. You'll end up here.'

The Metropol was closing down. The lights went on. The dregs dragged themselves towards the exits. God was millions of people and some of them needed to sleep through Sunday.

14 *All the fun of the fair*

I was walking up the Unter den Linden, an anthology of new German poetry in the left-hand pocket of my bronze raincoat. It was a beautiful morning, too hot to be wearing a raincoat, but this was the only garment I possessed with pockets large enough to accommodate the hardback book I had promised to deliver to Wolfgang, screenplay writer and occasional poet and, I suspected, occasional spy.

Unlike those journalists who specialise in clandestine meetings with east-block dissidents, I do not pretend there was anything heroic in this mission. This book of poems published in the west, bulging somewhat in my pocket in the east, placed me in no personal danger whatsoever. Had I been searched and interrogated at the border, I would simply have said the poems were destined for Georg Karger, noted musicologist, etc. The official would have checked with his superior, a telephone call would have been made and finally the official would have apologised for the delay and told me to enjoy my day in East Berlin. The raincoat had expedited my progress through Friedrichstrasse checkpoint, that was all, but now I was sweating beneath its black silk lining. People were staring more intently than usual and, I must admit, I was quite enjoying the suspicions aroused by the unnecessary raincoat. I tapped the cultural contraband, making sure it was still there in the left-hand pocket.

I had seen too many raincoats in too many films about detectives and spies. I fired up a Marlboro. It wasn't raining.

Dashiell Hammett was a communist who fell foul of McCarthyism. He was a jailed dissident. He died broke and broken, though it never mentions this in the paperback blurb. I continued on up the tree-lined avenue which had seen the flags come and go. Its reddish tarmac surface was so smooth even the Trabants and Wartburgs glided across it like arrogant limousines. Double-decker tourist coaches from the west cruised slowly up and down, their passengers taking photographs through the clean windows. The trips most popular among western tourists were those where the coaches had no scheduled stops, like the bullet-proofed coaches taking tourists round Harlem and the South Bronx, motorised cinemas for paying spectators.

Across the street from the Opera House students were sunbathing on the freshly-mown lawns adjoining Humboldt University, *like students anywhere*, it was tempting to write, as if it were somehow surprising that students in the communist block should sprawl on the grass in between lectures, chatting and flirting and flicking through magazines. The man who gave his name to the university where students were now sunbathing was Wilhelm von Humboldt, friend of Goethe and Schiller and a learned philologist whose most important work was a study of the Kawi language spoken in Java.

On a cobbled street behind Humboldt University I watched a woman pushing a steel pram, a longish-haired man alongside her, his bare arm around her, a young family unafraid of declaring their corny love.

Humboldt University acquired these three-storey neo-classical premises on the Unter den Linden (the former residence of Frederick the Great's brother) in 1810, two years after the university was founded. Offhand I couldn't think of any royal residence in Britain which had fallen into productive use.

I crossed the Marx-Engels bridge to Museum Island, walked up the hill past the restored cathedral and found Wolfgang on the crowded terrace of the Palasthotel.

There were no free tables on the terrace so we had to make do with a window-seat indoors. I passed the anthology of poems under the table. Wolfgang smiled, a confident white smile, the product of regular visits to a dental hygienist who spent her days scraping away tobacco stains.

Wolfgang, like me, was overdressed. He had been at home writing for the last two days, he said. He hadn't realised this morning how hot it was outdoors. He was wearing a faded Levi jacket and two days growth of greying stubble, the cultivated shabbiness of the sixties bohemian. I noticed he was barely acknowledging most of the people who tried to say hello to him. What did that mean? Embarrassment at being seen in public with a westerner? Concern about the book I had given him? Fear of being seen to know too many people? He had already told me on a previous meeting that he had no social life to speak of and hardly ever went out. Tommy was one of his few friends, he had said. So who were these people trying to say hello? Only the richest of East Berliners could afford to drink at the Palasthotel. After one coffee he suggested going elsewhere.

'Losey died yesterday,' he said, walking back across the bridge over the Spree. 'In London.'

I said I hadn't heard, I wasn't reading the newspapers these days. I said I liked *The Servant*.

This coming Friday, he said, he was going to a special screening of two Wim Wenders films: *Lightning Across the Water* and *The State of Things*. Wenders himself was going to address the GDR film workers. Wolfgang was excited about it. Maybe that was the reason he had cultivated me: he just wanted more contact with the west. We were walking past the Opera Café.

'Before the war,' Wolfgang said, 'there were fifty cafés between Friedrichstrasse and the Unter den Linden. How is the Kurfürstendamm these days? Is that not nice?'

No, I said. It was just an expensive tourist hang-out: chintzy bars, car showrooms, porno nightclubs, street hustlers. He nodded, his mouth downturned. He was in an odd mood. He said he was going to take me to the site of a Jewish school opened by his hero, Moses Mendelssohn, on 4 January 1786, he had the exact date in his mind. We left the main drag and fifteen minutes later were walking down a narrow alley past Salon Wagner, the premier gay hairdresser's of East Berlin. Homosexuality was legalised in East Germany in the fifties.

Moses Mendelssohn arrived penniless in Berlin in 1743, made his fortune and established his reputation as one of the leading

lights of German rationalism. A friend of Lessing, he believed that
Jews should stop regarding themselves as a separate people and
should play their part in German intellectual life. (He set in train
the process which terminated in Jewish intellectuals like Georg
Karger having no truck whatsoever with their inherited Jewish
identity.) Moses Mendelssohn's salon attracted the most famous
talents of his time and made Berlin an animated forum of the
European Enlightenment. His daughter, Dorothea, was a feminist who followed the example of her father and ran a literary
salon. His grandson, Felix, became the well-known composer,
conductor and pianist.

The day Moses Mendelssohn walked through the city gates the
customs officer wrote in his logbook: 'Today there passed six
oxen, seven swine and a Jew.' Mendelssohn was now remembered by one street in East Berlin, none in West Berlin. Known
only by its surname, there was no way of divining whether
Mendelssohnstrasse honoured grandfather, daughter or grandson. Maybe it was killing three birds with one stone.

Faded lettering on the first floor of a stucco house at a
crossroads marked the site of a vegetarian restaurant popular in
the twenties and thirties. The green words were now too pale for
the restaurant's slogan to be legible against the shit-brown
plaster.

'My grandfather was treasurer of the Nazi Party in Leipzig,'
Wolfgang said, pausing to light a Club. 'Fortunately he died in
1933. But we have some photos at home that were taken at his
funeral. Hitler himself was there.'

I told Wolfgang that Ulrike had learned nothing of Nazism at
school. I added, by way of conversation, that all the postcards of
pre-war Berlin on sale in the west claimed to have been
reproduced from photographs taken in 1929, never any later, *but*
that Mark Reeder, eagle-eyed, had spotted the inconsistencies on
the soldiers' tunics and proved the dates on the postcards to be a
lie. Wolfgang was intrigued by my story of the Englishman
obsessed with the Nazis. He wanted to know how it was that a
boy from Manchester could develop such a strange hobby. I explained as best I could.

'Of course in our country the children are taught about

Nazism,' Wolfgang said. 'But they learn it from the particular perspective of orthodox Marxism: the construction of German capital and it structural relation to Nazism. They learn nothing of the connivance of the communists in securing the Nazi electoral victory. They learn nothing of Nazi art and architecture, Nazi youth culture, Nazi propaganda methods. They learn nothing of the Nazi-Soviet Pact. As far as I am concerned, you cannot study fascism without also studying Stalinism.'

This was why he was currently compiling an anthology of poems written in praise of Stalin, a portrait of the artist as brown-noser. Even Brecht had penned one.

By a circuitous route we had reached the school opened by Moses Mendelssohn on the date Wolfgang had committed to memory. It was built in sandstone, flush against the street at the front, a courtyard behind. It had latticed windows shaped like mitres. A friend of Wolfgang's had fought to get Mendelssohn remembered on the plaque that was now nailed to the wall, he said. I recalled my editor at *New Society* fighting for a George Orwell plague in Camden Town, another story of memory against bureaucracy, but I was sure that this friend of Wolfgang's was in fact Wolfgang himself. Had it been a friend he would have told me something of this person: who, how and why. Yet why should he lie? Maybe I had just been over-influenced by Astrid telling me to treat Wolfgang with suspicion.

Adjoining Mendelssohn's school was a Jewish cemetery. Desecrated in 1943, Wolfgang said, scrunching across the gravel track that wound round the defaced tombstones. A young couple on a wooden bench had come to this green and silent garden, kissing and petting among the dead. They sprang apart when they heard the footsteps on the gravel.

Wolfgang was writing a screenplay, which he did not expect to be realised in a film, about a Jewish novelist who had survived five years in a concentration camp and become something of a celebrity in the GDR after the Second World War. This man had lost everything in the war. All his family had perished in the camps. He remarried and had another family, but they were killed in a car crash. By now an old man of seventy-five, he was completely alone again until he met a thirty-year-old gangster, a wild and talented misfit who had spent his childhood in an orphanage and grown up to become a black marketeer. The Jewish novelist wanted to be a father to the boy.

'The film is about the relationship of two generations,' Wolfgang said, still walking round the cemetery that was a regular haunt of his. 'In the end the young guy is killed by two other gangsters. For me, the story is also about these old anti-fascists who are all dying off now, one after the other. In the fifties and sixties these people were still heroes. Now they are almost forgotten and fascism is a growing force among younger Germans. This gangster in the film, he is attracted to some fascist ideas, as are many young intellectuals. It's not just the Nazi skinhead workers. Intellectuals these days are into Nietschze and the celebration of the irrational and of nature, like the Greens in West Germany with all their talk of the beauty of the German woodlands and mountains. The Nazis also wanted to return everyone to the peasant state.'

'But it isn't fascist to want to protect beautiful landscapes from acid rain and nuclear power stations,' I said. 'You've read Rudolf Bahro.'

'Sure. But now he speaks too much of God and Germany and nature. It's a dangerous alchemy.'

Further down the street from the Jewish cemetery was a small, dim-lit café with baroque wooden furniture and purple velveteen wallpaper. Wolfgang said he needed a drink. He chose the table furthest away from the other customers. Having ordered two beers, he asked me if I knew anything about a book which concerned a quest for Nazi gold. He had heard it was a best-seller in Britain. Yes, I said, and there were many such books.

'In Britain the swastika is a powerful marketing device,' I said.

'The state here is so scared of the symbol. That is why some stupid young people write it on the walls.'

I had taken out my notebook and was writing things down. Wolfgang was looking anxiously all around, his shoulders twitching. I asked if the notebook bothered him? Of course not, he said, why should it? I felt uncomfortable and put the notebook away. Wolfgang immediately seemed more relaxed.

'Did you ever hear about this fictional account of Goebbels's diaries that was published here in East Germany immediately after the war?' he said, his eyes shining like a boy about to make mischief, like Mark Reeder in fact. 'The book was a big success, then in 1953 its author was sent to jail by Walther Ulbricht and, after a big protest, he went to West Germany. Goebbels was a liar, you see, even in his diaries. So this is Goebbels's diary written as if he had told the truth about himself and about the system. It's really fantastic.'

Wolfgang flashed his milk-white teeth.

It was time for lunch. Wolfgang said we should go to the Metropol, another of those five-star hotels where guests had to pay in foreign currency. He paid the bill at the café and we walked through the sunshine beneath the curious glances of the old men and women sticking their heads out the windows of their tenement flats.

Wolfgang was born on 10 January 1951. Like everyone else in Germany born before 1955 he could remember exactly what he was doing the moment he discovered the Wall was being built. It was the German version of the Anglo-American question which had spawned a million magazine features: what were you doing when Kennedy was shot?

'It was a beautiful Sunday,' Wolfgang was saying, approaching Friedrichstrasse. 'In front of our house there was a bicycle race through the streets. I was sitting out on the balcony, watching the race. Suddenly my mother came out to the balcony. Quick, she said, come inside. Something has happened, it's on the radio. I went inside and listened to the radio report about the construction of the Wall. Only three days before I had been with my family in West Germany. Many years later my parents told me they had intended fleeing to the west and staying in West Germany, but for some reason they had second thoughts and came back to East Germany. I still remember that day very clearly. I didn't really understand, but I knew something very special had happened.'

August, I said, had been a busy month in the post-war period: VJ Day, Hiroshima, the building of the Wall, the occupation of Czechoslovakia.

'I was in Warsaw that day,' Wolfgang continued, 'the 21st of August, when the Russian tanks arrived. I was put in jail for twenty-four hours. It was the first time in my life I had been to jail. I was there with two guys from West Berlin who were active in the student movement. It was a Friday. We decided to go and see a film about Chairman Mao. We took our little red bibles and our literature about Mao and China to the cinema. It was a three-hour film. There was this sequence in it showing Mao swimming across the Yangtse river. Thousands of people followed him, including many who couldn't swim, so hundreds died. After we came out the cinema we heard about the invasion and went to the Czech Embassy in Warsaw with many others. We lay down on the steps of the embassy and ten policemen came and arrested us. In my pocket I had two Mao bibles. We spent twenty-four hours in jail and then we were released. The next day I went to the Czechoslovakian Cultural Centre and laid flowers at the door. I wrote Viva Dubcek on a piece of paper and stuck it on the window. I thought I would have problems when I returned home to the GDR, but nothing happened. Officially, I had been in Warsaw with a young tourist group so I suppose the head of the group hadn't informed on me.'

I had the impression Wolfgang told a good many lies, not cruel or cowardly lies, but enough lies to plug the gaps in his stories, to add appropriate touches of drama and heroism. A common enough conceit, normally it didn't bother me at all, most people who could relate entertaining anecdotes were deadpan liars, but in Wolfgang's case I always felt there was a more troubling reason for the untruths. He seemed professionally enigmatic.

From the emerald plastic ceiling of the Café Metropol hung glass light fittings shaped like laboratory flasks. Four white-haired gentlemen in cream dinner jackets, white shirts and black bow-ties were on a small half-moon stage playing the tune to the song which goes: I can't help falling in love with you. Wolfgang ordered the coq au vin. I had a Spanish omelette.

'Ah,' Wolfgang said, filling the two glasses with Hungarian white. 'The band are playing a piece called "Northern Romance."'

I looked out the window to the International Trade Centre across the street, a black skyscraper framed in white and built by the Japanese. The sun had disappeared, the wind had got up and an hotel employee was tying up the orange parasols on the terrace outside.

This afternoon, Wolfgang said, he had to take care of his daughter, Lilli. He was going to collect the two-year-old girl from her kindergarten and take her back to his flat (which was so close to the Wall he could see the Kaiser Wilhelm Memorial Church from his bedroom window). A reluctant father, he had never lived with the mother and didn't believe in marriage, but he loved Lilli, and because of her, he said, he would stay in the east. But it was unusual for him to take care of Lilli during the week. He was mostly a Sunday afternoon father, like millions east and west.

Tonight, he said, he was going to a pop concert at the fairground in Treptow if I wanted to meet him there. He had heard some of the city's punk rock groups would be playing. It sounded unlikely to me, underground gigs were invariably held in churchyards as a result of the special cultural space granted to the church by the state, but I agreed to go along anyway. For some time I had been meaning to visit the Treptow fairground. Al and Mark Reeder had both recommended it. Al had told me the haunted house there had a real live ghost: a permanent fairground employee paid to hang around in the shadows pouncing upon unsuspecting punters. *That's a job I'd like*, Al said.

One of the violinists had flown the coop, but the band kept things going with a polka, reminding me of a television play about an old married couple who returned to the seaside hotel where they had spent their honeymoon. Sanguine men in dinner suits were still playing the same tunes up on the stage, young waitresses still scurried beneath the crystal chandeliers, but the couple had decayed, their bodies and their spirit. The husband was haunted by the memory of the first paranoid imaginings of his wife's infidelities, his imagination preparing his stomach for the pistol shots of sexual jealousy he would later endure. I drained my glass.

The bill came to 64 marks 96 pfennigs. Wolfgang refused to let me pay in western marks. 'Don't waste them on this,' he said, pulling his wallet from his denim jacket. I said I'd see him at the entrance to the fairground at 6.30 sharp.

Carrying the anthology of new German poetry in a plastic bag, the enigmatist went to collect his daughter who will be eighteen in the year 2000 when I will be forty-seven assuming Lilli and I survive bombs, bullets, disease, deadly drugs, deathly depressions and drunken drivers. I ordered another coffee. While everything was still fresh in my mind, I scribbled some notes in the made-up shorthand that was illegible to everyone but myself and sometimes defeated my own powers of decipherment. The violinist who had gone AWOL returned to his post. A man sitting alone three tables away was crushing sugar into his tea. I felt his eyes all over me like hands.

The notebook was to blame, the red-and-black hardback notebook, made in China, size A5, big enough for 300 words per page and small enough for a raincoat pocket. Writing in cafés in West Berlin, I was always resolutely ignored. A notebook in West Berlin was perceived as an appendage of style: he thinks he is some king shit literary type so I must not give him the stares he so clearly craves. (I am a westie and this is also my reaction to scribbling poseurs in cafés and bars: ignore the fuckers.) But in East Berlin a notebook was a sign of either enmity or stupidity. In East Berlin I must either be a Staasi or a western agent or a complete idiot for recording my thoughts in public and if I am none of these things then it must be some kind of double bluff: I want people to think I am so ingenuous it has never occurred to me anyone would think writing in public constitutes grounds for suspicion, hence keeping secret my true identity and the gravitas of my mission. In cafés in East Berlin this complex process can often issue in conspiratorial smiles: I have sussed you out, but it's okay, your secret is safe with me love.

In this case, however, I figured I could wait a long time before receiving a smile from the steely-eyed tea-drinker three tables away. He smelled a rat or maybe a bourgeois reporter researching another propagandist piece about the bleakness of life under the despotic Marxist totalitarian tyrannical regime, an I-was-there account recording the fear in people's eyes, the uniformity of the clothes, the queues for fresh vegetables and the bugs in hotel rooms plus interviews with teenagers offering over the odds for the reporter's blue jeans and biros and ending with tear-jerking homilies about the divided city and the grim horror of that Wall, I could write that kind of stuff in my sleep, but I decided to get the bill and pay up quickly, keep the change, before that tea-drinker approached my table and went through his good-citizen routine: who are you? and are you here on business or pleasure? and I'm sorry to ask these questions but you do realise the GDR has many unscrupulous enemies? I distributed my belongings in my raincoat pockets. The soothing strings were playing a slow waltz, whose steps I had mastered at Park Grammar when it was too wet for double games and the boys and girls had compulsory dancing lessons in the assembly hall and I was too shy ever to ask a girl called Gaynor when the teacher said to take your partners for Strip the Willow or the Dashing White Sergeant. Gaynor's older sister once approached me in the corridor saying Gaynor liked me and did I like Gaynor? I was surrounded by sniggering second-form boys and so I said no, I didn't like her, thinking I'd find some private moment to tell this older sister the romantic truth, but the opportunity never arose and I think Gaynor started going out with someone else and that was the tragic story of my first crush coming back to me, walking out the Metropol pursued by the eyes of a cantankerous tea-drinker.

Across the street from the ten-storey Metropol I noticed for the first time a plaque marking the site of a house inhabited by Engels between 1841 and 1842. The house had been destroyed by bombs dropped from British aeroplanes named after dukes: the Lancasters and Wellingtons that had seemed so glamorous when I was a boy. I also kept my eyes skinned for the tea-drinker, but he had evidently decided against tailing the enemy through the streets. I had once been followed all the way from Friedrichstrasse station to the Alexanderplatz by a man in dark glasses and a leather jacket, too laughably caricatural to be taken seriously, I had decided, though it was remarkable how often characters in real life aped their fictional realisations, this being particularly true of unloved professions like journalism and the police.

Sidestepping through the hurry-skurry of Friedrichstrasse station, I made my way to the iron pedestrian bridge leading across the Spree to Café Trichter on Schiffbauerdamm, once the haunt of Bertolt Brecht.

A small rectangular bar, it had a bluish mural of its most honoured customer smoking a cigar against an industrial landscape of factories and chimney stacks. Every time I had been here the same waiter had been on duty, a lugubrious gent with greying hair and a pencil-thin black moustache. He wore a barathea dinner suit with black bow-tie and white dress shirt, circulating the tables with beers held high on a silver tray. Straight-backed and deadpan, he carried himself with the superior deportment of one who had waited on tables in more genteel times and was unimpressed by the rabble requiring service in the current epoch. He never spoke, but always arrived at exactly the right moment with the silver tray of fresh beers. Because beer was the only thing on the menu at Café Trichter he never needed to speak. When you arrived he placed a glass before you on the white tablecloth. When it was empty he brought another beer. When you asked for the bill he totted up the beers and wrote down a number on the small A6 pad he carried in his barathea dinner jacket. He acknowledged tips with a perfunctory bow. He reminded me of Dirk Bogarde in *The Servant*.

Silently, he set six beers before the six soldiers drinking at an adjoining table, moving on to collect the empties from a self-consciously intellectual gathering of men in their mid-thirties sporting close-cropped beards and spiky haircuts. Two of them wore thick-rimmed round spectacles identical to those worn by Brecht in one of the framed photographs on the wall. Maybe those men worked at the Berliner Ensemble, the Brechtian theatre fifty metres down the street on Bertolt Brecht Platz?

A man drinking alone in the corner of the café had looked in my direction a couple of times. I snatched a glance back and realised I had met him here before, in the company of Wolfgang. I couldn't remember his name, I knew him only as *the fallen DJ*. Once the most celebrated radio DJ in East Germany, he had lost favour with the authorities following the Russian occupation of Poland and was now editing a small-circulation entertainments magazine. I caught his eye.

Forcing his face into a smile, he came to join my table.

We asked each other how we were and we both said fine. I said I'd had lunch with Wolfgang. He said he'd come here to escape his lousy fucking magazine. I said his magazine didn't sound too bad, as jobs went. He said I should try doing it for a few months. I said any job became boring in time. He agreed. Chit-chat. Another beer? The German Jeeves arrived on cue.

Tall and broad-shouldered, the fallen DJ hunched over his beer. In a low, tobacco-cut voice he related the story he must have told to hundreds patient enough to listen. His parents were born in Poland. It was because of his Polish blood, he said, that he felt so outraged when the Red Army crushed Solidarity. He made his views known and lost his job. His mother was now dead and his father had fled to West Germany. All his friends had gone to the west too. There was nothing for him any more in East Berlin, he said. He was divorced. He saw his three-year-old daughter at weekends. He drove a Renault and lived in a fancy apartment just off Karl Marx Allee. By East German standards he was still very well off, he said, but that was no consolation. He had loved being a radio DJ.

It was this removal from the limelight, I thought, which had occasioned his greatest sadness. This judgment may have been unkind, but there was something ugly and familiar about his self-pity. Straightforward career failure was often re-written as political persecution, east and west, drunks down on their luck bitterly denouncing the vile conspiracies that caused their fall from grace, woebegone casualties talking themselves into heroes while the Dutch courage coursed through their veins. Success had made them happy and failure made them sad, an emotional carousel turning on the same mechanical axis, grinding out the same tune. Success and failure were two painted horses on this same merry-go-round. One rider had PRIDE tattooed on his forehead, the other SHAME. Both riders collaborated in the same stupid dream and finally were drowned in the same successpool. I neither liked nor trusted the fallen DJ.

'I have applied to leave East Germany,' he said, scratching his beard. 'But so far permission has been denied.'

When I later reported this story to Pint, he laughed out loud. '*Apply* to escape?' he said. 'That's rich.'

Meantime, I fielded the fallen DJ's questions about the pop music scene in Britain and the USA, questions designed to parade his own piecemeal knowledge, I thought, the poor sod. The Beatles and the Rolling Stones had meant a great deal to him when he was a teenager. He had become a famous DJ. Trying now to keep abreast of new names and fashions was his nostalgic tribute to the glories of his own youth. The pathos of the fallen DJ was the pathos of all the ageing hipsters hearing ever more faintly the rock and roll beat and hopelessly denying the evidence in the bathroom mirror. I was thirty-two and nearing the point of no return, the wrinkled Peter Pan measuring out his days in lapel widths and pop singles. We had lived in a time when it was good to be young in these cities of the north.

The bearded and bespectacled intellectuals rose up from their seats. The fallen DJ raised a palm in vague farewell as they trooped out the café. We talked for another hour then the fallen DJ left abruptly, saying he had to get back to the office. As the afternoon wore on the six soldiers in uniform became progressively noisier, the toasts more exaggerated, the laughter more raucous, the arguments fiercer, the eyes redder, but I suffered none of those feelings of apprehension I had experienced in the company of pissed-up squaddies in West Berlin bars and British Rail trains. Soldiers in the National People's Army never attacked strangers for the sheer fucking hell of it.

The soldiers had drunk their fill and were about leave, straightening their uniforms and replacing their peaked caps. One of the six approached my table. He said nothing, but smiled broadly and held out his hand. I stood up and shook his hand. The soldier returned to his mates. He turned around to wave as he walked out the door. I waved back.

I spent some minutes thinking about the handshake and wave. It was easy to forget that most of the soldiers were conscripts who probably hated the bloody army. My clothes and cigarettes marked me out as a westerner. For the soldier I was a symbol. He had decided to make his own symbolic gesture.

The handshake said: don't be fooled by the uniform.

The handshake said: safe journey.

The handshake said: another time, another place.

The wave said: everything is possible.

The wave said: walls come tumbling down.

The wave said: remember the handshake.

It was half five. Café Trichter was filling up with early evening tipplers, men having a quick one or two before going home to kiss the children goodnight and watch West German television. I left a decent tip for Dirk Bogarde. He nodded impassively, slipping the notes inside the right-hand pocket of his dinner jacket.

Treptow Park was on the same line as Grünau, where the Kargers lived, so I knew where to board the train. The carriage was half-empty when it left Friedrichstrasse, but it was standing-room only after the Marx-Engels Platz stop. Leaving Alexander-platz station the car was as crowded as the Northern Line in rush-hour. As in London it was essential to have something to read to avoid the clamour of eyes. I pulled *Welcome to Hard Times* from my raincoat pocket, the seam had torn slightly under the strain of the cultural luggage. The pockets had been built for hands and cigarettes not hardback notebooks, poetry anthologies and paperback novels. I was so engrossed in the book that I missed my stop, alighting from the train at Plänterwald, some two miles down the line from Treptow. A guard at the station said I could walk back to Treptow through the park, along the banks of the Spree. I thanked him for his trouble.

I walked through the park till I came to the banks of the broad river and continued walking for what seemed like miles along a tarmac footpath, slowly increasing the pace as I realised I was getting seriously late. Wolfgang would be waiting.

On the opposite bank were factories and a power station belching smoke. The nightshift would have taken over by now. Every so often I passed courting couples on the riverside benches, tracksuited joggers, men taking their dogs on early evening constitutionals, but where was the fucking fairground? I stopped one of the joggers to ask directions. Running on the spot, he pantingly informed me I had to leave the tarmac footpath and head through the forest. I followed the line of his finger along paths of dried mud through the woods. Eventually I came to the Café of Youth. It was closed down, but I could see the tip of the big wheel above the trees. I ploughed on. The big wheel disappeared from sight, the trees were too tall and close, but I started hearing the music. A live band was playing. Blown by the breeze, the amplified music fell unevenly among the trees.

The fairground was buried in the middle of the forest like a dream. The faint rhythm of the music sounded familiar, blue-eyed reggae, early Police? It was Jessica. Christ, I couldn't pop behind the iron curtain without encountering the GDR's fastest-rising pop group, launched to fame by a lad from Manchester. I hurried through the trees. Sometimes life seemed scripted. Who needed to invent things? I understood why people believed in gods and star signs. Fate was more glamorous than co-incidence.

Wolfgang was standing by the fairground turnstiles, anxiously examining his watch, scraping back his slightly thinning hair. I apologised for being half an hour late, explained what had happened: *Welcome to Hard Times* and missing the stop and everything. Wolfgang had changed. He was now wearing a long black leather raincoat.

'Where did you get the Gestapo coat?' I said.

'No,' he said. 'Gestapo coats were green.'

'So much for the punk rock groups,' I said, indicating Jessica on the stage.

Wolfgang held out his hands like a preacher or a method actor. He had been given duff gen. He apologised profusely, but in truth he lived at too great a distance from the punk underground for his information to be anything other than duff, which was why his apology had such a defensive ring. East and west, film writers in their mid-thirties liked to think they were in touch.

No matter, I said. Despite the absence of rebel music, the fairground customers constituted a rainbow alliance of minority groups: alcoholics, hippies, punks, skinheads and a smattering of teenagers wearing DIY versions of the designer chic they had seen on pop videos broadcast from Munich. The fashion tribes of East Berlin had taken Treptow fairground to their hearts, I had heard this before from Al and Mark Reeder.

A beautiful chaos of pointless colour and pleasure tech-nologies, fairgrounds were the natural home of urban dreamers east and west. Police looked silly in fairgrounds. (I am talking about old-fashioned fairgrounds with dodgems, big dippers and coconut shies. I am not talking about Disneylands and theme parks and other modern variations on the fairground principle.)

Coloured lights were strung between the trees. Customers staggered windblown from the roller-coaster and came giggling from the exit of the Haunted House, where the professional ghosts must become weary towards the end of their shifts, jumping on people all day for a living. The music of Jessica crackled through the Tannoys.

Watched by their parents, small boys and girls, eyes wide as saucers, clutched the steering wheels of miniature fire engines, jeeps and saloon cars, travelling in slow circles beneath the brightly coloured steel umbrella of the clanking carousel.

Long-hairs and skinheads were mowing down ducks at the shooting gallery. 'This is typically German,' Wolfgang said, sneering, addressing a finger at the marksmen.

'No so,' I said, explaining that in British fairgrounds the punters also shot down ducks to win furry toys, plastic trinkets and goldfish swimming in plastic bags of water. The guilty Germans never believed that the follies of their own race were mirrored abroad in quite the same way. I knew Germans who routinely lied about their national identity when taking holidays overseas, when faced with smug Britons picking fights in English with guilty Germans on beaches in Greece and Spain.

Unfortunately, the big wheel was out out of commission. No one knew why. An orderly queue was waiting for a turn on the dodgems. A fairground employee stood in the middle of the track, the shiny cars proceeding in slow collision-free circles around him. It didn't look much fun. This was more typically German.

Wolfgang suggested we went and listen to Jessica down by the stage. I pulled a face. I had seen Jessica four times. I knew their repertoire by heart, I said, including the numbers sung in ersatz English. They tried too hard to please, they were too boy-next-door. I told Wolfgang I had much preferred the fuzz-box nihilists screaming their drunken messages in the Lutheran churchyard the summer before (NO NAZI PIGS IN EAST BERLIN), the moustachioed Staasis standing by in their tight white T-shirts, arms folded in disapproval, the punks dancing around open fires, awestruck mouths pressed against the windows of the S-Bahn trains that ran alongside the churchyard, the *Observer* photographer leaving the gig early because he thought the Staasis might confiscate his film, although I reckon he was just chicken-shit and, the thing was, he missed the blues band playing afterwards inside the church and the sixteen-year-old girl holding a faded photo of Neil Young she had bought for five marks from a black marketeer hawking his wares along the pews, I told Wolfgang the whole story. The girl didn't even know who Neil Young was. She just knew she'd bought a photograph of a western pop star. It seemed a poignant detail at the time.

'How did you find out about that gig?' Wolfgang said.

'*Contacts*,' I said, doing a high-camp version of the hard-nosed hack protecting his hard-earned sources and attaching further allure to a profession he knows is considered glamorous by many outsiders (in the next scene the reporter gets the girl), but I went on to tell Wolfgang the truth: that it was a stroke of luck, that I'd made an appointment to interview a couple of punks round at Tommy's flat and when they arrived they said, we got an interesting programme for you tonight.

'Pure chance,' Wolfgang mused.

'That's right.'

There was no booze on sale at the fairground, but most of the punters had brought their own, half-bottles of GDR vodka stuffed in the pockets of raincoats and parkas, secreted in PVC handbags. At the open-air café I had bratwurst served on grey cardboard and a plastic cup of lemonade which was not clear and fizzy but lime-coloured and still, tasting of lemons, a delicious lesson in etymology. Wolfgang looked sceptical when I told him how good it was.

We sat down on a low wall right underneath one of the Tannoys broadcasting Jessica across the fairground. Two beautiful girls wearing the bobbed haircuts and black clothes that were standard in the Djungel stood at the café's Formica bar vaguely watching Jessica. The lead singer was break-dancing.

Two black-leather punks with practised lower-lip sneers were trying to impress the girls, pushing each other around in mock battle.

Scruffy men in green parkas, wobbling from the drink, exchanged the kind of insults that pass for badinage among drunken men the world over.

A skinhead was explaining the internal rationale of his cult to two nervous hippies.

Shouting above the din of the Tannoy, I managed to persuade Wolfgang I was genuine in my desire to take a ride on the roller-coaster. I loved roller-coasters: *ice-cream-cone railway mountains.*

Wolfgang reluctantly concurred, his thigh pressed against mine in the bull-nosed rail-car painted red, clutching the cold steel safety-bar made shiny by thousands of expectant hands, being ratcheted up the ice-cream-cone mountain, tension building, sons smiling hopefully at fathers, girls giggling and boys feigning cool, this cargo of paying pleasurers poised now on the brink, the point of no return, here we go: sheer thrilling descent, riders yelling with fear or delight, white-knuckled fists hanging on for dear life, a blur of colour through the noise tunnel, the two-second fall filling the eyes with tears, reason abandoned in the *whoosh*, the crash that never comes, the red and blue cars decelerating now along steep-banked hairpins and jerking to a halt by the wooden platform crowded with the next cargo.

Grinning from ear-to-ear, exhilarated passengers extracted themselves with difficulty from the cars, dizzily negotiating the wooden steps that led back to solid earth. The next cargo noted with satisfaction the livid faces of the last. Wolfgang and I lit our cigarettes. In order to avoid post-carousel gloom, I suggested we needed a drink. Wolfgang said he knew a place.

Outside the fairground turnstiles, a scuffle had broken out between two boys with eyes for the same girl.

We walked along Puschkin Allee as far as Elsenstrasse, crossing the bridge over the Spree by the S-Bahn station where I should have got off on the way up here. Treptower Park station was less than 1,000 metres from the fishermen of Kreuzberg 36, who would be packing up their rods about now. It must have been nearing nine. The last of the blue was escaping from the sky.

'Have you heard about the sport at the West Germany Embassy?' Wolfgang asked, leading the way down a footpath between the green and the blue, between the trees and Rummelsburger Lake.

'I heard something,' I lied.

It had all started, Wolfgang said, when a 25-year-old man tried to set fire to himself outside the Embassy. Officials dragged him inside while he was still soaked with petrol, before he lit the match. Subsequently, he had been joined by another forty-five would-be émigrés. They had been waiting inside the Embassy for a month. Nine more arrived yesterday, Wolfgang said.

'Oh,' I said, distracted by the familiar beat of Laura Branigan. The source of the music was the basement of a white mansion that must have been a private residence before the war. I peeped through the half-open door. The basement was packed with sweating teenage dancers.

'Some kind of youth club,' Wolfgang said. 'I never saw anything going on there before.'

On the gravel car park outside the white mansion was a motorcycle-and-sidecar painted black and red, garnished with eagle decals. Wolfgang walked all round it twice.

'Beautiful,' he murmured.

'Were they German eagles or Yankee eagles or just regular common-or-garden eagles?' I said, back on the footpath.

He shrugged. He said you didn't see many motorbikes like that in this part of the city. I told him I had once seen a 1934 Indian at a party in East Berlin. Its owner was a sculptor's technician called Fritz. His girlfriend drove a 250 cc Awo, the 1959 model. She was a costume-designer for an unofficial street theatre group and earned her living by selling home-made op-art mini-dresses and punk jewellery on street markets. Wolfgang looked sceptical again. He had never met such people here in East Berlin, he said. Where was this party anyway?

I told him I couldn't remember.

The place Wolfgang had in mind was an eighteenth-century garden restaurant that had been re-built during the fifties in the Stalinist style.

'The zuckerbäcker architecture,' Wolfgang said, approaching the frilly white building. 'I hate it.'

I said I quite liked it.

A white-coated waiter said if we hadn't booked, gentlemen, he was sorry but a table was simply out of the question. We said we only wanted a drink. The waiter said he was still sorry: they were only serving dinner at this time of night. Wolfgang cursed under his breath. He said we might as well cut our losses and head back into town and maybe we could get something to eat later on? I said I couldn't be too late tonight. I wanted to go and see the Psychedelic Furs at the Metropol. I wanted the best of both worlds. East was day and west was night in the schizophrenic city where sleep was such a waste. I was greedy for all these eastdays and westnights, the chance might never come again. I had arranged to meet Laura at the Metropol. Al and Mark Reeder had said they might come along too. It was going to be another late westnight. Tomorrow I had to present myself at the British Army's Olympic Stadium headquarters at 10 a.m. I wanted my bread buttered both sides. I wanted jam on it, as my father said. I didn't know I was born, as my mother said. Neither of them would ever make it to Berlin. My father's dream was the Himalayas and my mother's was the Caribbean and probably they would never make it there either.

We waited for the train at Ostkreuz station, the oldest S-Bahn station in either Berlin. The cobbled platforms and wooden waiting-rooms were for Wolfgang a charmless cliché. Ostkreuz had been photographed and filmed to death, he said.

'Years ago I thought it was beautiful,' he said mournfully, though I suspected he was acting. Writers often enjoyed acting. Laura said I was a good actor. She usually chose bad times to say it. *I loved you*, that would be the worst thing she would ever say, worse even than the time she would get me muddled with her new lover and call me by the wrong name. *I really loved you*. The past tense was a killer, that cruel little d-sound, the tongue hardly touching the skin above the teeth.

It was six stops to Friedrichstrasse. In the empty carriage Wolfgang told me a story about a boy from East Berlin whose hobby was collecting car numbers. In his early twenties he escaped to the west, setting up home in West Berlin. He was puzzled by western ways and rarely left his small apartment, but once he ventured out and came upon a demonstration. Idly watching, he wrote down the numbers of cars, as was his habit. It did so happen that he wrote down the number of a West German agent's car. He was taken away and beaten up so badly he went to hospital for a week.

'For many years he had written down car numbers and nothing happened,' Wolfgang said, smiling. 'The first time in West Berlin, he ended up in hospital.'

We walked from Friedrichstrasse to the Café des Artistes, right next to the Wall by the Brandenburg Gate, but the hat-check girl took one look at me and said the Café des Artistes was off-limits for foreigners.

'No artists go there any more anyway,' Wolfgang said, deciding we should go instead to Ganymed on Bertolt Brecht Platz. 'Was a time in the early seventies when it was a genuine hang-out for the city's artists and stayed opened till three in the morning, but a while ago it was all done up and these days the only people who go there are well-placed Party men and their wives or mistresses.'

Wolfgang was writing his own part as he went along, the political parable of the man who collected car numbers immediately followed up by an anti-apparatchik anecdote. He was strolling through his own mysterious film, choosing his own locations: the Palasthotel, the Metropol tea-rooms, the school opened by Moses Mendelssohn, the desecrated Jewish cemetery, Treptow fairground, Ostkreuz S-Bahn station, the Café des Artistes and now Ganymed, the plushest and priciest restaurant in East Berlin.

Its high ceiling was turquoise and cream, plaster patterns of complex flowers picked out in gold-leaf. Polished silver chandeliers cast soft lights across fresh linen tables glittering with silver cutlery and crystal glass. Immaculate waiters wore blue cotton jackets with shawl collars, the shade of blue known as royal in England.

Ganymed positively pampered its western clientèle. Dining in the same room as Wolfgang and myself were an American soldier in uniform, his wife in mufti, and two French officers. From a nearby annexe I could hear a hubbub of posh English: port-thickened bass and cut-glass soprano punctuated by general guffawing and shrieking and occasional cries of *hear, hear*, like the Houses of Parliament on the radio.

'Home from home?' Wolfgang said, extracting the white wine from the ice bucket.

After a light starter of eggs mayonnaise I went to investigate (on the pretext of taking a piss). It was a British regimental dinner.

The officers were in ceremonial uniform: bright red tunics and brass buttons, navy strides with thick red stripes down the side. Their spouses mostly wore pastel-coloured full-length gowns with accessories of pearl, silver and gold. They must have started quite early; they had reached the port and liqueurs phase of the party. Two waiters patrolled the rectangular table freshening the glasses. In other circumstances I would have approached this gathering, hail-fellow-well-met, jacking up the accent, Ian Walker *The Observer*, small world, jolly pleased to meet you, etc, in order to discover what the fuck they were doing holding regimental dinners here. But for various reasons (I was looking somewhat seedy, I was with Wolfgang, I had a date the next morning with the British Army PRO) I decided against attempting any fraternisation. Ganymed's oblong room, a waiter told me, often played host to British regimental dinners. The fact of the matter was (I subsequently realised) that splendiferous shebangs were impossibly expensive in the capitalist quarters of the occupied city. Changing deutschmarks into ostmarks at the black market rate of 4:1 the officers and their wives could enjoy cut-price luxury here at Ganymed, whose cuisine and ambience compared favourably with the best available in the other half of Berlin. And whereas many of the glitziest restaurants in West Berlin (the Paris Bar, for example) would feel uncomfortable entertaining the peacock remnants of the British Empire (other customers might complain, it could damage their regular trade), the Ganymed management was flattered to accommodate these imperial relics. East Berliners enjoyed contact with the west, however eccentric the contacts. I returned to Wolfgang with my news.

My main course had arrived: lamb chops in a kind of blackcurrant sauce. I tried not to think of the animals while I ate. I decided to introduce the subject that had been half on my mind all day: espionage. I related to Wolfgang an anecdote told me by a scientist called Hans who was discovered in the boot of a car when he tried escaping to the west. After many hours of interrogation a Staasi said to Hans, 'Of course, you realise that here in the GDR we have the second-best security service in the world.'

'Oh,' replied Hans. 'You mean the GDR's spies are second only to the comrades in the Soviet Union?'

'No,' said the interrogator.

'The Israelis,' Wolfgang said, interrupting the anecdote. 'Yes, I have heard that before. The Israelis have the best intelligence service.'

'That's right,' I said. 'That's what my friend was told.'

We drank in silence. We were both enjoying the game now, the unspoken sub-text of the conversation.

'There is a new system of spying now, in foreign affairs,' he said, taking a Marlboro from my package. 'They do not succeed in the dramatic moment, like in the spy films, the dramatic unmasking of double agents and so on. They succeed by years of painstaking work. They collect all the information they can from western Europe. Some of the information they find in ordinary newspaper reports. It is the *weight* of information from as many different sources as possible. That's what counts, collecting the thousands of pieces that make up the puzzle.'

'I've heard that,' I said, waiting for him to continue. A blue-jacketed waiter filled our white china cups with coffee.

'Here in East Germany, anyone can be called a secret service man,' he said quietly. 'If I don't like somebody I can say, I'm sure he's a Staasi. Everyone will believe me. There are some people who say I'm a Staasi. Everyone believes their neighbour can be an informer. The atmosphere is so destructive.'

'But why would people say you were an informer?'

'I'm too critical and I speak out too much, that's what they say. It's hard to explain, I don't take it too seriously. It's more like a game. But Germans have no sense of humour. *Everything*, they take very seriously.'

I was thinking about Kim Philby. I had recently re-read his autobiography, *My Secret War*, with the foreword by his friend Graham Greene. I said to Wolfgang I regretted not speaking in more detail to Babu about her mother, Litzi Friedman, who helped convert Philby to communism during the Vienna Uprising of 1933. Babu was now living in West Germany with her orthodox Jewish husband.

'You know Philby lived here in East Germany for some time? I once met someone who knew him well,' Wolfgang said, pausing as the waiter brought the bill to the table on a silver dish.

'There is a sentence written by Roland Barthes which I very much like,' Wolfgang continued, running his eyes across the bill. 'All I claim is to have lived to the full the contradictions of my age, which may well make sarcasm a condition of truth.'

I knew the quote, it came at the end of the foreword to *Mythologies*, Barthes's most commercial book, but what meaning had Wolfgang plucked from it? Was he saying that this whole conversation, this whole day, from the delivery of the poetry anthology containing two works by Wolfgang to the reception of the bill for 159 ostmarks, had been built around a kind of joke? Was the quote a warning or another piece of disinformation? Or had Roland Barthes provided Wolfgang with the ideology with which to pursue his contradictory life as film writer and spy, dissident and informer? I paid the bill, equivalent to a tenner in British currency. From the oblong annexe the cackles, guffaws and shrieks had grown steadily louder. The officers and their wives were now banging the long table demanding *speech speech*.

For some reason Wolfgang was talking about the difference between Bhagwan and Marxism. I told him I had to dash. The Psychedelic Furs would have begun their set by now.

As was the custom, Wolfgang escorted me to Friedrichstrasse station. As Pint said: *spies can be nice guys too*.

Getting out of the U-Bahn train at Nollendorfplatz, twenty minutes later, I heard glass breaking and high-pitched Cockney curses. Some off-duty squaddies were having a ruck. At the Metropol the thirty-seventh in line to the throne took my ticket and I ran up the stairs towards the music.

Al and Mark Reeder said Laura hadn't arrived yet, but I'd only missed four or five numbers and they thought it was going to be a long set. Pink and blue smoke had engulfed the stage. Slowly it dissipated and the lead singer stood there in a black robe tied with rope at the waist, like a Franciscan monk on smack, his made-up eyes two black holes in his ghost-white face. He went goose-stepping across the stage. The guilty Germans nervously applauded. Al and Mark Reeder sniggered. The next song was called 'President Gas'.

Here come cowboys, they're no fun at all.

Here come cowboys, here to save us all.

His voice was a cracked wail negotiating the melody like a drunk staggering the street clutching at the railings, falling away from the tune then finding it again. I had never seen the Furs live before, but I had become addicted to one of their records three years ago, feeling low in London, staring through the sash window of my flat to the Thomsons office block across the street, heads bent over desks and stuck to telephones, this hoarse singing voice generalising the melancholy. The LP had been bought by an Argentinian girl who had fled the military junta when she was sixteen. She was living in my flat during the Falklands War when my romance with Laura was less complicated, when I was still enthusiastic about my job at *The Observer*, when I had no real reason to be depressed. Songs were like the pages of diaries.

No tears . . .

Talk about the rain again.

He sang that song for his first encore. Laura arrived in time for the second. She had brought Ulrike. Murat was babysitting again. After the gig we all went to a nightclub called Backstage. Its proprietor had also been in the Metropol, so the dancing began with the Furs. The barman bought us tequila on the house. A regular at the Metropol on Saturday nights, he was wearing the same psychedelic shirt and flared trousers he always wore to the hi-energy disco. The dancing continued through Tamla Motown and concluded some time around four with the one-off hit by Nancy Sinatra, 'These Boots are Made for Walking'. Laura got so drunk she pissed herself, making a heart-shaped stain on the black cocktail dress her mother had worn in the sixties. Just above knee-length, the dress had a black silk butterfly bow at the bosom. People pretended not to notice the stain on the dress that had touched two generations of women's lingerie and men's hands.

15 Toffs and tommies

I stood at the Gneisenaustrasse Imbiss, one elbow on the white
Formica shelf. I dunked the chips in the glob of mayonnaise, took
tongue-burning swills of bitter coffee and hoped I would feel
better soon. I was already half an hour late for my date with
the British Army. No matter. First things first. I needed some
breakfast. Dogs prowled the traffic island, looking for scraps. A
pale girl sat crying by the entrance to the U-Bahn. Drunks glugged
the first Schultheiss of the day. Kreuzberg was wiping the sleep
from its eyes.

I walked twenty metres down the street to the taxi-rank. The
driver perked up when he heard I wanted to go all the way to the
westernmost edge of the city, to Olympic Stadium in the British
Sector. He wore sunglasses and printed cotton shorts and said
what a nice day it was, the second sunny day in a row. It was a
25-minute drive to the British base.

I presented my credentials to the West German MP. He gave
me a slice of plastic to wear on my jacket.

The PRO, David Prior, was waiting outside the monumental
building. He was in a flap, his wrist shooting up and down for the
time like a mechanical toy. It was five to eleven. I was almost an
hour late. I made the apology as fulsome as I could, hoping the
sheer volume of terribly sorries would remove the need for any
specific excuse. It didn't work.

'What happened?' he said abruptly.

You cannot say you got slashed at the Psychedelic Furs gig

and danced till four in the morning and had some trouble getting a taxi home. Instead, you manufacture intricate lies. You embark upon a long ancedote involving a loved one's job interview in London (a wife, even better), the problems of arranging flights at short notice, the absolute necessity of accomplishing all this before setting out for the British base at Olympic Stadium. Lies furnished with enough elaborate detail begin to breathe a life of their own. You feel quite sorry for your own plight by the time the narrative is concluded. You can tell from the more relaxed attitude of PRO David's face that he has more or less bought the story.

PRO David was a civilian, an employee of the Ministry of Defence. He wore a brown checked suit and oatmeal tie over a cream shirt. He smoked Benson and Hedges. He had spent some years working on an evening newspaper in Northampton before being hired by the MoD. It was something the Russians found absolutely incomprehensible, he said, civilians working for the army.

'They think we're all spies. It's quite frightening really, how the Soviet soldiers are indoctrinated, you know, fed the Party line,' he said, walking across the marbled floor between square granite pillars.

'Classic piece of Nazi architecture,' I said.

'It's a fake. Complete fake. Funny really. These pillars are not granite at all. They're concrete made to look like granite.'

I slipstreamed him as far as the public relations office.

'He was late because he had to arrange transport to the UK,' PRO David said, introducing me to his boss, Captain Something, I didn't quite catch the name. We shook hands. He was younger and posher than PRO David. He picked up a baton and addressed himself to the maps on the wall, switching into automatic like a guide on a pleasure-cruiser.

'Potsdam, British Sector . . . Ultimately responsible for law and order . . . Eastern part, the Soviet Sector. Can create certain difficulties.'

He was tip-tapping the maps with his stick. His blond hair had a knife-edge side-parting, his eyes were blue, his voice sonorous, his manner blithely arrogant: the innocence of the privileged.

You never know whether to laugh or cry. There were black-and-white photographs of black and white boxers on the wall by the maps. The office was further decorated with pictures of polo players, military parades and Chieftain tanks painted in the urban-camouflage style peculiar to Berlin.

'In West Berlin there are something of the order of 15,000 Brits. About a third are expatriate. Nothing to do with the army or the various consulates.'

Captain Something's spiel had the exaggerated rhythm that was a function of saying the same things too often: dumb-dumb-dumb, du-dumb du-dumb du-dumbity-dumb. The rhythm represented the battle against boredom.

'There are 3,500 servicemen in the British garrison. Total official presence is around 10,000 including wives and children. Of course with the trend towards shorter hair the chaps don't stick out like they used to. You have to look out for the tattoos.' (Laughter.)

'Most of the servicemen will be here for two years. Nearly all of them that are married will bring their wives, depending of course on the availability of accommodation. The Royal Hampshires took over from the Royal Irish Rangers last December.'

I moved my face in concert with the rhythm. PRO David remained dutifully silent.

Captain Something was saying that British military parlance distinguished between the Wall and the Wire: the Wall was the border between West and East Berlin, the Wire was the border between West Berlin and East Germany. Although East Berlin was the true capital of East Germany, the western powers still drew a distinction between East Berlin and East Germany. In reality, the Wall and the Wire were part of the same circular structure enclosing West Berlin.

'The Wire patrols go up to the Spandau Forest and as far as the Ice Keller.' Tip-tap.

Main function of the British Army in West Berlin?

'Showing the flag and checking the border.'

He told me about the plethora of Anglo-German friendship societies and the good works performed thereby. He said no restrictions whatsoever were placed on the lads' social activities.

He said in fact that *considering everything* (by which I took him to mean the social conditions spawning the squaddies) the lads were very well behaved.

'I think that's about it,' Captain Something said brightly. 'Cheers.'

I later learned that the Captain had telephoned *The Observer* immediately after my briefing. He spoke to the editor of the colour supplement. He explained he had just met someone claiming to be a reporter from *The Observer*, someone whose dress and general demeanour had – how could he put it? – aroused a certain amount of suspicion in the Captain's mind. The Captain described me over the telephone. I was that Wednesday morning wearing a beige zipper jacket (a bum-freezer, my father would call it), an un-ironed white shirt, a thin blue-and-black checked tie kept in place by the Berlin Brigade tie-pin costing $6 at McNair Barracks, navy blue Staprest parallels (ex-GI issue) and brown Dr Martens. The editor said I did sometimes dress somewhat eccentrically, but that I was indeed in Berlin. He did not know exactly what I was up to. I was in Berlin on unpaid leave researching a book. I was not on assignment for *The Observer*. Captain Something left me in the sound hands of PRO David. A little tour had been arranged.

A West German national sat behind the wheel of a white Ford Transit. He turned off the radio as PRO David slid open the door. The German was told in English to drive to the Russian war memorial by the Brandenburg Gate.

'Tomb of the Unknown Rapist, they call it,' PRO David said, chortling. He seemed pleased to have got the formalities out of the way. I suppose from his point of view it was quite a cushy day, better than being stuck in his office making telephone calls. He lit a cigarette.

'Of course some of our chaps find it a bit confusing when they first come to Berlin. To start with it isn't in West Germany, as they'd thought, and whereas the Russians are our enemy in most places, here in Berlin they're our allies, officially,' he said, adding that we had been lucky with the weather.

The gods were indeed smiling on us, I agreed, going on to mention the PR tour arranged for me by the Yanks. (PRO David had already called them Yanks, so I figured that was okay.) I said I had been most impressed with Doughboy City.

'We've got one too. Actually much bigger than the Yanks'. Called Ruhleben Fighting City. That's where we have our war games. We invite the other armies over sometimes. Brits against the Yanks and sometimes the Frogs join in too, have a good old blat. Kind of thing they do is split up into groups of seven or eight men and develop techniques of taking houses. In the fastest time possible with the least number of casualties.'

PRO David's eyes lit up while he was describing these mock battles in Ruhleben Fighting City. He knew more about the military hardware (the *kit*, as they all call it in their scoutmasterly fashion) than most army personnel. He was quite endearing, still stuck in the *Eagle* comic conquests of his boyhood, rat-tat-tatting through the streets as he runs that fast snake-pattern through the enemy fire whipping up dust at his feet, diving into a doorway, biting the safety catch from the grenade and lobbing it with deadly accuracy into the enemy's third-floor window. Aaaaaagh! Enemy bodies and weapons come flying out in all directions. Nice work Dave, old Scottie says, taking out his pack of Capstan Full Strength. The closing frame shows our two modest heroes sharing a smoke amid the wreckage of their victory.

But no, he said. It was extremely doubtful whether I would receive permission to make an official visit to Ruhleben Fighting City. No chance, in fact. He was quite happy, however, he said, to answer any queries about the place.

'Who fights who in the war games?' I said.

'Well our forces represent Ruritania, that's what we call it. The enemy forces represent Fantasia. Sometimes it's also called Blue Force against Orange Force, the goodies against the baddies.'

'Why orange?'

'As close as we can get to red without upsetting our allies. But we do put blue and red tape across the two sides' vehicles.'

I asked PRO David what scenarios the war game strategists imagined leading to an outbreak of hostilities between Ruritania and Fantasia?

'Well, Fantasian forces have massed along three miles of the border with, or within three miles of the border with, Ruritania.

Ruritanian forces have moved into full mobilisation. Then, you know, Fantasian forces have embarked upon full-scale invasion, that kind of thing.'

'Are the men briefed on this background to their war game?'

'No,' PRO David said, amused by my naïvety. 'The soldier on the ground can't be told such things. You just say to him: the enemy's in there, go get 'em.'

The white Transit was approaching the Victory Column. PRO David told the driver to slow down. He pointed to the gold angel atop the memorial.

'There used to be gold cannons up there too,' he said. 'They were taken down by the Russians. They melted them down, only to discover it was gold-leaf paint. There are replicas of those cannons, though. The Queen was given one. She declined to accept a second one, in her polite way. Kennedy got one.'

The white Transit joined the queue of tourist coaches waiting to complete the slow U-turn up to the Brandenburg Gate and back. PRO David said a man recently drove full-pelt into the Wall here and killed himself.

'He had a history of pyschiatric disorders and attempted suicides,' he said glumly, pulling on his duty-free Benson, the brand that hid gold packages in paintings of dreams on roadside hoardings.

Behind the Russian war memorial, guarded round-the-clock by a Red Army soldier, was a small white house where the Russian soldiers took it in turns to kip. At 3.30 every afternoon the Royal Military Police escorted the Red Army guard back across the border and the new shift was escorted in, another scene in the daily pantomime of the occupied city.

'It's a cocktail party story,' PRO David was saying, 'that shortly after the war a British senior officer and a Russian senior officer were chatting over a glass or two. Wouldn't it be nice to have a permanent memorial to our dead? the Russian officer said. No problem, old boy, said the British officer. There's a little plot of land right next to the Reichstag. The majority of the building was done in the next twenty-four hours. And that is how we came to have a Russian war memorial in the British Sector. Tomb of the Unknown Rapist, they call it. Oh, I told you that already, didn't I?'

The white Transit followed the tourist coaches to the graffiti-spattered Wall and completed the funereal U-turn. Ruhleben Fighting City was so authentic, PRO David said, it even had anti-imperialist slogans on its walls and housefronts.

Driving north up Moltkestrasse, named after General Field Marshal Helmuth Count von Moltke, a Prussian general in the time of Bismarck, the white Transit turned right into Scheide-mannstrasse and came to rest on the gravel before the Reichstag. West German schoolchildren were sunning themselves on the grass. A few teachers' pets took photographs of the graves planted by the Wall in memory of those who died trying to escape in the sixties. PRO David didn't know where to go next.

'I suppose you've seen most things, haven't you? *Checkpoint Charlie?*' he inquired hopefully.

I nodded.

'Oh well. Might as well go back to the Officers' Club. I haven't booked a table, but you can get very nice bar-snacks.'

Crossing the Spree at the bridge named after the afore-mentioned Prussian general, he said three-quarters of all goods imported to West Berlin arrived by waterway.

'Berlin is still the biggest manufacturing centre in West Germany, you know,' he said. 'You've got BMW, Siemens and Siemens . . .'

His list ran dry. He was right, of course. Some 178,000 worked for capitalist manufacturers in West Berlin, people who got up early and lived in the suburbs and took dogs for walks. West German workers were offered over the odds to re-settle in West Berlin. Ordinary people didn't want to live in this rundown madhouse encircled by neon and watchtowers. I watched a British army truck pull up at a red light. The soldier at the wheel had his shirtsleeves rolled up, his tattooed arm jutting out the window, his pale pock-marked face fixed in a vague smile. He probably felt lucky too, lucky to be in Berlin and not Belfast on such a fine day.

The Berlin Officers' Club was formerly the Berlin Tennis Club, *the* hang-out for Wehrmacht officers in the thirties. The building was white as snow, its entrance grandly announced by wide steps and white columns. PRO David said it was miles better than anything the Yanks or the Frogs had got following the carve-up of

Berlin. By far the nicest officers' club in town, he said, moving towards the bar. It was just gone noon and the place was still empty, the white tableclothes in the dining room laid with silver cutlery and upturned wine glasses. PRO David ordered two pints of subsidised lager and 200 cigarettes. The bill came to around four quid.

The sun was still hot so we repaired to one of the tables outside by the swimming pool, taking our seats beneath the parasol. All around the turquoise swimming pool young officers' wives were splayed out on towels, oiled like chips, eyes closed against the sun. A transistor radio was playing inside a kind of beach-hut bar serving cocktails and bar snacks.

'*Toastie!*' The cry from the bar echoed round the pool at regular intervals. Women rose dazed from the sun and staggered across the grass to collect their toasted sandwiches. PRO David gazed with evident satisfaction all around him: the young bodies in bikinis, the well-tended grass, the tall trees, the pool in which two women were floating on their backs.

'Nowhere else in the world where the British army can offer an officers' club quite like this,' he said, raising the chilled lager to his lips. 'Well, maybe Hong Kong. I don't know, I've never been there.'

'Belize?' I said.

'Certainly in Europe there's nothing to compare to this.'

I said the ambience was indeed most agreeable.

Leaning back in his white chair, PRO David made sweet moan. He was pleased at the prospect of becoming slightly heady in the midday sun. Entertaining journalists from the UK, he was entitled to relax of a lunchtime. He was on expenses. It was one of the good things about his job. I bought the second round.

'I wonder what's happened to Julian?' he said languidly.

Julian was a captain in the Yorkshire Regiment. He was joining us for lunch. He was a good bloke, PRO David said. Down-to-earth. Not stuck-up like some of the officers. PRO David was grammar-school-boy provincial. Most officers were still old-money public school. It was a class question, the difference between pleased-to-meet-you and how-do-you-do.

Julian was a stout red-haired Yorkshireman in his late

twenties. He had gone to Bradford Grammar School and Oxford. He was wearing his army greens and black boots.

'Pleased to meet you,' he said, shaking my hand, taking off his cap.

I bought him a pint. I told him my father had tried to get me into Bradford Grammar School, but the headmaster wouldn't have me so I had gone to Prince Henry's Grammar School in Otley instead. Julian knew Otley. Pretty little mill town, he said. Our eyes held their own conversation. In two months' time Julian's regiment was going to Northern Ireland, but Julian would not be going with them. He was getting out of the army. He was hoping to get into journalism. My eyes said yes and his said right.

'Hello, John,' PRO David said to a fortyish man in sunglasses and short-sleeved blue shirt, carrying his towel towards the changing-rooms.

'He's a spy,' PRO David whispered when the man had disappeared. 'He's the closest you can get to MI6 in Berlin. But officially he's a schoolteacher, a civilian.'

Julian and I avoided each other's eyes and gulped back our giggles. The transistor radio at the bar was playing 'Hi-Energy', currently number one in the West German charts.

'It's strange,' Julian said. 'You'd think that given the shared language we'd be very similar to the Americans, but they're as foreign to us as the Russians. Out of all the soldiers here the Americans are the only lot who actually believe all that nonsense about the evil commies. They really do. They think communism is a kind of disease. The French soldiers I've met have all been conscripts, a bit sceptical about the whole thing, and the British don't believe any of it. I don't think the Russians believe they're involved in a struggle against evil capitalists and imperialists either. Its just the Americans who go along with what they're told.'

'Yes, there is a difference between us and the Yanks,' PRO David said.

'I mean, have you heard all those adverts on AFN?' continued Julian.

I nodded, giving a brief impersonation of the corniest one I could remember.

'We all crack up when we hear those,' Julian said. '*I just want to tell you that the folks back home are all real proud of you.* None of the Brits think that. They know that no one back home gives a toss about what they're supposed to be doing in Berlin. They don't think that people *should* give a toss either. They think it's quite right that people don't give a toss. It would be their attitude too.'

I said the last time British soldiers really believed in what they were doing was the Second World War.

'Yes,' he said. 'But all this stuff about the British soldiers and their heroic battle against the Nazis, that was a load of rubbish too. They'd have fought anyone as long as they were foreign. They'd certainly have enjoyed fighting the Russians. And they're the same lot today.'

'Hope it stays like this,' said PRO David, squinting up at the sun.

'In the eighteeth century,' Julian said, warming to his theme, 'soldiers were press-ganged into service from the slums and the backstreets. But they fought perfectly well.'

A heretic gleam in his eye, Julian dared me to differ. Not me, sir. I was out of the same mould. PRO David asked me exactly what it was I wanted to write about the army. I said I wasn't sure, thinking this kind of thing would do fine: lunch at the Officers' Club with a disillusioned wag from Bradford and an overgrown schoolboy from the MoD with bit-parts for spies masquerading as schoolteachers. Julian was enjoying my evasive response to the PRO's question. He had me sussed. Of all the officers in the British Army, why had Julian been chosen to spend the day with me? It was either a set-up or a cock-up. My money was on the latter, but you could never be sure about such things. Maybe Julian was leaving the army for the intelligence service. Journalism was good cover for agents.

'One toastie! Two steak and chips!'

Our order was ready. PRO David went to collect it. I asked Julian if he had met many Russian officers during his two and a half years in Berlin.

'A few,' he said. 'Usually on the train duties. Escorting trains through West Berlin to the border there's usually a wait of around fifteen minutes while the British captain hands over authority to the Russian captain. It's always very polite and formal, sometimes very affable too. Once I got chatting with a Russian captain who grew up in the Don valley. He was interested that there was a River Don in my home county too. The Scottish translator said he had also grown up near a River Don. That sort of broke the ice.'

PRO David returned to the table with my toasted ham and cheese and the steak and chips twice.

'A Russian captain is an important and respected person,' Julian said. 'Unlike in Britain.'

We downed our third pint. My hangover was mellowing.

Julian said the first time he travelled into West Berlin he was offered a cap badge by a Russian at the border.

'I refused. I thought I'd be shot. It was my first time in Berlin.'

I reckoned he had a decent collection of cap badges by now.

He said most soldiers enjoyed getting hold of cap badges from other armies. It was a heartening detail somehow, thousands of British and Russian soldiers swapping their cap badges, an illegal wordless exchange of metal remembered by both parties all their years, thousands of grandchildren listening in the future to an anecdote which could be told many different ways, though I liked to think that at least some of the grandfathers would tell it as a kind of parable, you know, I looked at this Russian and he unhooked the catch on his cap badge and slid the badge across the counter towards me. I did the same and we both smiled and, it's funny, but I've never forgotten that. I wonder what that bloke's doing now? You see, the lads on the ground never really hated the Russians. We'd been brought up to hate them, but when you met them, had some kind of contact, you realised how daft it all was. They were just ordinary blokes, same as us. I've still got that badge upstairs.

'We have a lot in common with the Russians,' Julian said, sawing his medium rare steak, a smear of blood on his serrated knife when it completed the cut. 'The Russians are a very conservative people. Margaret Thatcher would get along well with the Russians, if only she knew it.'

By way of illustration, PRO David referred to the Russian reaction to British and American officers at checkpoints on transit roads leading from West Berlin to West Germany. The Russians respected the formality of the British officers, who consequently had a lot less hassle at the checkpoints than the Yanks in their blue jeans and T-shirts, he said.

'There's only one superpower,' announced Julian, laying down his cutlery on the blood-splashed plate. 'All this talk of the superpower balance is nonsense. The Russians know that too. They can only keep up the arms race by being on a permanent war-time economy. The Americans can do it on a peace-time economy.'

'Which is another reason for the Americans to intensify the arms race: to bankrupt the socialist countries,' I said, throwing caution to the winds.

'That's right,' Julian said.

PRO David was looking frankly baffled. He glanced at his watch and said oh God was that the time? Two thirty. We were running late.

The white Transit was waiting in the car park.

'Smuts Barracks,' PRO David said to the driver.

'Yesterday I was in East Berlin with a film writer whose grandfather had been a well-known functionary in the Nazi Party,' I said. 'Hitler went to his funeral.'

'Interesting,' said PRO David. 'I suppose in a way it's like being a member of a union. In times to come the children might say, but why were you a member of the union? The answer of course is that you just had to be. There was no alternative.'

Julian suppressed a smile. I concentrated hard on looking out the window. It wasn't worth arguing. Outside the gates of Smuts Barracks a small queue of squaddies had formed at the Go-Go Grill.

'Always a queue there. Any time of the day or night. A gold-mine,' said PRO David, showing his ID to the MP and explaining who I was. Julian said we had an appointment to see the Colonel. We were waved through. Julian returned the salute.

'There's been a military barracks on this site for 400 years,' he said, stepping out of the Transit.

From October 1935 to April 1945 it housed the 1st Battalion of the 67th Infantry of the Wehrmacht. In May 1945 it was occupied by the Red Army victorious in the Battle for Berlin. The British assumed ownership in June 1945.

'It's a good solid *soldierly* kind of place,' Julian said, inhaling deeply, tightening his lips and casting his eyes around the familiar redbrick square. Smuts Barracks was the same gloomy red as Spandau Prison right across the street. Tucking in his shirt and tugging down his cap, Julian led the way to the Colonel's office. Bare-topped men were playing football on an Astroturf pitch. Wednesday afternoon was games afternoon in the British Army.

The Colonel jumped up from his desk and bellowed his introduction: how do you do? His was the loud voice of egotistical authority, the loudness convinced of its own truth and unused to voices raised in opposition, the loudness purpose-built to scare off and drown out the weaker talkers. I made small-talk about sport, having heard previously from Julian that this was a subject close to his Colonel's heart.

'Sport is important,' he pronounced. 'To play it successfully. To play it well. Encourages the right kind of attitudes. Toughness. Competitiveness. This regiment is second to none on the sportsfield. Isn't that right, Julian?'

'Yes sir!'

The Colonel was brisk as brisk can be, possessing the brittle staccato delivery that always sounded in the military mouth like an unconscious echo of the battlefield's *rat-tat-tat*. But the Colonel's remarks about sport should not lead me erroneously to believe that regimental life in Berlin was all beer and skittles, he said.

'Our job is to train for war. Nothing more, nothing less. Isn't that right, Julian?'

'Yes sir!'

I could see why Julian was getting out of the army.

Behind the Colonel's desk was a framed photograph of Prince Charles, the Prince of Wales who couldn't speak Welsh. The Colonel was eyeing me suspiciously. I addressed his eyes and didn't look away until he did.

'Hope you're going to set the record straight with this book of yours,' he said.

'How do you mean?' I said.

'This stupid idea that Berlin's a morbid grey city,' he said. 'To me Berlin is lakes and rivers and marvellous forests. Boat trip I'm going on next week with some Germans, for example. It's all bloody good fun. And it's important we're seen by the people. Isn't that right, Julian?'

'Sir!'

At least Julian had dropped the yes. Why did the Colonel have to conclude each little speech with this ritual humiliation of his Captain? I said I certainly intended to dispel some of the myths about Berlin, including this general ignorance about its landscape and wildlife.

'Most people understand it to be an evil kind of place. But there are wild pigs and deer in West Berlin. The city fathers have very strict rules about the preservation of their wildlife and trees and we have to be very careful not to break those rules when we are out training. But they are right to have strict rules. So would London if Londoners had nowhere to go,' the Colonel said.

'Absolutely,' said PRO David, reminding everyone he was still in the room.

The Colonel said he had to dash. Important meeting. Look after him, Julian. Be intrigued to read this book of yours. Cheerio.

A black Ford Cortina was waiting for him outside his office, the motor running. In his haste to hurl himself on the back seat and shut the door all in one dextrous moment, the Colonel's cap fell off. He replaced it with as much dignity as he could summon in the circumstances. He stuck up an imperious finger and his limousine swept out of the base.

The Colonel's briefing had sobered us all up, but the comical incident in the Ford revived the post-lager euphoria. The moment the Colonel's cap fell off, he became a slapstick clown from cartoon-book England. Like Tony Hancock playing some pompous patriot, he was betrayed by the endearing mishap. *We are here to prepare for war. Nothing more, nothing less.* The cap falls off and the studio audience split their sides.

'Where now my love?' I sang to Julian.

'Where do you want to go?' he said.

'Anywhere. Just wander round and meet some of the lads.'

'Okay,' he said, walking towards a crowd of soldiers setting up tables and chairs beneath a green canvas marquee. 'Mmm, this looks interesting.'

'It's a company social sir,' said the soldiers' spokesman. 'Thirty Yanks are coming too sir.'

'And we've got fifteen hundred cans of beer. We might make a slight profit,' said someone wearing a sweatshirt printed with an anti-tank device. 'The Yanks are coming down tonight for their tea.'

'And then you're all going to get pissed?' Julian said.

'That's right sir.'

'One thing I can't do in life is sunbathe,' one soldier said to another.

Continuing our stroll, past the Astroturf football pitch, Julian said the barracks were shared by his regiment and the Royal Hampshires: 'When I first heard about that I thought, Jesus Christ, there'll be a massacre. But actually it's worked out quite well. There was a bit more trouble when we shared with the Royal Irish Rangers. We recruit from Bradford and Hull. Basically. That's it.'

Inside a dark garage tattooed mechanics were working on a tank, their hands black with oil, their bare torsos smeared with sweat and dirt.

'A punchy bit of kit,' enthused PRO David. 'Notice the rubber pads on the tracks. Without that these tanks'd destroy the roads. The French are more blasé about that kind of thing.'

Julian stared down at his black boots. The radio in the garage was tuned to AFN.

'We ran a campaign last year: have a British soldier for Christmas,' PRO David said, shielding the flame to light his cigarette. 'It was quite interesting really. Quite a few of the families who offered their hospitality got requests from French and American soldiers, but the families wrote back saying they would much prefer to have a British soldier.'

'Why's that, do you think?' I said.

'Oh,' he said, with a knowing wink. 'It doesn't do to question those things too much.'

In his mind the notion that British is best was indelibly inscribed as the blue and red designs on a squaddie's forearm. The

ideological equivalent of lasers stood no chance against such
ingrained smugness. What was to be done? Have a British soldier
for Christmas. Carry On Up The Spree. Farther along, a small
group of soldiers were crawling over an armoured carrier known
in armyspeak as a pig. (I had come across the term and the vehicle
in Northern Ireland. Walking down the Falls Road one time a
soldier had hurled a brick at me from the turret of a pig, believing
me to be a dirty Fenian bastard.)

'That vehicle has a 30 mm calibre gun, a fairly punchy piece of
kit,' said PRO David.

'These are some of the brightest guys in the battalion,'
whispered Julian. 'They patrol the Wire.'

'One six hundred. Woman on balcony.'

The gunner was lining up a woman sunbathing on the balcony
of a block of flats overlooking the barracks.

'Woman in bikini. I think she's knitting. Probably knitting a
bra.'

Ho-ho hollow laughter. Function of male solidarity. Exchange
of sniggering expressions. Thoughts of brassières. White lace
black lace falsies too. Twanging them in the playground.
Unhooking them one-handed Saturday nights and boasting
afterwards to your mates that you got to number 6 which was
feeling the tits *inside* the bra. Number 1 was holding hands.
Number 2 was having an arm around. Number 3 was kissing.
Number 4 was French kissing. Number 5 was feeling the tits
outside the bra. Number 7 was feeling outside the knickers.
Number 8 was feeling inside the knickers. Number 9 was sex with
a johnny. Number 10 was sex without a johnny.

The gun in the pig had a range of 2,000 metres. The sergeant
supervising this training exercise wore Adidas training shoes and
a white T-shirt. He had often met East German soldiers on his
patrols along the Wire.

'I've tried to talk to them. About anything. But they don't want
to talk to us,' he said. 'The only time one of them ever spoke was
when I was on patrol along a bit of the Wire that runs under a
railway bridge. There was just this yellow line on the road, like a
no-parking line. I walked over this line and the guy said in perfect
English, "Would you mind getting back into your own country."
I didn't realise that the yellow line was the border.'

'Oh, it's well known, that yellow line under Staaken railway bridge. I've often taken journalists there,' boasted PRO David.

Everyone talked about this for a while: this one short section of the Berlin Wall that was a thin line of yellow paint on a road beneath a railway bridge. Just goes to show, really.

Men were cleaning their weapons in the afternoon sun, whites from Bradford and Hull shooting the breeze with blacks from the southern states and the northern ghettoes. The Americans had spent the day on the firing range with the Brits. Together they were going to drink 1,500 bottles of beer at the company social tonight. I got talking to a nineteen-year-old boy from Leeds who thought Berlin was a great town for civilians.

'But in the army you've got so much ceremonial you don't get a minute's peace,' he said. 'And I can't go out on the piss down discos and clubs and that because I'm getting married. I send most of my money back to England.'

His name was Andrew Parkinson. He was due to get married the coming August. This was his first tour of duty. He had never been to London. He was dark-haired, freckled, young for his age. What he enjoyed best of all, for an occasional treat, he said, was going to East Berlin in uniform at the weekend.

'It's great if you go through on a Saturday night,' he said, still rubbing down his rifle. 'You go to a restaurant and get a right good feed, very cheap. And if you walk in as a squaddie you go straight to the top of the queue. It's brilliant. Get champagne and everything, sir.'

The 'sir' was tacked on because Julian had wandered across to hear what his private was saying. I asked Private Parkinson why he thought squaddies were taken to the head of the queue at restaurants in East Berlin.

'They like squaddies there, sir. Everyone's dead friendly and that, even though not many speak English.'

Squaddies, like guestworkers, were barred from many places in West Berlin. Squaddies, like guestworkers, snatched a glimpse of the good life when they travelled across the border. They ate with the toffs, drank the best Russian champagne, danced with the prettiest girls and briefly tasted the luxuries enshrined in the western television commercials. Andrew Parkinson and the rest of the lads would be off to Northern Ireland at the end of the summer. Everything but the local British Legion bar would be off-limits. They would spend their nights watching pornographic films in the TV room and drinking at the NAAFI and doing night patrols shit-scared in hostile neighbourhoods and writing letters to their girlfriends and wives and boyfriends, saying they wanted to get the hell out of the army, settle down in civvy street. For the squaddies the cold war was a cushy number.

Some of the soldiers saluted when Julian walked past. Others straightened their backs and dangled their arms down by their sides. Julian seemed faintly embarrassed by it all. 'How are *you* today?' he said, pleasantly enough, to all and sundry.

There was no one in the TV room. The carpet was spotted with cigarette burns. The NAAFI was empty too. Everyone was enjoying the sunshine. I told Julian I'd like to see one of the rooms where the lads lived. He knocked on a few doors until a voice answered 'come in'. A squaddie called Paul was bulling his boots in the tiny room he shared with two others. Every available inch of wall and ceiling space was covered with colour photographs from *Playboy* and *Penthouse*. Paul was from Bradford. He was applying the final shine with a rag. PRO David had long felt there was some secret to the spectacular sheen soldiers achieved on their boots. He had asked before, he said, but the secret had never been divulged. He asked again.

'It's just layers and layers of polish plus bags of elbow grease, sir.'

PRO David humphed.

Helping me out, perhaps thinking of his own possible future in journalism (could I do this kind of thing? would I enjoy it?), Julian asked the private if he was enjoying his time in Berlin.

'Yeah, it's great sir. I've been all over, exploring on the U-Bahn. Squaddies in uniform can travel free. There's loads of lads don't want to leave, sir.'

Julian smiled ruefully or maybe guiltily.

The number of soldiers going AWOL from the British Army in Berlin could not be plucked from the clenched teeth of the public relations office (Captain Genser, my guide round Doughboy City, said the Brits were pastmasters at obfuscation and that he had learned a whole lot from the Brit PROs since coming to Berlin) but I was prepared to bet that at least a few boys from Yorkshire would never make it from Berlin to Belfast. Stories about British soldiers going AWOL never appeared in British newspapers, though Al had told me about that one in *Stern*. A window-cleaner I knew in London had been in Smuts Barracks between 1958 and 1960. An ex-fisherman from Godshill in the Isle of Wight, he had later been involved in a shoot-out with the Red Army Fraction in a forest near Hanover. He was demoted from his rank of tank commander when he was caught smuggling seven catering-size tins of coffee and 600 cigarettes into East Berlin. At his trial only two of the tins and 200 of the cigarettes were produced in evidence. He had a girlfriend in East Berlin. He told me lots of stories about blokes going AWOL. Talk to any squaddie in sufficiently relaxed circumstances and you hear stories about men going mad, taking drugs and helicopters for joy-rides, killing for fun and running away for love.

Despite massive evidence to the contrary, most British journalists – the objectivity sales force – still believed they had the best and freest press in the world and were terribly snotty about the Yanks' lack of interest in foreign affairs, to name but one point of international comparison that reflected rather favourably upon ourselves wouldn't you say? Words failed me and I probably failed them.

Walking to the officers' mess, I quizzed Julian about what kind of journalism he intended writing when he left the regiment.

'Of course it's very tempting to use your experiences in the army and write about that,' he said, raising his eyebrows, indicating we were still being tailed by PRO David. 'There's so much scope, I can tell you.'

I know, I said, trying to encourage him in this project.

'But I don't know.' He shook his head. 'I think it would be disloyal, somehow.'

This was also how things were kept secret in England.

The officers were reading *The Daily Mail*, *The Sun* and *The Telegraph*. They drank strong tea from china cups. Some also ate toast spattered with raspberry jam and fresh cream. Hung on the wall was an oil painting of the Battle of Culloden. The regiment was commended at Waterloo, Julian said. Engraved silver cups and shields were displayed in glass-fronted cabinets. Sitting alone, not reading any newspaper, was a black officer from the US Army, he must have been about six-foot-four. No one made any attempt at conversation with him. The English officers were all white. Julian said he had a great view of Spandau Prison from the window of his room. I said I would like to see it. We told PRO David we wouldn't be long. Fine, he said.

Julian led the way up a broad spiral staircase, his boots clip-clopping on the stone. His room, on the top floor, was large and untidy, strewn about with clothes and books. Lying on the carpet was an LP of military music. British Grenadiers marched in red tunics on its cover.

'This is the best view of the prison you'll find anywhere in Spandau,' he said proudly, standing at the latticed window.

Beyond the Go-Go Grill and a garage called K. and Z. Werkstatt was the gloomy Gothic prison housing its single symbolic Nazi, its red bricks the colour of dull red wine.

'Hess's cell is behind those trees on the other side of the jail,' Julian said, pointing. 'The guards aren't allowed to talk to him. Sometimes you can see the old rascal walking in the garden.'

Looking bored, French guards promenaded the walkway connecting three green watchtowers behind the red prison wall. Next month Hess would be guarded by Americans, then the Brits, the following month the Russians, and so on and so on until the scapegoat was dead.

'At the end of each picket duty the army in question puts on a big dinner and officers from all the allied armies get invited,' Julian said. 'The French dinner is the one everyone tries to get an invite to. But the Russian one is okay too: caviar and Russian champagne.'

Spandau was a German army military prison in the 1880s, mainly for political prisoners and Jews. It was good, Julian said, and satisfying, this continual reminder of history through the window.

'It's so close,' he said softly. 'When the Russians are on picket duty you can hear the watch calling out to each other on the hour, 12 o'clock and all's well kind of thing in Russian, the cupped shout passing all around the prison.'

This was a traditional form of watch-duty evidently approved of by Julian, who spoke with odd affection of the Red Army, as if it was one of the last great armies, accorded proper respect in its country, a sleek force with a strong sense of purpose and decent pride in its traditions. He stood silent by the window. The shadows had lengthened and the sky was a more fragile blue.

I could now understand some of the excitement Julian felt in his early days in uniform at Smuts Barracks. Everyone in their own way was captivated at one time or another by the thrill of the past. Some feeling for history was the closest many of us got to the feelings others had in church. Soldiering was Julian's handle on the past.

'You get a good mist in the winter,' he said. 'Then it's really creepy.'

'The ghosts of prisoners past?'

'Yes.'

I shook hands with Julian, told him to be sure to contact me if he thought I could help him with his journalistic career, contacts and stuff. He never rang.

PRO David gave me a lift to a junction where he said I could get a bus back into town. When the bus finally arrived, after a thirty-minute wait, it was bound for Wannsee. *Wannsee?* What the hell. I liked travelling around. I sat on the top deck by the front window, kerbside, green boughs slapping against that window as the bus negotiated the narrow country lanes. I remembered boughs slapping excitingly against windows when my grand-mother took me to the seaside in a bus one time. I wondered again how I was going to organise all this material. An odyssey through the two Berlins and the fractured state of my own consciousness? *Berlin has meant a great deal to you*, Johnny once said. *You must explain why*. How am I doing, Johnny?

16 Here's Johnny!

My name is Johnny. In East Berlin John was prounced Yoan so I always insisted on being put down in the school register as Johnny. Johnny Weissmuller was playing in *Tarzan* at the time. People could handle Johnny better.

I am trying to imagine what a western audience would see as the highlights of my life. That I was a minor pop star in the sixties? That I met Paul Robeson when I was ten years old? My father was acting as his translator. I have a photograph showing me standing next to Paul Robeson. He was a big man. I didn't even come up to his waist.

Usually when I meet people at London parties and say I grew up in East Berlin they feign interest – how *fascinating*! – but look somehow panicked and don't really know what to say next. Their eyes wander. If I had grown up in New York City, or really anywhere in the west, the next questions would flow with routine ease. Where in the city had I lived? What was my job? How long had I been in London? Did I miss my family and friends? But I come from East Berlin and no one knows what to say next.

I was born in Vienna and came to East Berlin with my mother and father, Florence and Georg, when I was two and a half. I am thirty-six now, working in London as an architect. Officially, I am still married to Juliana, who has been travelling the world for the last five or six years as the manager of Nina Hagen. Some of my friends said it was only a passport marriage. Juliana wanted to get out of East Berlin. We went first to Vienna and later to

London. I suppose I am still in love with Juliana, but that's the way it goes. Time heals the wounds up to a point, but there remains a kind of melancholy. My own mother never really recovered from a love-affair she had with a hard-living Welsh journalist who died in tragic circumstances when he was thirty-odd and Florence was in her early twenties. (Since my teenage years I have known my mother and father as Florence and Georg.) I am in fact named after this Welsh journalist.

In London during the war Georg worked for the Communist Party. He was a cultural officer at the Austrian Centre, which was a Communist Party front. He went back to Vienna in 1946. The Red Army was still stationed there and it looked for a while as if the communists would help form the government. But their influence waned, they did badly at the first elections and, as a known communist, Georg had no prospects of getting a job in Austria. That's when his invitation came from East Berlin, where suddenly he was an important person. Florence wasn't, which was a problem.

Florence was shocked by the conditions she found in East Berlin. It was still a completely ruined city. Later she told me about the first day we arrived, standing in a crowded S-Bahn during the rush hour. I was at my mother's feet, crying, and she didn't know what to do. There wasn't even enough space for her to bend down and pick me up. She looked all round the carriage, hoping for some help, and all she could see was this sea of grim faces.

In those first weeks Georg spent his days walking round the ruins looking for a building he could convert into the conservatoire he was supposed to be establishing. I remember him coming home at night with his trousers covered in dust. Florence was stuck at home with me, not speaking the language. Must have been pretty miserable. We were staying in a small flat in Schöneweide.

Meanwhile, they were building the settlement in Grünau to which we moved in 1952. All the neighbours were writers, artists, actors, or else they were directors of factories. Florence became friendly with an American woman named Edith whose husband was director of one of the big publishing houses. Both Florence and Edith worked for the International Women's Congress. They went to the conferences as interpreters. Florence also got a job as a translator for ADN, the East German news agency. Later she worked for Radio Berlin International. She also did editing and proof-reading for Seven Seas Books, the English-language publishing house run by Stefan Heym's wife.

I went to kindergarten, learned how to sew and cook. We played instruments too. I have fond memories of it. I learned how to read and write there. At the first school I went to I was the fastest runner and the tallest, those were the two most important facts. I was a member of the Young Pioneers, the Party equivalent of the wolf cubs. I wore my blue Young Pioneers scarf to school, I was very proud of it. I remember my father when I was six, taking me to be registered at the school. The director asked if I wanted to attend religious lessons (which didn't take place at the school, incidentally, but at a nearby church). Georg, in his liberal way, asked me if I wanted to attend these religion classes. I was outraged that he should even ask such a reactionary question. I think about 90 per cent of the kids were members of the Young Pioneers. If you weren't a member it was quite clear your parents belonged to the old bourgeoisie.

One afternoon a week the Young Pioneers met to sing songs and go for walks and cycle rides. We also had summer camps. At one of these I learned to shoot, with an air-gun. I was fourteen by then. I used to like going to Pioneer's Park, which was just a few stops away on the S-Bahn. They had a great miniature railway, sports grounds, theatre and concert halls, all for the children. A white shirt and a blue scarf, that was the Pioneers' uniform. I can also remember clearing the ruins of central Grünau, opposite the post office, cleaning the bricks and piling them up. My parents also took part in that. Another major activity of the Young Pioneers was collecting old bits of metal, paper and wool on house-to-house collections, also bottles. You delivered them to the Young Pioneers headquarters and got a little stamp you stuck in a book and then you'd be proud of how many stamps you'd collected. You also got a little stamp for each hour you worked on the ruins.

Sometimes I went to the centre of Berlin to pick up my mother from work. I travelled up on the S-Bahn and met her outside ADN. Sometimes we went to the opera. The old Comic Opera had somehow survived the bombs and was still in its original building. But the Alexanderplatz was in ruins. At the station in the A-platz you had to go through underground tunnels past all these heaps of rubble in order to get on the S-Bahn. The Stalinallee was in the process of being built. Maybe I wanted to be an architect because I had grown up with all these ruins round me.

I also used to love these building games that you could get. Made of compressed dust, the bricks were like a GDR version of Lego. I was only child and maybe a bit spoilt, so I got loads of these bricks. I built entire towns. I always wanted to be an architect.

My parents named me Martin John, thinking Martin was a name that could be used in both English and German, but I always hated Martin and, anyway, I was always proud of being a foreigner, being different, I didn't want to hide it. I had one enemy at my high school, where I went when I was ten. This enemy was the son of the vicar. He had blond hair. Half the class were behind me and the other half were behind this vicar's son. It got so bad I went home in the evenings and did press-ups to build up my muscles for the big fight I felt sure was coming. There was never an actual fight, but there were plenty of other incidents. The one I remember most vividly is this vicar's son standing up in class and saying, why was it that the Jews were always favoured, why did they always get the best deal? While he said it, he was looking at me and I didn't really know why. Georg was Jewish, but he had never once talked about it and I was only very vaguely aware of it. His being Jewish was of no significance to Georg. He was a communist and an atheist and that was all that counted.

Once I asked Georg what he had done in the war, why he hadn't been in the army. He said it was because he had a bad heart. He never went into it in any way and, to this day, he still insists that being Jewish is of no consequence to him. Quite a few of the Jews in Germany and Austria before the war had become Christians. The ones who came to England from Poland and Russia at the turn of the century were quite different. Even if they were atheists they still might do the Friday night candles routine or hold a barmitzvah for their son, whatever, but a large percentage of bourgeois intellectual Jews in Germany and Austria completely ignored all that. For the Jewish intelligentsia in Berlin in the twenties and thirties, being Jewish meant nothing to them. Quite a lot had served in the First World War and considered themselves to be good Germans. My father belonged to that kind of tradition.

Anyway, after what the vicar's son had said at school, I went back to my father and asked him: 'What is this Jewish thing?'

Georg explained and, from that time on, I started noticing things. I noticed that when kids were shouting and fooling around on a tram, some people would say, 'It's just like a Jew's school.'

In those days East Germany was still full of reactionary anti-semitic bastards. One of our teachers, a guy of maybe sixty, told us about his war exploits with pride. I remember him telling us what a fantastic time he had in Italy. He was a real old Nazi. He would describe us as strong young oaks that would one day grow up to be fine Germans. He would invite us to his house and show us photographs and cuddle the little girls on his sofa. I started going to school in 1956, just eleven years after the war. How could they have eliminated all the Nazis from the professions?

My best friend at high school was called Christoph. He was the son of a famous German actor who also lived in Grünau. One of the GDR's first film stars, he died when I was sixteen. He had a younger, beautiful wife. She liked me and I got on with her. I called her Inge and *du*, whereas Christoph called my mother Frau Karger and *sie*. He had an unusual name, Christoph, very arty. The family was very trendy. Christoph's marks actually weren't good enough for him to get into the Oberschule, but his mother made a big fuss and he was allowed to go. Only about 15 per cent went to the Oberschule. In the class book at the junior school there was another column after our names where it said either A for *Arbeiter* or I for *Intelligenz*. The idea was a kind of positive discrimination in favour of working-class children. Christoph's marks weren't good enough and, also, he was the son of the intellectual class. But his mother could make a fuss precisely *because* Christoph was the son of a famous actor. I later discovered that I was guaranteed a place both at the Oberschule and also at the university of my choice, a special privilege granted to former exiles from Nazism like Georg.

Like a lot of middle-class families in England in those days, I suppose, we never had television. I had one friend at school whose father was the caretaker at one of the sports clubs on the waterfront at Grünau. The family lived in a little flat attached to the sports club. I used to go there and watch television. We only watched programmes broadcast by West German TV. I became intrigued by it and went there more and more, although my parents disapproved. In the early evening, before the news, six to half six, they had this programme which consisted of adverts with snippets of cartoons in between. That was the real favourite in East Berlin. Everyone loved watching the western adverts. That guy was my first working-class friend. All my other friends were sons and daughters of my parents' friends.

I went to England with my mother before I ever went to West Berlin. I was a good communist and, politically, it was not the done thing to go to West Berlin, although of course it was quite easy to go before the Wall was built. When I was about eleven I remember kids started walking round with transistor radios that had pictures of Elvis stuck to them. I didn't get into pop music until a couple of years later. I was still a political snob, an intellectual who went to the opera with his parents rather than listening to Elvis on the western radio stations.

I flew to London with my mother for the first time in 1958 in a Polish airliner. I was very impressed by London. I loved the cars. The people seemed okay too. After a couple of days we went to visit my Aunt Mavis and Uncle Jack in Thetford. Jack was Florence's favourite brother. He sold vegetables off the back of a lorry for years and eventually saved up enough money to rent this general store. I loved working in the shop. I used to help myself to the sweets. The school bus left from just outside the shop and, at certain times, the shop was full of all these English schoolchildren who I found quite intriguing. They used to take the piss out of my English accent, which was not too good in those days. I was completely bilingual when I was three or four, but then my mother had TB and had to go to a sanatorium in the southern part of East Germany. She was there nine months and I forgot all my English. It wasn't until I was fourteen or fifteen I made a conscious effort to improve it.

I went to West Berlin for the first time about a year later when I was thirteen. I was completely astounded. It was just like London and right on my doorstep. All it meant was getting on the S-Bahn and not getting off at the last stop. Just going on one more stop. Most of my schoolmates had already done it. I went with Christoph. We didn't have much western currency, just a few marks. All we bought were some black-and-white chequered decals for our bicycles.

It was a big secret. I couldn't tell my parents about the visit or show them the decals, nor could Christoph. Both our parents were in the Party and in those days it was frowned upon to even watch western television. We got told at school we shouldn't watch the western telly. People would notice if your aerial was directed in such a way it could receive the western stations. I had a really bad conscience about going to West Berlin.

Later that year I went to England again with Florence. In London we stayed at a huge villa in Potters Bar where some friends of Florence lived: a Norwegian diplomat, his wife and their son, David, who was my age. I remember being aware that the parents were communists doing sensitive work. Florence had warned me on the aeroplane not to talk about politics with David. She said he didn't know anything about his parents' views. So David, to my eyes, was a real naive kid: he just didn't know what communism was. He was mainly interested in toy pistols and Dinky cars.

The day the Wall was built I was in England. After a week in Potters Bar we had gone to Thetford where I worked in Uncle Jack's shop again, selling sweets. I had been reading stories in the newspapers about streams of refugees leaving East Berlin and I was convinced that when I got home my classroom would be empty. One boy in my class belonged to a family that ran a shop in West Berlin. I was sure that he, at least, would be gone. I was quite influenced by the propaganda in the English newspapers, where I read about the building of the Wall one Sunday. To be honest, I wasn't really that surprised and it didn't mean that much to me personally, apart from the worries about my schoolmates. I had strong memories of the smugglers crossing the border on the S-Bahn. It was always quite a significant moment when the train stopped at Friedrichstrasse. About 80 per cent of the people in the carriages got off at Friedrichstrasse and those that stayed behind always looked embarrassed, avoided catching anyone's eye. Often those who stayed on the train, to go a few stops further to Zoo Station, had big bags loaded up with stuff. People stuffed things under their coats, too. Meat, eggs and butter were the main things they took to sell in the west.

So I didn't see the building of the Wall as a tragedy or anything like that. I didn't have any sympathy with the smugglers. And when I got back to Grünau nothing had happened. No one had left, not even the boy whose family ran a shop in West Berlin. The boy never talked about it and I never found out what happened to the shop.

I suppose I must have boasted about these trips to England when I got back to East Berlin and I suppose some people must have resented my privileges. My parents had insisted on me having an Austrian passport because of their fear that their position in East Berlin was only temporary.

We never had net curtains on our windows and friends always used to ask me about that. My mother used to say we weren't really settled here, we just moved here temporarily. I think it was just an excuse, she hated net curtains, but it was probably also true that she didn't want to settle down permanently in East Berlin. She got terribly homesick. Anyway, I always loved my passport. It was very important to me, one of my most treasured possessions.

I got involved in the band during my second year at Oberschule in Köpenick. The band was called Team 4. One of my friends at the Oberschule was this boy called Thomas whose father was one of the top light music composers in the country. He lived in one of the big villas built in the thirties for industrialists. The place was called Wendenschloss, the other side of the river from Grünau. This friend's villa had a big garden and his father had a huge sound-proofed study with double padded doors and beautiful bookcases. A bit *nouveau riche*, you know, but he'd really made it. The son, Thomas, was also very musical and, as I said, we became friends. In the second year at school there was a youth festival and we heard this band from Czechoslovakia. (This was 1963, the Beatles had their first hit.) We thought, well, we can do that. There was another boy in the class we persuaded to become the drummer. I was taking guitar lessons and Thomas was quite good on the piano and guitar. Thomas had another friend, they'd written poetry and songs together. This other friend became quite a famous poet. He was a complete reactionary but somehow made this career as a progressive poet and now is one of the top functionaries in the Free German Youth movement. He's run to fat, someone sent me a photograph of him the other day. Anyway, we just borrowed instruments and started to play. Later Thomas's father gave us some money to buy Czech guitars and I got some strings in London. We used the sound-proof study. We tried to imitate the Beatles. We really worked hard at getting that sound right, the jangly guitar sound, and we tried to shout like Lennon and McCartney. We also wrote our own songs. Mostly we sang in English but there were a couple of numbers we did in German. We made two records, I've still got the singles at home in London.

This all happened at the time when the state discovered there was such a thing as youth culture, that you couldn't give fifteen-year-olds the same kind of music and theatre as you could thirty-year-olds. So there was the first programme on television for teenagers. And they played a Beatles record. Maybe it was 'She Loves You', one of the first Beatles records issued in East Berlin. They showed it on the programme with flashes of photographs and stuff. We wrote this letter to the programme, saying, 'We may not be as good as the Beatles, but at least *we* are from the GDR. And why don't you put us on your programme?'

So they did. We had to perform first in front of this editor who didn't like our own songs at all and advised us to do the cover versions. By this time we did lots of Stones covers: 'You'd Better Move On', 'Play With Fire', 'Get Off My Cloud', 'Satisfaction'. It was the time of the 'Rubber Soul' LP and we also did 'Baby You Can Drive My Car'. So this editor tells us we can do two covers, but the embarrassing thing is, well, at this time too the GDR was making films about cowboys and Indians. Of course they were progressive and everything, more true to the facts, they'd studied the American-Indian culture and all the rest of it, but they were previewing one of these films on the programme and we had to sing our first song right after the preview. *So they dressed us up as Red Indians.*

With the help of Thomas's father we made two singles. And we played in FDJ (Free German Youth) club houses. Five years later there were some bands that became quite famous in the GDR, but in those days there was no one like that. We played at a youth festival in Karl Marx Stadt on an open-air stage and we played school carnivals. At the festival in Karl Marx Stadt I met the first love of my life, Tatiana. She was into western folk music, American progressive, protest songs, Dylan, that kind of thing. There was a Canadian singer called Perry Friedman who played the banjo. He organised a club in a small room above a Berlin cinema and about fifty people went there once a week.

There wasn't a hit parade in those days, but our songs were played on the radio a few times. At our high school we had to do a proper apprenticeship for two months in every year. We could choose which factory or trade we worked in. Because I wanted to become an architect I insisted on becoming a bricklayer. The problem was you always damaged your hands laying bricks and you weren't allowed to wear gloves. Too cissy. You had to wear wooden clogs and white pyjama suits, but I had to be really careful not to damage my long finger nails and the foreman was really contemptuous of that. Then one lunch break, one of my songs was on the radio. The foreman was *very* impressed. After that he stopped teasing me about my finger nails.

I left the band when I went away to college at Weimar, but the others carried on, found a new bass guitarist. They had to change our old name because Team was considered too English. They became one of the top ten bands in the GDR.

The summer before starting at college we had to build cow-sheds in a little village near East Berlin. We went to Weimar in October and were given beds in dormitories, eight to a room, terrible, I was determined not to stay there for long. But that's where I met Tommy. When I came into this dormitory he was lying in bed smoking a cigarette. It turned out he remembered me from the entrance examinations. He remembered I hadn't cut my hair whereas he had. We became instant friends.

In Weimar in 1966 we didn't know very much about Rudi Dutschke, the student revolutionaries or Kommune 1 and 2. We didn't have television and were quite unaware of the things happening in West Berlin. The only politics we had had was really dogmatic Marxism, the lessons we'd had throughout school. Right from the beginning we'd had classes called Citizens' Knowledge, which was mainly about politics. Later we were taught Marxism and the history of the working class, but it was all taught by *non*-Marxists. They were teachers who just repeated what they'd read, so our understanding of politics was really quite superficial. We knew nothing about Trotsky. We had no context to put the student revolution in. To us, the students in West Berlin were just being disobedient, irreverent. We didn't understand what it actually meant.

For us Czechoslovakia was more important than the West Berlin student movement. None of my friends were unaffected by Dubcek. We all instinctively felt that he represented something important and progressive. Obviously we'd all started to have our doubts about the way the state operated and there was the revelation: the Prague spring. That was our main political experience of those years.

I was in Italy at the time of the invasion of Czechoslovakia, hitch-hiking with an English friend. Sitting in some market square, we saw the newspaper vendors, it was a special edition. I felt confused and angry. Perugia, that was the name of the town. I went along to some CP meetings there. Some peasants turned up and there were some lively discussions, which made me feel a bit better.

Instead of going straight back to Berlin as planned, I went to Vienna to meet an old friend of my father's, Walter Hollitscher, a Marxist scientist whose main work was popularising, through his writing, the scientific view of the world from a Marxist position. Unfortunately he has remained an old Stalinist, my parents have since quarrelled with him, but he was someone I wanted to talk to. From Vienna I took the train through Czechoslovakia to Berlin. I saw the tanks round Prague. I stayed on the train.

One of the first things that happened at college was everyone was supposed to sign a statement supporting the invasion. I talked to a few friends before we were called into this meeting and we agreed we'd ask questions and start up a discussion. In the end our entire seminar group of about twenty-five people never signed the statement. The authorities gave up, it was just too awkward. Also they were worried about the student movement in West Berlin. After one particularly large demonstration in West Berlin a few Party members in my seminar group were called out during a seminar. Afterwards one of them told me the authorities had been warned there might be an influence on GDR students from West Germany and that Party members should be alert and report anything that went on. In 1969 they decided to reform the college, to restructure everything. We had open sessions where we discussed the way the course was run. One day I went to the refectory and there was a poster on the noticeboard advertising a meeting to discuss the formation of a socialist student organisation separate from the FDJ. Everybody thought it was a brilliant idea and I remember some teachers supporting it too, but within a day it was forbidden by the Party. You can't break up the FDJ, you know, this is the unified socialist youth organisation, blah-blah. But the first meeting took place and the guy who gave the main speech was chucked out of college.

I was able to go to West Berlin when I was back in Grünau for the holidays, so I was able to keep in closer touch with the western student movement. Sometimes I bought *Konkret*, the magazine Ulrike Meinhof used to work for, which was an odd combination of Marxism and pornography. There was very strict control whenever I came back through the border. A few times they caught me with *Konkret* and confiscated it, but I was a passionate architecture student. The books I bought in the west were mostly about architecture.

I was one of the main sources for records too. I can still remember buying the first Captain Beefheart LP. We had a nice student club in Weimar that was run independently of the FDJ. It was in a corner tower of the old city walls, five-foot-thick walls they were. In the basement we had a circular bar and above that the dance hall. On the next floor we had another bar and a lecture room. We painted the dance hall with abstract murals. By this time I was living with three other students in a squat, a semi-ruin which had one tap and a toilet in the yard.

I came back to Berlin in 1972 and it took me a few months to find a job. I met Juliana through a gay friend of mine called Eduardo. She had this flat in the centre of town which belonged to her mother. She was working as an interpreter and earning loads of money. She wanted to study film but for various reasons, the most important of which had been her involvement in a pro-Dubcek solidarity group in East Berlin, she was unable to. She was really pissed off, but earned a hell of a lot of money. We didn't know what to do with all the money, so we ate in the best restaurants, Ganymed and the restaurant on the top floor of Hotel Stadt Berlin. That was such a snobbish place. I remember a waiter asking somebody whether he wanted his fish flambéed in French cognac or German Weinbrand.

I immediately moved in with Juliana, despite the protestations of her mother. I married Juliana on April Fool's Day 1973. We were late for our 10.30 appointment at the registry office. We didn't have any witnesses and we didn't have a ring either, but we got someone from the waiting room to be our witness. It was a Saturday. We didn't tell anyone about the wedding. Afterwards we went to my parents' place and giggled a lot, but didn't tell them anything. Later Florence told me she guessed something like that had happened.

I had been working for almost a year as an architect in East Berlin, a team of ten involved in the renovation of Prenzlauer-berg. We were all straight out of college and our boss couldn't handle us, so we spent months and months just messing around. Each architect was responsible for one tenement block of twenty flats. There were loads of cock-ups. We designed the kitchens and bathrooms around units that were supposed to arrive from Czechoslovakia by train, but the units never came and the plans were scrapped. I remember spending days and days without any work to do. Juliana and I left for Vienna two months after our marriage, at the beginning of the summer.

Vienna had a film school where Juliana was keen to study and I had some connections at the town planning department, where I managed to find a job. Juliana had to sit the entry exams for film college the day after we arrived. She also got a job as assistant to a director who was making TV commercials.

Towards the end of our time in Vienna I got a letter calling me up for military service in Austria. I wrote back saying that my primary residence was East Berlin, that I was only in Vienna temporarily. They wrote back saying, *so what*? You still have to present yourself at this time and place for interview and medical examination. So for the last two weeks in Vienna I went underground. I left our apartment and stayed with a friend. I was shit-scared. We drove from Vienna to Stuttgart, where we stayed the night with a former lecturer of mine. We had all our possessions in the back of the car, including a dog called Shushka who had to be put in quarantine at Dover.

We arrived in London on 1 October 1974. Juliana got a place at the London Film School and I found work at Solon, the architects' co-op in south London. At first we stayed with two people from East Berlin and later with a Canadian couple in Clapham, a place advertised in *Time Out*. After a year I was offered a flat on the top floor of Juniper House, a five-storey walk-up block in Peckham that had been turned into a tenants' co-op. As far as my marriage was concerned, it was the beginning of the end. Juliana soon went her own way and I was left with the dog, Shushka, the most intelligent and rational dog I have ever come across. He would disappear for nights on end, presumably engaged in some kind of sexual activity, and then return to my front door on the fifth floor where he would bark just once, economically, like he was ringing the bell. It was Juliana who had really loved the dog, but after she left I took care of him for obvious and sentimental reasons.

Sometime later I met Ian in the squat on Drummond Street which was the office of *The Leveller*. He was the magazine's only full-time worker. I wrote a couple of things, but mainly I used to help out on the design side, doing layouts and stuff. Ian and I shared interests in politics and pop music and films, the usual things, but really we aren't very similar, as I found out most dramatically when he lived in my flat for a few months. He was useless round the house and he never lifted up the toilet seat when he was taking a piss. The final straw was that time him and one of his drunken friends got so wrecked they smashed up my JVC record-deck at about five in the morning, accidentally of course, nothing much ever happened to Ian on purpose, or so he liked people to think. To be honest I always felt kind of paternal about him. I think I once admitted to him that I like to play that part. I like surrounding myself with people who are more chaotic than myself, Juliana came into that category too.

I loved it when Ian started going to Berlin and meeting my friends, east and west. It was a kind of link between my lives, the German and the English, the communist and the capitalist. Things seemed less separate, less accidental. When he said he was going to write a book about Berlin, I liked that idea too. People in England really are so ignorant about eastern Europe, almost everyone here is a child of the cold war, and I knew Ian would do his best to break down the prejudices. But more than that, I liked the idea of a friend writing about myself, my family, my friends. Partly through him I realised that what had happened in my life was of some interest. It meant something. I often went with him on his Berlin trips. I had more adventures that way.

I've been in London almost ten years. God, how time flies! Ian once said that by living first in Vienna then in London (after I had left East Berlin) I was retracing the family steps, familiarising myself with the cities where my parents had separately spent their formative years, till they were brought together in London as a result of Nazism and the war and my mother's romance with the Welshman I was named after. But I don't know about all that. I can't speak with authority of my own subconscious and I've never been in analysis, though I've noticed it's becoming more fashionable in London now, getting as bad as New York, where I also have a few friends. That's one advantage of having parents who led nomadic lives. You have friends and contacts all over the place.

I still go back to Berlin at least once a year, to see my parents and friends, to remember certain things. I don't think I ever felt at home anywhere.

17 *The birthday party*

Laura drew two androgynous people, thin and bald, wearing square glasses, smoking slim cigarettes, sparse tufts of hair at their armpits. These drawings were turned into party invitations at Andreas's design studio. Laura, Ulrike and Uschi did the shopping and cooking. Uli, the taxi driver wanted by the police, helped Andreas clear out the basement and fix up ambient lighting. The owner of the Saint Bernard that was a great favourite with Charlotte, he brought along his disco equipment and spent all day installing it. We hardly knew him, I think he must have fancied Laura or Ulrike, maybe both of them. Al and Mark Reeder each made a party tape. Al's was soul, Mark's hi-energy. Al and I went to Friedrichstrasse for the booze, buying as much GDR vodka and Russian champagne as we could carry on the smugglers' express back to the west. Looking back, Laura's party was the last great collective action undertaken by the Mittenwalderstrasse household. Everyone did their bit.

Everyone came, too, apart from Johnny, who had gone back to London by now. There was a big contingent of East German émigrés. Pint brought Sonia, his girlfriend. Astrid, who was still working as a cinema usherette for DM 12 an hour and taking photographs of skulls in bizarre locations, she came along with her boyfriend, Pius, an architect who had been a contemporary of Johnny's at Weimar. Pius's flatmate, Hans, he was there too. Pius and Hans had met on the Praktika camera production line of an East German prison. Hans was a theoretical physicist. He told me something about a new job he had got, he had left his lectureship at the Free University of Berlin and was now working for some upmarket environmental group specialising in alternative energy or something, I didn't quite catch it, the music was so loud. Tutu, the most glamorous of the East German expats, arrived dressed like a sixties cover girl with her pretty teenage boyfriend, who was affecting the new romantic mode, a trifle demodé, as I bitchily remarked to a few people. Tutu's career as a fashion designer was going from strength to strength, the way she told it. She was spending a lot of time in Manhattan. Tutu had once been in love with Tommy, the one who stayed behind, who knew all these people and would have loved to come, I thought a few times during the course of the chaotic night, trying to see the party through his eyes.

Al was wearing the blue short-sleeved Free German Youth shirt he had bought on Frankfurter Allee that day in East Berlin. The joke went down well with the GDR émigrés, although it was lost on most of the other guests, especially the BMW-driving dope-dealer who once boasted to me that he had never visited East Berlin in all his seven years in West Berlin. Ulrike was making eyes at him periodically. She had given up on Pint. She couldn't understand what he saw in that awful fat-arsed floosie Sonia, she whispered drunkenly in my ear sometime after midnight. She said she had overheard Sonia saying something which confirmed Ulrike's thorough dislike of the woman. Sonia had allegedly said, 'And to think, I once licked that guy's arsehole!'

Both of Uschi's current boyfriends came, the father of her nascent baby, the ex-butcher's boy who drove the beaten-up white Mercedes and had a kind of grown-out skinhead haircut that made him look quite tough, and the other one who was much younger, druggier and sweeter and gave Laura a Michael Jackson cassette as a present, except he was so embarrassed he gave it to me instead. 'For your honey,' he said in English.

Mark Reeder was wearing his demob suit again. I think he realised some of us felt uneasy about his uniforms. Well, personally it didn't bother me, he was a friend, but I knew others would immediately think he was fascist had he worn one of the uniforms. He brought with him four or five teenage beauties, fellow regulars at the Metropol on Saturday nights. The 37th in line to the throne never made it, but I was pleased to see that the gay barman at the Backstage, the one who always wore psychedelic shirts and flared trousers, had somehow got to hear about the party. He spent the whole night on the dancefloor, his anti-fashion statement puzzling the more orthodox hipsters, who debated whether the flared trousers were being worn by accident or design. If it was accidental it was just sloppy, no excuse. If it was deliberate, if he had *thought* about the consequences of such a controversial action, it was okay, cool even. Maybe flared trousers were on the way back, they concluded. Everything came back in time.

The other mainstays of the dancefloor were George's mates from Sri Lanka, about a dozen of them, who danced enthusiastically throughout the ugly cacophony of rap, hip-hop and funk that was monopolising the turntable, never less than one track playing at the same time.

'It's like they just discovered mixing yesterday,' Mark Reeder said scornfully. And it was true, West Germans tried so hard to be hip it was painful at times. They still had this idea that newest was hippest, that the march of fashion was inexorable, scientific, as the march of Progress generally. The music had been hijacked, that was the problem, by three high-tech trendies I had never seen before, sitting at a battery of tape and record decks wearing headphones. It was an occupational hazard of party-throwing. Every now and again Al and I stormed into this high-tech zone demanding 'Stoned Love' or 'I Second That Emotion' and these guys said, sure, no problem, the track after next, I like that too, but the rap continued unabated, the jack-in-the-box laments of New York street-life.

It was definitely the worst feature of an otherwise excellent party, Al and I decided, drinking GDR vodka like Tizer and fantasising about the Motown tracks we would most like to hear, *right now*. I said 'I Can't Help Myself' by the Four Tops. Al insisted on 'Stoned Love' and I began to think the track held some sentimental significance for him.

Laura of course was loving every minute of it. She didn't have such set ideas about music. She was wearing the black cocktail

dress that had once belonged to her mother. The heart-shaped
stain had been removed at the dry cleaner's. She wore a white silk
bow in her burnished brown hair. I didn't spend much time
talking to her. That's another thing that happens at parties.
Spouses go their own ways. Also, it was her birthday and she had
to be the circulating hostess. In reality, I knew more people there
than she did, so I had to do a certain amount of polite circulation
too, at least while I was still relatively sober and conscientious.
Laura had been given enough flowers to open a funeral parlour. I
was happy for her. She would remember this party all her life,
even though she might not have realised that just at the minute.

Parties were punctuation marks making chronological sense of
the grey slabs of prose. Parties were memory-makers. No matter
how drunk you got you could always remember some of the
people who were there, what they were wearing, a few of the
tracks played, a few of the more outrageous indiscretions, some
amusing remarks, some people who met for the first time that
night and fell in love, some others who finally fell out of love that
night. Parties crystallised the moment. You could remember
more or less how old you were, how much money you had, the
state of mind you were in. However horrible parties were at the
time, they came in handy afterwards. I had been to more parties
than Laura and I was beginning to be able to see my life as a series
of chapters decorated with different kinds of parties, a continuum
of music and ideas and drink and love, clothes and confessions,
being happy and feeling sick.

Murat was wearing the cloth cap which I subsequently realised
from the films of Guney was standard garb for the Turkish
worker. He got very drunk and tried to engage people in
conversation about the spiritual malaise of German capitalism.
Murat, as always, wore flares, but that was okay, the fashion
snobs decreed, because he was third-world. It was an authentic
detail, dovetailing with the cloth cap, the shiny red shirt with
huge lapels, the black moustache, the mystic eyes. I wondered
what kind of music Murat would play at his own parties, if he
ever lived in a room big enough for a party.

In respect of the number of personnel and the merry-making
graph, the party peaked around two, when there were about 70

people dancing, 40 or 50 talking around the dancefloor and another 30 or 40 in the garden. The last of the food was being devoured by people who suddenly realised how pissed they were and thought they ought to take some ballast on board. I always forgot to eat at parties, always the next day blamed my helpless drunkenness the night before on this lack of food. I had spent around £200 on booze and most guests had brought a couple of bottles so there was no danger of the drink running out, which was always the death of parties. I remembered that I had invited Florence and Georg Karger, the two of them of course being free to travel to the west whenever they wished. I think they had been flattered to receive the invitation, but had decided against coming, which was probably just as well. The air was sweet with the tang of marijuana. And, here and there, guests were huddled around tiny mirrors upon which white powders were being chopped and scraped into wispy lines by razor blades, people taking it in turns with rolled-up DM 20 notes, one nostril then the other, passing on the slightly snot-stained cylinder. Florence and Georg would have disapproved. Georg would have been composing speeches about the decadently self-destructive tendencies of western youth for some weeks to come. Florence would have worried that her own son moved in these circles. Drugs was the main reason western parents didn't get invited more often to their children's parties.

At around 3.30 Al and I launched a successful raid against the high-tech trendies and seized control of the music for a blissful twenty-minute interlude of sweet soul sounds, in which Al danced with his eyes closed and I danced with Laura, near Laura anyway, I didn't like dancing permanently facing someone, that kind of possessive dancing much favoured by husbands and cruisers. I also believed that smiling and dancing were separate and distinct activities and felt vaguely ashamed when, one time, I found myself surrounded by the dancing Tamils, who smiled and laughed so unselfconsciously through each number.

The black American DJ who sometimes dropped by for a shower, he was dancing with the woman who gave free aerobics classes to the house once a week or whenever she could make it. The thin man with the goatee beard who played classical guitar in the garden on sunny afternoons when Ulrike was holding court, he was unsuccessfully chatting up one of the teenage beauties who had arrived in the Mark Reeder entourage. Her face was a study in boredom. Soon she would be telling him she had to go to the toilet or the bar. The toilet was better. He could offer to accompany her to the bar.

Ulrike kept rushing by saying I must meet this or that musician or painter, she had told them all about me, etc. but no such introductions were forthcoming and I can't say I was sorry. Ulrike was in her element. She believed in parties. She believed successful parties were a model of what could be achieved in the social struggle against boredom. If she had an ideology at all, it was that life should be one long party. There were worse ideologies.

She looked magnificent, her Berlin bob swept back and glistening with oil, her hour-glass figure subtly exhibited in a green dress that was just loose enough, just tight enough, the seams of her stockings two vertical lines above her black high heels. Ulrike knew she looked magnificent too.

That was one critical difference between her and Laura, between self-knowledge and innocence. Ulrike was secure in her sexiness, but wary of the dangers, streetwise. Laura, in the years to come, was going to feel more and more oppressed by her beauty, slowly realising that most men were talking to her mainly because they wanted to fuck her, till all she could see around her were hypocritical animals, men who said one thing and did another, women who connived in the sickness. She would end up believing everyone was motivated only by money, sex and fame, the holy trinity of glamour. I understood the desperation that was growing inside her. I sympathised with nihilists. I knew why people became junkies, too, it was all so obvious. Ulrike, however, had known all along how dirty the world was. She was therefore better equipped to survive. I remembered talking over some of these matters with Pint.

Sonia came and stood next to us, yawning theatrically. Pint said okay I suppose it's time to go home. I said I'd see him tomorrow. Thomas had invited me to a party in East Berlin and I had invited Pint. He hadn't been to an East Berlin party since trying to escape in 1970. Family get-togethers didn't count. I shook his hand and kissed Sonia's cheek. The party was thinning out.

Two Polish newly-weds were still here, however, plus the brother of the bridegroom. The two brothers had in fact been flirting with Ana, the Peruvian otherwise pursued by magicians, all night long. Ana was wearing the tightest shortest dress on show. Her face was painted like a doll. She had been out in the garden for the last hour with the two Poles. The recent bride was in a state of high dudgeon, I didn't blame her. It augured ill for the union. She was complaining angrily to Ulrike, who tried to soothe her with remarks about the generally despicable behaviour of men at parties, drunken men particularly. Ulrike always knew the right thing to say. Later, too, when it all started getting out of hand, the Poles taking it in turns to neck with Ana in the garden, Ulrike personally intervened, told the brothers they should be ashamed of themselves, and looked daggers at Ana, who actually wasn't aware that one of the men she'd been kissing had a wife in tow. Poor Ana, I had never seen her so lively and sociable before. The evil magicians had been temporarily expiated. The three Poles left the house all screaming at each other.

It was gone four. Someone who went out for cigarettes said you could hear the party clear as a bell outside Gneisenaustrasse U-Bahn station. Anywhere in London someone would have rung the police by now (whether or not the police came depended upon the neighbourhood), but Kreuzberg residents bore such inconveniences philosophically. You had to take the rough with the smooth.

Laura carried all her flowers into the bedroom at 4.30. She was sad to be going home in two days' time. She had a job interview: trainee cameraperson with Thames Television. There was a grain of truth in the lie I told PRO David. I stayed up talking to Al. Laura and I had stopped going to bed at the same time. That was another bad sign. Al and I helped the Saint Bernard owner to dismantle his disco equipment and load it in the van on the street. The sign outside the Karibik nightclub, NETTE GIRLS, was still flashing on and off. We considered going in there for a nightcap, but there was something intimidating about the place. You had to ring a bell and wait for someone to come to the door, which meant you couldn't get out in a hurry either. We talked ourselves out of it. Back in the house, everyone else had gone to bed.

We sat at the kitchen table surrounded by the wreckage of the good times, the usual aftermath of fag-ends in wine glasses, paper plates caked with food, the floor carpeted with bottles and roaches and empty packets of cigarettes, the map-like stains of spilled alcohol, all the usual shit that seemed so sordid in the hungover morning light but was still okay in the drunken grey dawn.

I picked up a cassette at random from the pile on the kitchen sideboard, slotted it into the Hitachi. It was a compilation of Velvet Underground-like guitar bands, a hypnotic dirge rendered even muddier by the age of the cassette. It suited our mood.

'I used to love this kind of thing,' Al said.

'Me too,' I said.

18 Nightshifts

Walking along Bismarckstrasse next morning, I said it was a pity they didn't let people through the border on bicycles. Yes, said Pint. You can go through on cars, motorcycles and mopeds, but not bicycles.

'Don't ask why. That's the rule,' he said, holding up the manic finger. For him most rules had a problematic relation to reason. If you must have rules, make them as daft as possible. What do you want, *sensible* rules? At the border a guard took me into a small room where I had to empty all my pockets. Alarmed by the yellow laminated press card, he checked it said journalist in my passport. The press card was stuck inside an NUJ plastic envelope which I used as a kind of wallet. The guard pulled out all the items in the wallet: two DM 20 notes, two minicab cards from Manchester and one from London, an out-of-date membership card for the Seven Dials Club in Covent Garden, an Islington library card, a ticket to the Red Raggers Christmas Review at Barrow Labour Club starring B.A.R.D. and Loony Left, an £8 cheque payable to myself (non-redeemable as the cheque was over twelve months old), a restaurant bill totalling £43.80 from L'Escargot in Greek Street and a seven-digit telephone number written on the back of a West Berlin bus ticket. None of it meant much to the guard. Some of it didn't mean a great deal to me.

Pint was waiting for me outside Friedrichstrasse. A short distance from the station a policeman carrying two wooden baskets of strawberries dropped one of the baskets. Strawberries scattered across the clean paving stones in a radius of five metres. The cop chased after them on all fours like a child. Oblivious to all the sniggering pedestrians, who took care not to squash underfoot any of the precious fruits, he remained on all fours till every last strawberry was returned to the wooden basket.

Going past the State Library on the Unter den Linden, Pint said he had worked in there once. It was in fact the last job he had before trying to escape to the west. A nice easy-going sort of place, he said. Most of the people who worked there were drop-out intellectuals who had been unable to go to university for one reason or another. Pint had spent most of his working days reading books. He had pleasant enough memories of the library.

Although it was a beautiful day, the open-air section of the Opera Café had been cordoned off. *Don't ask why*! Pint recited, the admonishing finger in the air again.

Inside, a four-piece consisting of violin, electric guitar, xylophone and drums was playing a tune that sounded like it could have been a hit in the twenties or thirties. The musicians wore powder-blue blazers and the expressions of stoic boredom characteristic of musicians providing background noise in restaurants the world over.

'Where can we check our coats?' Pint asked one of the white-coated waiters.

'In the cloakroom,' replied the waiter, the suggestion of a sneer in his mouth.

'So where's the fucking cloakroom?'

The waiter languidly pointed in its general direction. Pint stormed off cursing. Personally, I preferred sulky waiters to sycophantic waiters. I preferred the honest rudeness of Aeroflot air hostesses to the phony bonhomie of American Airlines. Rich people should be grateful enough they can eat in restaurants and travel in aeroplanes. Insisting also on good service was to want the bread buttered on both sides. I put this point to Pint when he returned from the cloakroom.

'Of course,' he said, 'but I know these fucking guys too well.'

The waiter was taking the rap for all the policemen, interrogators, jailers, bureaucrats and time-servers who had prevented Pint from becoming a doctor, forced him into exile and left him feeling out-of-place everywhere, even here, this city where he had grown up, drunk his first beer and tasted his first kiss. Pint swallowed his Weinbrand violently in one.

'Let's get out of here,' he said, springing up from his chair.

I left the waiter 15 per cent.

Mounting the steps of the Deutsche Museum, Pint said he had last been here as a schoolboy on a school trip, those excursions dominated by the strategic desire to sit next to a particular person on the coach home. The Max Beckmann exhibition was on the third floor. This was Max Beckmann's centenary year. The two-faced city was fighting over the artist's memory. Most of his famous paintings were hanging in a rival exhibition in the west, but the Deutsche Museum had still managed to amass a respectable quantity of drawings of drunkards and lechers, whores and hustlers, fat cats and preachers, pained intellectuals and café revolutionaries. Through Beckmann's eyes, the city was nothing but varying textures of shit.

I wondered if Beckmann hated himself, too, for being part of what he loathed, for desiring some of the things craved by the hypocrites he drew.

'Sure,' said Pint. 'Like everyone. But he was an angry man living in hard times.'

After lunch in the self-service at the foot of the Tele-Tower (meatloaf with red cabbage and roast potatoes) we sat in the sun by the water display outside, watching the Saturday afternoon lovers and idlers, the skateboarders and magazine-readers, the punks and skinheads trying to look threatening, the family men trying to keep children happy with ice cream, the western tourists stabbing their fingers on the buttons of Japanese cameras, looking at their exposure numbers to see how many shots they had left, hoping they wouldn't run out of film. Pint remembered walking around this area holding his father's hand when the whole of the city centre was dust and ruins, his father describing what it used to be like before the war.

We talked about the night I had taken out Pint and his father in London. *It's all over with me and the flags.*

His father had returned from a POW camp in the Soviet Union in 1948. My father had sailed the killing fields of the North Sea, delivering supplies to the beleaguered Russians. My father had lost some good friends on those convoys. His father had turned to the church in his later years. We talked about our fathers, walking nowhere in particular. My father was now in the habit of writing letters to his MP and the PM, as he called her, registering his protest at all the terrible things. I said it was a shame we had never managed to arrange a meeting of our fathers. That would have been something, Pint agreed, a kind of private anti-war congress.

I showed Pint the gay barber's shop near the Moses Mendelssohn plaque and the old Jewish cemetery.

'Now you know East Berlin better than I do,' he said.

I was flattered, but it was untrue, I said. He said he couldn't remember where things were any more, and anyway everything had changed so much. All he could remember was the smell of the petrol, the taste of the ice cream, the colours of cars and streets, the sound of trams and trains, he said. He had deliberately blocked out much of the detail, he said. What remained was a kind of vandalised library of the senses.

We had arranged to meet Wolfgang and Sonia, Pint's girlfriend, at Café Trichter. We got there in good time. The same waiter was on duty, the same lugubrious gent wearing the same barathea dinner suit and black bow-tie, striding upright with the glasses of beer held high on the same silver platter. He set two of these beers before us. Was there a flicker of recognition in his stony eyes? I looked hard, but he gave no sign.

Wolfgang swept through the bar in his long black leather overcoat. I introduced him to Pint and the two men shook hands, polite but wary. Sonia was late and Pint began to get agitated in that over-protective way men do. Wolfgang said the party was in Köpenick, Pint's home town. Pint shuddered. His sister lived in Köpenick with her husband, a Party official. Sonia, the painter of pricks, arrived with her apologies and we walked across the dark old bridge over the Spree to Friedrichstrasse, catching a train immediately.

We were in luck tonight, we said.

On the wooden S-Bahn seats Pint and Wolfgang spoke of the new German cinema and asked each other questions about their work. I was looking out the window at a long train of maroon cars. Wolfgang saw me looking and said it was the Moscow Express.

A girl in her late teens or maybe early twenties had her head sticking out of the window, the Moscow Express slowly picking up speed, clanging across the points. It was like the opening scene of a Mills and Boon romance: *her long hair blew across her face like a corn-coloured veil* or something.

She was happy in that undiluted way you can only know when you are young and at the start of an adventure. The low sun showed up the dirt on the maroon cars. Her face shone with anticipation. She was so happy she was waving randomly at strangers, including me. I waved back. My companions were still talking about films. The girl on the train couldn't stop smiling however hard she tried.

I remembered an overnight train from Kiev to Moscow, a beautiful train of wood panels and brass fittings, a party in the compartment, a drunken encounter with a feminist film-maker. The Moscow Express branched off down another track.

I said Moscow's underground system was deep enough to double as a fall-out shelter, so they said. Wolfgang said he loved Moscow. It was a proper metropolis, he said. It had the most beautiful prostitutes in the world. Pint and I looked down at our shoes, Sonia looked curiously at Wolfgang. He was a handsome bastard, no doubt about that. I could have sworn, however, that on a previous occasion Wolfgang had told me he was banned from visiting Moscow on account of his contacts with dissidents.

Passing the Tele-Tower, I said how much I had grown to like the concrete pillar topped with its silver sputnik.

'Really?' Wolfgang said. 'For me it is a monument to the sexual frustration of the Germans.'

The Dom was also ugly, he thought, continuing this commentary upon buildings passing the window.

'Formerly it was more ugly,' I said. 'Some of the frills were left off when the cathedral was restored. I've seen the old photographs.'

'That's right,' Wolfgang said. 'Did I ever tell you the story about the day I saw the flying angel?'

We shook our heads.

'I'd been visiting some friends who lived on the top floor of that modern apartment block on the A-platz. I was sitting at a window, drinking a beer and suddenly this golden angel comes flying past. One second later I realised that the angel was suspended from a wire and was being transported across to the Dom. It was like that bit in Fellini's *Dolce Vita* when Jesus Christ rides over Rome in a helicopter,' Wolfgang said, lighting up a Club. 'A magical moment.'

He smiled the kind of smile we used to call a toothpaste lie. Sonia was charmed, I could see. Pint remained deadpan.

Dusk was falling as we reached Köpenick. It started raining. We walked through the silent town to some riverside cottages built in grey stone. There was some confusion about the precise address and we spent twenty minutes trailing up and down before finding the right cottage. Wolfgang said they had planned to hold the party in the garden, but it looked like the weather was against them, he said.

Rain has never much bothered me. I liked the idea of everyone getting drunk and dancing in the rain in a garden that gave on to the Spree.

The party was being held in honour of a woman shortly to depart the GDR. It was her farewell party. She had married a Dutchman. It was impolite to ask whether she loved the Dutchman or whether she had married him for his passport, but I asked anyway. She smiled, shook her head this way and that: a bit of both, a bit of love and a bit of paper. The Dutchman had returned to Holland. The bride's name was Barbara. She had short dark hair and traces of gold glitter round her eyes. She wore silk stockings and a waisted cotton dress. She was a photographer. She said she hadn't worked for some time in East Berlin. She couldn't face working for newspapers and magazines and she had neither the contacts nor the money to organise exhibitions, she said. Her most recent work had been on the theme of reflections in windows and mirrors. I said East Berlin's profusion of reflected-glass buildings was perfect for such a project. I said you could see the cathedral reflected in the Palace of Culture on a fine day.

I had spoken to Barbara a few times on the telephone. Her

number was given out by Wolfgang. She passed on messages for him. She had sounded nice on the telephone. I imagined she and Wolfgang had once been lovers.

The party was in its self-conscious pre-dancing phase, all the guests congregated in one smallish downstairs room cluttered with china dolls, toy steam trains and racing cars, a 1930s Cigarren sign in swirly yellow script, old matchboxes and cigarette packets, pre-war maps of Berlin and Germany.

'Some years ago this kind of clutter was fashionable in West Berlin too,' Pint whispered, adding that now the vogue was for white walls, empty space, Bauhaus furniture. Sentimental hoarding was out of tune with the cool austerity that chic westerners had decided was the key to the eighties.

This cottage was not the home of the hostess, Barbara. It was rented by a tall graphic designer whose brown hair fell six inches below his shoulders. He had a wide open smile, big white teeth, clear eyes. I wasn't sure whether you could trust a smile like that, so replete with self-confidence. He dabbled in photography in his spare time and was a member of the unofficial peace movement, he said. Recently he had helped organise a protest of 200 cyclists who had just pedalled along together, without flags or placards, without singing or chanting, a silent procession of pacifists from Köpenick which got broken up by police before it reached Berlin.

'You see, even just cycling in large numbers is seen as some kind of threat in our country,' interrupted Wolfgang, always suspiciously keen to underwrite anecdotes with their obvious political conclusion.

I saw the fallen DJ across the crowded room. He came over, shook my hand and said he had been made responsible for the party tapes. He hoped I would find the music to my liking, he said. Fat chance, I thought, saying I would certainly be in the dancing mood after a few more bottles of this most excellent Budweiser from Czechoslovakia. Party talk.

Sonia was amazed, she was telling me. She had never been to a party in East Berlin before.

'What's amazing?' I said.

'Well, it's much more like parties in the west than I expected.'

'What *did* you expect?'

'I don't know. I didn't expect fashionable clothes and loud music. I didn't expect people to be so friendly with strangers from the west, to speak so openly. I don't know.'

Wolfgang was flirting with a young woman in a red mini-skirt. Pint was locked in conversation with an old schoolfriend, someone he hadn't seen in seventeen years. Sonia suggested we went upstairs to the dance room. 'Only In Miami', a salsa number, was followed by Smokey Robinson's 'Tears of a Clown' and 'Two Tribes' by Frankie Goes to Hollywood, the hit of the summer in both Berlins. The fallen DJ hadn't done such a bad job.

At ten past eleven Pint tapped me on the shoulder. I turned round sharply. He was holding out his watch.

'Don't you love Tina Turner?' the hostess said, her cotton dress twirling as she spun from one hip to another.

'Not bad,' I said. 'But I've got to go now. Thanks for the party. Good luck in Holland. Maybe see you again sometime.'

'Who knows?' she said.

Wolfgang said it was a shame I had to go, the party was just warming up. We shook hands. We said we'd keep in touch. We said we'd write. Pint and Sonia were waiting. Hurriedly, I pulled on my bronze raincoat.

Someone should write a pop song about the race back to Friedrichstrasse for midnight, I said to Pint and Sonia. It'd be a cold-war smash in West Berlin and a guaranteed samizdat success in East Berlin. Pint said Friedrichstrasse wasn't a very good word for a pop song, too many syllables. He reiterated his point that German was just not built for rock and roll. Rubbish, I said. Friedrichstrasse had the same syllable-count as San Francisco. I realised it was raining.

Pint said it was already too late to be able to take the S-Bahn and get to the border by midnight. The best bet was a Schwarzetaxi, he said, one of the illegal taxis that operated on Saturday nights. I ran ahead, my eyes peeled for Schwarzetaxis.

'How do I know which ones are the Schwarzetaxis?' I shouted this query thirty yards down the dim-lit street.

'You don't,' Pint shouted back. 'Stick out your arm at all cars driven by solitary men.'

It was raining harder now. For twenty minutes the three of us stood at three corners of a busy square in Köpenick, raising our hands at cars containing lonely men. No dice. Pint suggested we cut our losses and take the S-Bahn after all. Nothing much would happen to us at Friedrichstrasse if we were only half an hour late. Sonia and I agreed. We needed to take the number 86 tram to the S-Bahn station.

In any case, Pint was okay. He had a West Berlin passport; his visa was valid till 2 a.m. Sonia had a West German passport; her visa ran out at midnight.

The tram stop was at the corner of Lindenstrasse and Bahnhofstrasse. Teenage drunks were singing western pop songs. Two young lovers, oblivious to the din, ground their bodies against each other, their faces wet with rain and angry adolescent kisses, snatching the last seconds before the trams came to separate them for the night. I had done the same in bus stations and cinemas and when I got home my mother and father asked me if I had had a nice time and how was the film? and often I couldn't even remember its title. The cinema, like the bus station, like this tram stop, was just a dark refuge from the relentless glare of the dreary days.

The iron wheels of the trams chattered along the tracks, electric crackles and flashes of blue on the overhead cables briefly lighting the faces at the windows. The cobblestones shone blue and yellow in the rain. The cream trams disappeared into the night, enclosed in their world of blue electricity, spitting shards of colour at the sky.

There was still no sign of the number 86. Pint and Sonia were beginning to panic. I was too far gone to care. Things were coming to an end.

A Trabant pulled up at the tram stop, the driver asking a question with splayed fingers. Pint nodded vigorously in reply, jumping into the passenger seat for urgent negotiation.

'Okay,' Pint said, getting out of the car. 'Twenty-five marks to Friedrichstrasse. But he says he'll only take two. I'll take the S-Bahn. See you later.'

Sonia and I sat together on the back seat. The driver was about my age. Plump and balding, he spoke with a slight lisp.

'Is it really as bad here as they say on the western television?' he said.

'Oh no,' Sonia said.

The driver wanted to know what had brought us to East Berlin. Sonia explained, he seemed pleased. He offered us a cigarette.

'Most people in West Berlin couldn't care less about East Berlin,' he said, striking a match, holding the steering wheel with his elbows. 'They only come here if they have to, to visit relatives. Why do they never come here?'

'Oh, I don't know,' Sonia said. 'All the propaganda on the television. Some people probably worry that something might happen to them if they came here. It's also very expensive, you know, the money we have to change. Probably the people in West Berlin who would most like to come can't afford it.'

The driver was nodding. The Trabant juddered as he braked sharply for a red light.

'In the west it costs, eh?' he said. He rubbed his thumb and forefinger together, the way working men do in most cities, the common language of people who don't eat in restaurants or travel in aeroplanes.

'All that stuff they say about freedom and everything. Who cares?' the driver said, the Trabant whining in second as he accelerated away from the lights. 'What is freedom? Here you can live cheaply and well. In the west it's expensive to live well, but here you can be comfortable and it doesn't cost.'

He added that he didn't need to drive a Schwarzetaxi Saturday nights, he had a decent factory job, but a bit extra always came in useful and anyway Saturday nights weren't the same any more when you were married with children. It was okay to spend the night just driving around. He met interesting people.

'Like you,' he said, laughing.

The road was deserted, the countryside dark, the suburbs sleeping. Lulled by the rhythm of the engine ploughing steadily through the rain at around forty, I half-closed my eyes.

I was awakened by a blaze of light and the roar of machinery. The Trabant was driving past furnaces that looked like giant concrete women cut off at the shoulders and hips. A power station? Fluorescent tubes burned bright behind steel-framed factory windows. Bull-nosed trucks chugged in and out, the crush of headlights composing geometric criss-cross stars. The night-shift was in full swing.

'Unlucky for some. Working Saturday night,' the driver said.

Sonia murmured sympathetically.

I thought about the nightshift, the international community of nightshifts, all the metropolitan peoples toiling at nights to earn enough money for the basics plus one annual family holiday and maybe a car and some new furniture now and again if they were lucky. The driver had asked what freedom was. What was freedom for the nightshift? What was freedom for the women nightcleaners vacuuming office blocks in cities all across the west? The freedom to work all night and wait for the bus home at dawn? The freedom to fix breakfast and get the children off to school? The freedom to clean up the house and maybe catch a few hours' sleep before the children came home for their tea? The freedom to wait again for the bus that will return them to the deserted empires of the company headquarters that must be spick-and-span by morning for all the secretaries, clerks, accountants, PR people, designers, marketing and personnel managers, salesmen, lawyers and company directors, especially the place must be spick-and-span for the company directors, for all these armies of people busy making and selling useless things for fun and profit, the freedom to be part of this grand design? The freedom to enter polling booths, to inscribe twelve crosses during the course of a voting lifetime? I was thinking that people like the driver of this Trabant, people anywhere working on the nightshift, had neither the energy nor the inclination for silent bicycle protests of the kind described by the graphic designer of Köpenick. East and west, the same kind of people did these things. Dissent was also a kind of luxury. The driver of the Schwarzetaxi didn't give a fuck about freedom.

He would have felt out of place at the party in Köpenick. I had felt at home there. There was an international community of big-shots, of dissenters, of nightshift workers, all these little western worlds and eastern worlds holding up clean mirrors to each other. Big-shots in West Berlin lived in Dahlem. Big-shots in East Berlin lived in the suburb nicknamed Volvograd. Big-shots in

West Berlin were capitalists. Big-shots in East Berlin were communists. Big-shots said *we* and spoke for all their nation. I felt drained and drunk. I wanted to shout things from the rooftops, but the things got so complicated and the words just blew around like dust in the wind.

Travelling parallel to the Spree, the Trabant passed Ostbahnhof. It was 12.25. Brimful with pride, the driver was pointing out all the familiar landmarks: the Tele-Tower, the Palace of the Republic, the Opera House. *Beautiful*, he said, going down the Unter den Linden. Beautiful, we agreed.

This was his home. Most people were proud of their home. Most Americans felt good about America. Most Russians remained loyal to Russia. Most Germans supported whichever side of the argument they happened to have been born into. Treason everywhere was the most heinous of crimes. People were bound like mummies in flags. Truth, freedom, democracy, justice, these were the noises made by the big-shots. The big-shots were armed with the same words and bombs and different flags and national anthems.

The Trabant stopped at Friedrichstrasse station and Sonia gave the driver 30 ostmarks. He looked crestfallen. He must have been expecting deutschmarks, the big water-marked money, not these three thin, brown notes. Quickly, he put a brave face on matters. He wished us well and who knows maybe he'd see us again sometime, he said, maybe the next time we decide to come and get drunk in Köpenick, eh?

19 *Allied forces*

I stood on the Strasse des 17 Juni. It was Allied Forces Day Berlin 1984. Kind of our May Day, Captain Genser had said. Nine soldiers, three from each western army, were at the head of the parade. I was wearing a pair of brown brogues bought at a street market in a mining town called Castleford in Yorkshire. The shoes were in such good condition when I bought them I always imagined they had belonged to a working man who only wore them at the weekend. I imagined a miner driving the family out to the moors of a Sunday afternoon. I knew the shoes had belonged to a working man because the leather soles had been covered with the rubber stick-on soles you could buy at Woolworth's to save wearing down the expensive leather. The shoes must have been sold off with the rest of his possessions when he died. Probably, therefore, he was of an age to have fought in the war. Probably he would have felt odd if someone had told him that his brown suede brogues would one day stand on the street devised by Hitler as the showpiece entrance to the capital of the Third Reich, the street known in Nazi times as the East–West Axis, the street upon which the western armies of occupation were now parading their flags and guns.

Helicopters whirred overhead. Three black limousines glided to a halt outside the VIP enclosure and a British officer wearing a kilt showed the guests of honour to their seats. These big-wigs were the Commander-in-Chief of RAF Germany, the Commander of US Europe and a four-star general from France. (Generals were graded like petrol.)

A French troop wearing white turbans and flowing brown robes ran past at the double. In their white gloved hands they held sub-machine guns. They blew whistles and rang bells. In the public stand a little black and red flag was raised, the flag of opposition. It was angrily torn down by two burly men. A yellow balloon was tapped into the cordoned-off area by another demonstrator in the public stand. An American MP went dancing down the Strasse des 17 Juni after the balloon. For thirty yards the dancing balloon evaded his stamping boot. When he finally nailed it, people clapped and cheered.

Further yellow balloons were being blown up in the public stands and propelled towards the parade. The British MPs joined the American MPs in giving pursuit, the stamping polished boots time and again being fooled by the yellow balloons that bounded across the tarmac in such unpredictable patterns.

I watched an American MP discreetly raise the heel of his boot to see if any dogshit was smeared thereon. A minute later I was doing the same. Everyone, in fact, began examining their heels at around the same time, until it dawned upon all the spectators and soldiers and VIPs that the rank odour was part of the organised protest. Stink bombs had been secreted inside the yellow balloons. Each time an MP burst a balloon the foul smell was multiplied. The final phase of the demonstration was the simultaneous raising of thirty-odd banners and placards in the public stands. NO WEAPONS! NO WAR! TROOPS OUT OF BERLIN! People cheered as the placards, one by one, were scythed down by those who had come here to see the soldiers and the arms, to pay homage to the foreign armies protecting the freedom of Berlin. There were more balloons, more cries of *bravo!* as the MPs burst them. The marching resumed, the synchronised boots trampling the fragments of yellow that now littered the street.

It started raining. Three squaddies sitting behind me in the press box drank tea from Thermos flasks as the white wellingtons of another French unit came waltzing past, red tassels flying on their epaulettes.

I spotted PRO David. He was walking towards me. He was wearing his KGB raincoat, as his colleagues had dubbed it, he said. A voice over the Tannoy announced in English that due to the windy conditions the free-fall parachute display had been cancelled. PRO David was most fed up. That was the main reason he had brought along his Praktika, he said. The Red Devils had flown in specially from England, the Yank parachutists from Italy and the Frogs from Toulouse, he said. It was such a pity for all the wives and girlfriends who had come to Berlin from all 'over Germany to see their husbands and boyfriends on parade, he said. I made noises of condolence.

Eyes right, eyes left. Men bearing bayonets swivelled their heads in unison. Crimson stripes down blue trousers moved in parallel lines at 5 m.p.h. An American reporter in the press box had his press pass wedged in the band of his brown trilby like reporters in black-and-white films. The US Army, for obscure reasons, had graded its marchers according to height: basketball stars up front and dwarves bringing up the rear, a gentle gradient composed of bobbing black helmets.

'I see we had our traditional demo,' PRO David said, sighing. 'One year it was against the Yanks for Grenada. The next it was . . .'

He couldn't remember. Anyway, the point he was making was that these Berlin anarchists and lefties would always find some bloody thing to demonstrate about. The rain fell steadily. I wished I had stayed in bed. The French AMX13 tanks manufactured a shimmer of carbon monoxide.

'Here come our biggies!' shouted PRO David, beside himself. 'The Chieftains! In the urban camouflage.'

Like so many men exhilarated by weapons, he was a small boy in long trousers. I blame the parents. I once had a silver Lone Ranger pistol with matching bullet-belt and furry holster, one of my most prized possessions when I was six or seven. I had the complete outfit: black cowboy hat with silver sheriff's star, black embroidered waistcoat, black fringed trousers. Having loaded the pistol with green caps (it was always quite a hassle threading the thin coiled paper) I used to ride the dusty plains of my TV-fed imagination assassinating Red Indians, bandits and assorted ne'er-do-wells. I showed no mercy. With each shot the strip of green paper grew a further quarter inch above the gun until you had to tear it off, it looked more realistic when there was no paper showing. I loved *The Lone Ranger*, *Cheyenne* and *Rawhide*, they were the best programmes on television. When I outgrew *Beano* and *Dandy*, however, I did not progress to war comics. By that time I was into football, pop music, clothes and, secretly, girls. I suspect PRO David was a Meccano fanatic who had the *Eagle* delivered.

Tanks and jeeps, anti-aircraft guns and amphibious landing craft were still rumbling down from the Victory Column and proceeding solemnly to the Wall escorted by thousands of men and boys in hundreds of different-coloured uniforms like paid extras in a Cecil B. de Mille musical. I felt like death warmed up.

Hunching my back against against the drizzle, I lit a cigarette. A blond bloke was staring at me. I knew his face. It took me two or three minutes, sifting the possibilities, to recall that his had been the face at the wheel of the car taking myself and Captain Genser around Doughboy City. He was supposed to be a chauffeur. What was he doing in the press enclosure? PRO David was taking photographs of his favourite pieces of kit. In his KGB raincoat. I walked all the way home in my dead man's shoes.

The next day, Sunday, I accompanied Laura to Tegel airport. She was wearing her cream raincoat. I wished her luck with the interview.

'If you sleep with someone else make sure you use a johnny,' she said, kissing me and dancing off towards passport control, the cream raincoat billowing as she ran. I stood there watching. Her brown hair. Her blue stretch ski pants. Her black pointy shoes. I watched her with the hopeless eyes of an outsider. Before she disappeared she blew me a kiss. I blew one back. It was the last time I ever saw her at an airport.

She gets a job as a waitress at a nightclub on Great Queen Street. A smart move: late work. I lie awake at nights waiting for the putt-putt of her Fiat 500. It used to be her father's car. He once drove it all the way to Italy with his wife and three children. I know just how the car sounds. I will other cars to possess that sound, persuade myself that the car is indeed approaching. Any second now. I even write a poem about this, 'Waiting for Fiat 500'. I lose the poem. I am losing Laura too. I know the way all lovers know, the terrible language of hands and eyes. My mother rings up one night when I am alone drinking whisky in the flat. The usual conventions circumscribing telephone conversations with my mother are lost in drunken self-pity. I confess everything. I tell her what is happening. She tells me everything will be all right. She tells me Laura can't possibly meet someone she likes more than me in a nightclub. She tells me this with all the blind love of a mother. Afterwards, in the maudlin whisky night, I cry for the love of my mother too. Laura moves out the flat, saying it is not the end of the relationship, she just needs some time and space. Why do people always think lies are kinder than the truth? I don't know, I tell lies all the time too. Some weeks later she goes to Barcelona to live with Ulrike and Uschi, saying she will be back in London by Bonfire Night. I strike off the days on my Observer *calendar in the kitchen, but 5 November comes and goes and she is still in Barcelona. She returns at the end of November, saying it is just for a week. She wants to make her home in Spain. She wants to learn the language. She has another lover, I knew that all along in my stomach, but I know it for a fact when she calls me the wrong name by mistake.*

I consider killing myself. I couldn't care less about the cold war. I am fucking up at The Observer. *Features stop getting written, bills stop getting paid. All the plants in my house die. Friends start hinting I am drinking too much. I feel like a character in a morbid short story: the sudden crisis that tears away the veil. It doesn't take much, the veil is thin and flimsy, it gets torn away so easily. I become frightened. Sanity is a dreary category, a tawdry ambition, all well and good, but this time I am being made mad. I am not choosing madness. This is rather a big difference. I decide to flee to Central America. I wanted to go there anyway. Now there is no excuse. I can see George again. Every cloud has a silver lining. I prefer this to plenty more fish in the sea, which has a nasty imperialist ring to it. I repeat, time and again, in the mock-heroic cliché of these unheroic times, I am a survivor, another survivor who doesn't know the meaning of the word, I think, covering all my bases, chewing this thing up like a dog. Reason now has to resume some periodic occupation of my mind. I have to start talking about the weather again. Anyway, after a while the tears run dry or there are new tears for new reasons. I have to remind myself I am a lucky bastard. Love is a luxury. I fly away to Nicaragua. I write most of this book in Managua. I learn all kinds of things there. I know now with even more certainty that it is foolish and wrong to claim absolute moral supremacy for one kind of electric city over another when the billions of poor in the world's dusty periphery are still hungering for basic land reforms that will enable them to fill their bellies. The industrial revolution never happened in Central America, where the colonial countries plundered the gold, silver, tin, coffee, bananas, cacao and sugar and gave nothing back in return but war, starvation and disease. We should all carry this guilt. We are all guilty Germans now. I send Laura a birthday card from Managua. She sends me one from Barcelona. There is still some kind of romantic contact, I still think everything will work out okay in the end, but this is another illusion. The story has a few more details, but that's enough, that's already too much.*

I am back in London now, writing this, but I will be returning soon to Central America. In a way I am grateful to Laura for forcing me into exile. It's an ill wind. Everyone I know in London is worried about AIDS. My own doctor died of AIDS. It is a terrible plague and a political disaster, feeding people's self-obsession. People's nightmares become yet more parochial. In the communist cities now the talk is all of glasnost, the intellectuals are rejoicing. Gorbachev, it seems, is trying to dismantle the cold war. There is a real chance the apocalypse will be averted. Georg Karger, Johnny's father, is euphoric. For him, glasnost is the vindication of his entire communist life. He suffered horrible doubts during the dark days, the show trials, the invasions of Hungary and Czechoslovakia, but now he feels he can die content. He celebrated his eightieth birthday in January 1987, a big posh do at the Palasthotel. Johnny is in love now and his lover is expecting a child. He is trying to plant roots. I have torn up all mine. I have no real regrets, although sometimes I wish I could stop dreaming about Laura.

I caught a single-decker bus outside the airport. Coming back towards town down Karl Schumacher Damm, I remembered this was the day the French military opened its gates to the public. All the armies courted their subjects with one circus after another. Anglo-German Friendship Day was still to come. Many West Berlin police oompah bands had already been booked for the great day.

It seemed the French had had bad luck with the Berlin summer. A big wheel rotated in the rain in the base named after Napoleon. The flags were all wet. An Air France jet was coming in to land. I looked down at my brogues. The life of a shoe was full of surprises.

It was my last full day in the occupied city. I had no definite plans. I talked to Ulrike and Uschi about their forthcoming emigration to Spain. Charlotte was playing in the sandpit. The scab above her tiny pink mouth had healed. Ana was lying in Andreas's room, listening to the BBC World Service. Uschi was listening to Zara Leander and hoping it would rain.

I walked out the unlocked door, borrowed Uschi's bicycle for the last time and rode to the wide-open dereliction of Potsdamer Platz. I had a cup of coffee in the orange corrugated Imbiss and browsed among the stalls selling cuddly toys, painted mirrors of Elvis and Marilyn and James Dean, postcards of the Wall. A gruff-voiced drunk drew my attention to his watercolours of Berlin street-scenes. I said I was skint, I was just looking. He asked why I was writing things down in my notebook.

'For a book,' I said.

'About Berlin?' he said.

I nodded.

'That's beautiful,' he said, his purple face erupting in forced laughter. 'A book about Berlin! That's a good one!'

He slapped his thigh and shared the joke with the neighbouring stall-holder. Their jeers faded as I cycled away, parallel to the Wall, along Bellevuestrasse. I cycled past the ruins of the ballroom called Esplanade, its gold thirties lettering mellowed through the years to weak brown. It was just before five, a hot grey afternoon. I needed some breakfast, I decided. I knew a good café at the top end of the Kurfürstendamm, one of those places frequented by older women with hats.

The café had Louis XIV chairs upholstered in crushed velvet

the colour of wet roses. The tables were gold-leafed, the carpet grey. I ate my boiled eggs and toast. Tom Jones was playing softly across the PA.

And they'll all come to meet me.
In the shade of that old oak tree.
As they lay me, in the green green grass of home.

There was no escape. The Welsh miner went to Las Vegas and his voice went round the world. I finished breakfast quickly and jumped back on the bicycle. I had gone about 200 yards back down the Kurfürstendamm when a sudden gale, the storm's messenger, whipped up all the trash from the street. Panicked pigeons wheeled in the sky. Pages of newsprint clung to human legs. Men and women chased bouncing hats. Dogs slunk scared, tails between their legs. Glasses, cups and bottles flew from the café tables and shattered on the paving stones, where cigarette butts and sweet wrappings were trapped in manic little whirl-winds. Everyone hurried, hands shielding eyes against the stinging dust, their ears full of the wind's fierce music; the lowing of a million beasts and the singing of the sea.

The sky was rent with electric yellow and some people screamed.

The wind was banished by the thunder.

God turned off the lights and flung down the cleansing rain.

I got off my bicycle at the corner of Cicerostrasse and the Kurfürstendamm, seeking refuge beneath the blue canopy of a Peugeot showroom, together with a group of motorcyclists. The green C on the neon sign of a restaurant called Ciao sparked out.

Those already ensconced in the pavement cafés, dry and comfortable beneath the canvas, turned their chairs round to get a better view of the mayhem: the drenched and running people, skidding cars, fallen cyclists, wrecked umbrellas. They sipped their drinks and said nothing, like they were watching a rather boring disaster film which had the saving grace of some unintentionally amusing moments.

Wearing a lace shawl, seamed stockings and a black pencil skirt, one young woman was striding up the Kurfürstendamm as though nothing had happened. She must have been half-blinded by the torrential rain, but she had decided to disobey the general edict to run and hide. Why should she be scared of rain? Rain was the least of her problems. She let it beat uselessly against her pale face. She laughed and the rain beat even harder, filling up her eyes which ran with black tears. The rain did its best. It glued the cloth to her skin, tried to make her shiver. It filled up her laughing mouth. She was ankle-deep in the flood but she didn't once check her stride, her swaggering heroic procession up the main drag. Her skirt shone like fresh coal. I wondered who she was. She loved the rain. The rain had cleared the fucking streets. The rain was her friend. The rain had rescued the day, mocked the fragile city, washed the day into her memory, clear bright things that would not be forgotten. I watched her till she disappeared from sight.

Cars with dipped headlights patrolled slowly through the dirty rivers like they were looking for survivors.

Born in Birmingham, England, in 1952, Ian Walker has written for a number of English publications, including *New Society* and *The Observer*. He now lives in Nicaragua, where he is at work on another book.